Samuel Johnson
Updated Edition

Twayne's English Authors Series

Bertram H. Davis, Editor
Florida State University

TEAS 95

SAMUEL JOHNSON
Portrait by Sir Joshua Reynolds, now thought to be a copy of the original at Knole, Kent.
Reproduced by permission of the Tate Gallery.

Samuel Johnson

Updated Edition

By Donald Greene

University of Southern California

Twayne Publishers
A Division of G. K. Hall & Co. • *Boston*

Samuel Johnson, Updated Edition
Donald Greene

Copyright 1989 by G. K. Hall & Co.
All rights reserved.
Published by Twayne Publishers
A Division of G. K. Hall & Co.
70 Lincoln Street
Boston, Massachusetts 02111

Copyediting supervised by Barbara Sutton
Book production by Janet Z. Reynolds
Book design by Barbara Anderson

Typeset in 11 pt. Garamond
by Compositors Corporation, Cedar Rapids, Iowa

Printed on permanent/durable acid-free paper
and bound in the United States of America

Library of Congress Cataloging-in-Publication Data

Greene, Donald.
    Samuel Johnson / by Donald Greene. — Updated ed.
        p.   cm. — (Twayne's English authors series ; TEAS 95)
    Bibliography: p.
    Includes index.
    ISBN 0-8057-6962-5
    1. Johnson, Samuel, 1709–1784—Criticism and interpretation.
    I. Title.   II. Series.
    PR3534.G74   1989
    828'.609—dc20   89-33455
                                                                CIP

To John M. Lothian

Poverty of sentiment in men who considered themselves to be company for the parlour, as he called it,
was what he could not bear.

—Hester Lynch Piozzi (Mrs. Thrale),
Anecdotes of the Late Samuel Johnson, LL.D.

Contents

About the Author

Donald Greene is Leo S. Bing Professor Emeritus of English, University of Southern California. A native of western Canada, he earned his B.A. at the University of Saskatchewan and later received doctoral degrees from Columbia University, the University of London, and McMaster University. He has taught at the University of California at Riverside, Brandeis University, and the Universities of New Mexico, Toronto, and Wisconsin. A fellow of the Royal Society of Canada, Greene was twice awarded Guggenheim fellowships, a Canada Council Senior Research Fellowship, and a Fellowship of the National Humanities Center. He has served as acting editor of *Eighteenth-Century Studies* and the *Johnsonian News Letter*, and as president of the Johnson Society (England) and the Johnson Society of Southern California. His publications include *The Politics of Samuel Johnson* (1960), *The Age of Exuberance: Backgrounds to Eighteenth-Century English Literature* (1970), *Samuel Johnson: A Collection of Critical Essays (Twentieth Century Views)* (1965), Samuel Johnson, *Political Writings* (vol. 10, The Yale Edition of the Works of Samuel Johnson, 1977), and *Samuel Johnson* (The Oxford Authors, 1984).

Preface to the Updated Edition

Short but substantial books providing the novice with an up-to-date introduction to Johnson's writings are rare; such works as Leslie Stephen's *Samuel Johnson* in the English Men of Letters series (1878) and John Bailey's *Dr. Johnson and His Circle* in the Home University Library (1913), though highly readable, are hopelessly outdated in their facts and concentrate much more on Johnson as the "personality" presented by Boswell than as Johnson the thinker and writer. When my anthology of Johnson's writings in the Oxford Authors series was published in the bicentennial year of Johnson's death, and I cast around for a volume to recommend to readers unfamiliar with his work, I could find nothing more suitable, whatever its deficiencies, than my little *Samuel Johnson* (1970) in Twayne's English Authors Series.

When a new edition of it was proposed, I reread the book carefully and found little that I wished to change in the interpretations and judgments I give there; a good deal of what I have published on Johnson since 1970 is a set of extended footnotes to the book. So the bulk of this volume is the same as the earlier one, with a few small changes and corrections. In addition, however, a fairly full account is given of developments in Johnsonian studies since 1970. There have been many of them. A somewhat jaundiced reviewer recently wrote, "Why do people go on writing books and articles about Johnson?" They certainly do so, as my chapter on recent developments and the updated bibliography indicate. An answer to the reviewer's question might be "For the same reason they go on writing books and articles about Shakespeare." There is still much more of value to be learned about Johnson.

Donald Greene

Los Angeles

Preface (1970)

"Of every great and eminent character, part breaks forth into public view, and part lies hid in domestic privacy" wrote Samuel Johnson in his life of Sir Thomas Browne, the seventeenth-century physician, scientist, and moralist, who was so like Johnson in his inexhaustible curiosity about the world and its denizens, in the serious and penetrating insight he directed to its problems, and in the wonderfully poetic prose in which he set down his observations about it. No one knew better than Johnson how to explore the "domestic privacy" of an eminent character—he may well be considered the originator of modern, psychological biography. It was Johnson's ironic misfortune, however, that his great disciple in biography, James Boswell, learned his lesson so well that, for most people since his day, Johnson's domestic privacy has greatly overshadowed the part that was in "public view"—that is, his career as a writer. This loss is lamentable, for Johnson's writings, a major landmark in the history of English literature, are capable of affording exquisite "delight" and invaluable "instruction" (Johnson's—and Horace's—criteria of literary worth) to the intelligent reader of any age.

Although Boswell's *Life of Johnson* remains a great work of art, with which every educated person should be acquainted, the time is long past when anyone takes seriously the old quip that Johnson lives only because Boswell knew him. "The best part of every author lies in his book, I assure you," Johnson once said to a friend who was pestering him for an introduction to some fashionable writer. This statement is very true of Johnson himself (as it certainly was of Boswell), and the chief concern of the present account of Johnson is to introduce the reader to the fascinating variety, the intellectual stimulation, the continual freshness, and the rare artistry of his writings.

At the same time, we should continue to be aware, as Johnson always was, of how much the circumstances of a man's "domestic privacy" condition the part of him exposed to "public view." A knowledge of Johnson's life, and the personality and psychology of the man who lived it, can help to illuminate his writings, and the opening chapter attempts a sketch of it. For those who know Johnson only through Boswell, it ought to be pointed out that much has been learned about Johnson the man that Boswell did not know. By modern standards, Boswell's *Life* is by no means the superlative biography Macaulay thought it. It is a superlative *something;* but, in a sense, it is not a biography at all. It is a compilation from Boswell's enormous journal, kept ever since he was an adolescent, a synthesis of the passages dealing with the times when Boswell was in Johnson's company. This period, it has been calculated, was a total of only 425 days in all, a quarter of these during their joint trip to the Hebrides in 1773,[1] for Boswell lived in Edinburgh and came to London only during a few months of the year, and by no means every year. Boswell knew Johnson only during the last twenty years of Johnson's life, meeting him first in 1763, long after Johnson had become famous. Accordingly, his account of the first fifty years of Johnson's life is a very sketchy one, taken from reports at second and third hand; and sometimes it is quite inaccurate and misleading.

Besides, Boswell was at once too far from Johnson and too close to him to see him in proper perspective. Thirty years younger than Johnson, he belonged to the generation that is always more likely to patronize its immediate predecessors than subsequent generations are. This fact may account for the "quaintness" of the picture of "dear old Doctor Johnson"[2] that so many readers have got from Boswell's *Life*. Moreover, Boswell was a Scot, and he had been brought up in a severely Presbyterian atmosphere (against which he revolted at one point to embrace Roman Catholicism). Hence he was never thoroughly at home in the peculiarly English framework of Johnson's political and religious thinking, and he gives oversimplified interpretations of both that have badly confused many students.

A really satisfactory biography of Johnson by modern scholarly standards has still to be written. Fortunately, the first forty years of his life have now been carefully investigated, chiefly by the English amateur scholar, Aleyn Lyell Reade, who devoted the spare time of a busy life to tracking down the records of it in parish, town, and school archives, and by Professor James L. Clifford. But the busy middle years, from about 1745 to 1765, remain almost as much a mystery as the corresponding years in Shakespeare's life. We know that Johnson lived in London and wrote and published certain works, but we know extremely little about what he was doing from day to day during this time. For the last two decades, from the 1760s to the 1780s, we have the excellent pictures of him on social occasions given by Boswell and Mrs. Thrale. Yet even here there are gaps—long periods of time and important areas of his work and interests that have not been properly explored. And what the modern reader really needs, to illuminate Johnson for him, is some kind of history of his *intellectual* life: a systematic account of his voluminous and catholic reading, the influences on his thinking on various important subjects, the development of his ideas, and their relation to ideas that preceded and followed them.[3]

But before the student can undertake this, or any other serious inquiry into Johnson's mind and art, he must be familiar with what Johnson wrote; and to provide an introduction to what Johnson wrote is the main purpose of this book. The chapters, after the first, have a loose sort of chronological organization: that is to say, Johnson's career as a writer began with poetry, continued with journalism, and may be said to have culminated in his work as a critic. Likewise, there is some chronological organization within chapters. But essentially the arrangement of the book is topical rather than chronological. I have quoted copiously from Johnson, first, because many of the pieces I quote from—especially his journalistic writings—are difficult of access and seldom read, and, second, because Johnson's prose is so succinct and pregnant that an attempt to paraphrase it would take up more space than the original. I have not said much about the topic so popular in college courses, "Johnson and His Circle": there is really no reason to believe that Johnson had any more influence on the thought and work of the highly independent and original people with whom he associated—Goldsmith, Reynolds, Burke—than, say, Shakespeare had on his friend Ben Jonson or Milton on Andrew Marvell. Nor have I said very much about Boswell: this is a book about Johnson, and there is no lack of available books about (and by) Boswell. As Edmund Wilson has remarked, "That Johnson himself was really one of the best English writers of his time, that he deserved his great reputation, is a fact that we are likely to lose sight of"; it is the object of this book to call attention to that fact.

Donald Greene

University of Southern California

Acknowledgments

Think where man's glory most begins and ends,
And say their glory was he had such friends.
—Yeats,
The Municipal Gallery Revisited (adapted)

In this updated volume, I wish to recognize John Abbott, Paul Alkon, Bob Allen, Lionel Basney, Jack Bate, Fred Bernard, Skip Brack, Morris Brownell, Bob Carnie, Chester Chapin, Tom Curley, Bert Davis, Mary Hyde Eccles, David Fleeman, Bob Folkenflik, Joel Gold, Harvey Goldstein, Kathleen Grange, Jim Gray, Gloria Gross, Isobel Grundy, Jean Hagstrum, John Hardy, Ben Hoover, Nalini Jain, Shirley White Johnston, Tom Kaminski, Gwin Kolb, Paul Korshin, Mary Lascelles, Jake Leed, Fritz Liebert, Helen Louise McGuffie, John Middendorf, Daisuke Nagashima, Prem Nath, Fred Nicholls, John Riely, Pat Rogers, Loren Rothschild, George Rousseau, Dick Schwartz, Arthur Sherbo, Oliver Sigworth, Al Strauss, Mark Temmer, Ed Tomarken, Clarence Tracy, John Vance, Bob Voitle, Magdi Wahba, John Wain, Marshall Waingrow, Bob Walker, Howard Weinbrot, Kai Kin Yung, and all the other devoted laborers in the Johnsonian vineyard, bringing forth the fruits thereof.

Chronology

1746   Signs contract for *Dictionary*. Drafts *Plan of an English Dictionary* (1747; dedicated to Lord Chesterfield).

1749   *Vanity of Human Wishes*. *Irene* performed and published.

1750   Begins *The Rambler* (to 1752).

1752   Elizabeth Johnson (wife) dies.

1753   Contributes to *The Adventurer*.

1755   Awarded honorary master's degree, Oxford. *Dictionary of the English Language*.

1756   Edits *Literary Magazine*. Proposals for edition of Shakespeare.

1758   Begins *The Idler* (to 1760).

1759   *Rasselas*. Sarah Johnson (mother) dies.

1762   Awarded annual pension of £300 by government.

1763   Meets Boswell.

1765   Publishes edition of Shakespeare. Meets Mr. and Mrs. Henry Thrale. Honorary LL.D., Trinity College, Dublin.

1766   Assists Robert Chambers with Vinerian lectures on law at Oxford. Severe depression; recovers with help of Mrs. Thrale.

1770   *The False Alarm*.

1771   *Thoughts on Falkland's Islands*.

1773   Publishes revised editions of the *Dictionary* and Shakespeare. Tours Scotland with Boswell (August to November).

1774   Tours Wales with the Thrales. *The Patriot*.

1775   *Journey to the Western Islands of Scotland*. *Taxation No Tyranny*. Honorary D.C.L., Oxford. Visits France with the Thrales.

1777   Agreement with booksellers to write prefaces to works of English poets *(The Lives of the Poets)*. Unsuccessful campaign to reprieve the Reverend William Dodd, condemned to be hanged for forgery.

1779   First four volumes of *Lives of the Poets* published.

1781   Henry Thrale dies. Last six volumes of *Lives of the Poets* published.

1782   "On the Death of Dr. Robert Levet."

1783   Stroke, loss of speech. Recovers; during winter of 1783–84, ill and depressed.

1784   Religious "conversion," February. Dedication of Burney's *Account of Commemoration of Handel*. Dies 13 December. Buried in Westminster Abbey, 20 December.

Chapter One
The Man and His Life

On the surface, Samuel Johnson's was a dull, unadventurous life, like that of most professional writers of the eighteenth or any century. He was born 7 September (18, New Style) 1709, the son of a struggling bookseller in the small Midland city of Lichfield. He was given the usual grammar school education, and he spent a little more than a year at Oxford before poverty forced him to withdraw. There followed some years of fruitlessly trying to establish himself as a schoolmaster in the Midlands, culminating in a strange marriage to a widow twenty years older than himself, who had a few hundred pounds that he invested in a private school and quickly lost. Then, when Johnson was nearly thirty, came the move to London and many years of badly paid journalistic writing, which, however, enabled him to live. As his reputation as a writer developed with painful slowness, he had the mortification of seeing his former pupil and companion on the journey to London, David Garrick, rapidly attain dazzling success. It was not until Johnson was forty that his name began to be known, with the mild succès d'estime of his long poem *The Vanity of Human Wishes* and his blank-verse tragedy *Irene* (written long before and now produced only through Garrick's influence).

In the following decade (the 1750s) real and permanent fame did come. After his impressive series of *Rambler* essays and the great *Dictionary of the English Language,* Johnson could no longer be ignored, and he took his place as one of the most important literary figures of his time.[1] But, as he said in the astonishingly personal concluding paragraph of his preface to the *Dictionary,* the success came too late to give him pleasure: "I have protracted my work till most of those whom I wished to please have sunk into the grave." His wife had died three years before; there had been no children; the one remaining member of his immediate family, his mother, was now a very old woman, with only four more years to live. The fairly substantial sum he had been advanced for the *Dictionary* was dissipated during the seven years it took him and his assistants to complete it, and he immediately had to plunge into a number of new projects of writing—the abortive editorship of the *Literary Magazine,* an edition of Shakespeare which languished for many years, and the *Idler* essays. To pay the expenses of his mother's last illness, he dashed off "in the evenings of a week" the brilliant *conte philosophique, Rasselas.*

At last, when he was fifty-three, the new government of George III and Lord Bute freed him from the oppression of financial worry by granting him a moderate pension. This income also relieved him of a certain amount of incentive to effort; indeed, one of its effects may have been the severe intensification a few years later of his lifelong fits of depression, from which he was rescued by the attentions of his newfound friends Hester Thrale and her husband, the wealthy brewer. For the remaining twenty years of his life he cultivated social intercourse—perhaps as part of a campaign to bolster his mental health—spending much time in the company not only of such distinguished members of The Club as Joshua Reynolds and Edmund Burke, but of the young—the unsatisfactory but amusing Scot, James Boswell; the gay, aristocratic adulterer, Topham Beauclerk; the scholarly Bennet Langton; and, when he had the opportunity, of intellectual young ladies like Fanny Burney and Hannah More. He was always highly susceptible to feminine charm and more appreciative of the feminine mind than many of his contemporaries. He traveled a good deal, in striking contrast to the years of his thirties and forties, when he seems scarcely to have left London. He made almost annual visits to renew old friendships in the Midlands and at Oxford; he traveled to Wales and France with the Thrales; and, most remarkably, in his mid-sixties, made an arduous expedition with young James Boswell to the Highlands of Scotland, then an outpost of civilization.

He continued to write, now not as a task to earn his bread, but when occasion and impulse offered. Yet, for a man who remarked that "No one but a blockhead ever wrote except for money" and who, in his private diaries, continually lamented his sloth, the list of his writings during the last two decades is substantial: the much-delayed edition of Shakespeare; a series of four exuberant pamphlets on political issues of the day; a very fine work of social anthropology (*Journey to the Western Islands of Scotland*); and, in his seventies, the magnificent *Biographical and Critical Prefaces to the Works of the English Poets* (the usual title, *The Lives of the Poets*, is a misnomer), one of the greatest monuments of both biography and criticism in any language. Though suffering throughout his life from a multitude of ailments, and given to hypochondriac brooding over them and to self-diagnosis and treatment, Johnson had in fact a robust constitution—he laughed at poor Boswell's sufferings during the hardships of the Hebrides journey—and lived to the respectable age of seventy-five, dying on 13 December 1784.

On the face of it, one might wonder why such a life, conspicuously lacking, in Johnson's phrase, "those performances and incidents which produce vulgar greatness," has produced almost continuously for two centuries so much devoted and enthusiastic study and has inspired such excellent biographies, from Sir John Hawkins's and Mrs. Thrale's and Arthur Murphy's (all admirable works), through Boswell's great work of art, down to such fine recent books as those of Aleyn Lyell Reade, Joseph Wood Krutch, John Wain, James L. Clifford and W. J. Bate. The answer is perhaps that anyone who comes into contact with Johnson is bound to catch some of his passionate concern for humanity—for the condition of being a member of the human race, for human life as of profound value and interest whether that of a Frederick the Great, a humble individual like Johnson's friend Robert Levet ("obscurely wise and coarsely kind"), or Claudy Phillips, "an itinerant musician," whose epitaph Johnson wrote.

"Human beings are too important to be treated as mere symptoms of the past," Lytton Strachey has declared; but Johnson had said much the same long before: "I have often thought that there has rarely passed a life of which a judicious and faithful narrative would not be useful. . . . We are all prompted by the same motives, all deceived by the same fallacies, all animated by hope, obstructed by danger, entangled by desire, and seduced by pleasure." This is true even of authors, Johnson says with dry irony: "An author partakes of the common condition of humanity; he is born and married like another man; he has hopes and fears, expectations and disappointments, griefs and joys, and friends and enemies, like a courtier or a statesman; nor can I conceive why his affairs should not excite curiosity as much as the whisper of a drawing-room or the factions of a camp." It is not the outward but the inward events of an individual's life that Johnson finds of perpetual interest, as did his friend the great novelist Samuel Richardson, of whom he remarked, "Richardson picked the kernel of life; Fielding is contented with the husk."[2]

The husk of Johnson's life was unspectacular enough; but the fascination of the complexity and turmoil, even violence, of his inner life has made men like Boswell and Reade willing to devote years of minute and laborious research to gathering up clues, however small, that may help to unravel something of its mystery. And in doing so they are following Johnson's own recommendation. The methods of the psychoanalyst would have come as no surprise to him: "The business of the biographer is . . . to lead the thoughts into domestic privacies, and display the minute details of daily life, where exterior appendages are cast aside."[3]

The best biographer of Johnson turns out to be Johnson himself: although only a tiny fragment has survived of the autobiography he began to write in middle life, its method is one the modern psychologist must applaud, with its Proustian (and Wordsworthian) particularity about the memories that impressed themselves on his childish mind, and the bare simplicity of the style:

Sept. 7, 1709, I was born at Lichfield. My mother had a very difficult and dangerous labour, and was assisted by George Hector, a man-midwife of great reputation. I was born almost dead, and could not cry for some time. When he had me in his arms, he said, "Here is a brave boy."

In a few weeks an inflammation was discovered on my buttock, which was at first, I think, taken for a burn; but soon appeared to be a natural disorder. It swelled, broke, and healed.

My Father being that year Sheriff of Lichfield, and to ride the circuit of the County next day, which was a ceremony then performed with great pomp, he was asked by my mother, "Whom he would invite to the Riding?" and answered, "All the town now." He feasted the citizens with uncommon magnificence, and was the last but one that maintained the splendour of the Riding.[4]

Family Relationships

There can be little doubt that Johnson's massive psychological troubles in later life stemmed, like most people's, from his childhood relations with his parents, as they were affected by social patterns. Michael Johnson was descended from the humblest stock—"I have great merit in being zealous for subordination and the honours of birth," Johnson once remarked wryly, "for I can hardly tell who was my grandfather."[5] As boys, Michael and his brothers had had to be assisted by charitable institutions in Lichfield, which paid for Michael's apprenticeship as a bookseller. Eventually he achieved some prosperity as the only bookseller in the cathedral city and as one of the few in the whole Midlands. He was fifty-two and sheriff of Lichfield, as his son records, when the child was born. The prosperity did not last: Michael began to engage in enterprises, such as a tannery, that were evidently too much for his capital or his business acumen; and, before the boy was very old, the family seems to have been plunged into unremitting financial distress, such as Samuel was to know for the next fifty years of his life.

Samuel's mother, Sarah Ford (forty years old when he was born), was from a distinctly "better" family, the Fords of Warwickshire, who had produced numerous well-to-do tradesmen and professional men. The late marriage of a poor man of intellectual tastes with a respectable bourgeoise was not likely to produce happiness, and Johnson in his fragment of autobiography vividly records that it did not:

In the second year I know not what happened to me. I believe it was then that my mother carried me to Trysul, to consult Dr. Atwood, an oculist of Worcester. My father and Mrs. Harriots [of Trysul], I think, never had much kindness for each other. She was my mother's relation; and he had none so high to whom he could send any of his family. He saw her seldom himself, and willingly disgusted her, by sending his horses from home on Sunday; which she considered, and with reason, as a breach of duty [religious duty]. My father had much vanity, which his adversity hindered from being fully exerted. I remember, that, mentioning her legacy [£40, which probably sent Samuel to Oxford] in the humility of distress, he called her "our good Cousin Harriots." My mother had no value for his relations; those indeed whom we knew of were much lower than hers. This contempt began, I know not on which side, very early; but, as my father was little at home, it had not much effect.

My father and mother had not much happiness from each other. They seldom conversed; for my father could not bear to talk of his affairs; and my mother, being unacquainted with books, cared not to talk of any thing else.

When the boy was three, he was found to be suffering from scrofula (a tubercular disorder which apparently resulted in the loss of the sight in his left eye), and the conventional treatment of the time was recommended by his parents' medical advisers:

In Lent [17]12, I was taken to London, to be touched for the evil by Queen Anne. My mother was at Nicholson's, the famous bookseller, in Little Britain. My mother, then with child, concealed her pregnancy, that she might not be hindered from the journey. I always retained some memory of the journey, though I was then but thirty months old. I remembered a little dark room behind the kitchen, where the jack-weight fell through a hole in the floor, into which I once slipped my leg. I seem to remember that I played with a string and a bell, which my cousin Isaac Johnson gave me; and that there was a cat with a white collar, and a dog, called Chops, that leaped over a stick.

The child with whom Sarah Johnson was pregnant was Samuel's younger brother Nathanael. Little is known of him except that he died suddenly when he was twenty-five, just at the time Samuel was leaving for London. A letter of Nathanael's, written a short time before, has survived; it is full of bitter reproach against his brother for turning his mother against him and of something like despair about his own future.[6] It has been speculated, with some plausibility, that Nathanael's sudden death was a suicide, that Johnson may have guiltily recognized his own share in the responsibility for it, and that this incident accounts for what has seemed to readers the extreme sensitivity to the fact of human death that caused him to denounce Milton's *Lycidas* as unfeeling.

It becomes clear, as the details of Johnson's early life are studied in the light of modern psychiatric knowledge, that the person most directly responsible for Johnson's difficulties in later life was his mother.[7] This statement may come as a surprise to those who have read his very tender letters to her as she lay dying—"You have been the best mother, and I believe the best woman, in the world."[8] But Johnson had a large capacity for romanticizing persons, and institutions, with whom his direct contact had in reality not been very productive of happiness: his mother, his wife, and his alma mater, the University of Oxford. In spite of those wonderful letters, the fact remains that Johnson did not visit his mother for nearly twenty years before her death, and this neglect can hardly be explained on the grounds that poverty prevented him from making the not-very-arduous trip from London to Lichfield.

Sarah Johnson seems certainly to have been a woman with "character": her determination and business sense kept the bookshop in Lichfield in operation from her husband's death in 1731 until her own in 1759 and there must have been times in the hungry 1730s and 1740s when it was the only dependable source of income in the whole Johnson family. No doubt her son appreciated and admired these qualities in her; but along with them were the rigidity and narrow-mindedness that made her husband unwilling to spend more time at home than was necessary—also no doubt to the son's detriment—and a self-centeredness that made her unable to fill the emotional needs of her late-born children. Samuel and Nathanael were never able to please her, and so they were never able to please themselves. Samuel's deep conviction of his own basic unworthiness that tortured him all his life (and also deeply troubled Nathanael, as is seen in the one poignant letter to have survived) must be laid at Sarah Johnson's door. Nor did it help matters when this self-disesteem was reinforced with a Calvinistic emphasis on the pains of hell (the Ford's background was Whig and Puritan) that remained with Johnson throughout his life.

Still, it would have taken an exceptional parent to counteract completely the trauma that illness and poverty inflicted on the boy. One of his eyes lost its sight when he was small the other remained extremely shortsighted and he was early marked with the scars of scrofula and smallpox. In later life, what people first noticed about him was his strange convulsive muscular tic, which was no doubt psychosomatic in origin, but could be the object of cruel ridicule in the eighteenth century. Two schools rejected him for a post as teacher on the grounds that his actions "might become the object of imitation and ridicule among his pupil," and indeed one former pupil, David Garrick, caused much mirth with his imitations of them.

In fact, however, the boy grew up to be a powerful, big-boned man. When he wanted to, he could perform feats of physical strength that amazed his friends, who thought of him as a sedentary intellectual. "Johnson rides to hounds as well as the most illiterate fellow in England," one of them commented in surprise, forgetting, as Johnson himself pointed out, that his uncle Andrew Johnson had been a semiprofessional wrestler. (The average student's notion of Johnson as obese is probably derived from the too-often-reproduced 1765 portrait by Reynolds, which displays a puffiness of jowl not found in other portraits.) When, at twenty-nine, Johnson arrived in London to begin a career as professional writer, one bookseller glanced at his muscular frame and advised him to seek work as a public porter instead. For all that, his amateur interest in medicine and pharmacology and his willingness to practice them on himself, certainly turned him into something of a hypochondriac most of his life and he must have been painfully aware that his appearance was anything but attractive.

Poverty and Education

His father's poverty also helped to make Johnson feel set apart from the relatively prosperous middle-class boys who attended the Lichfield grammar school with him. It was a school with some tradition of distinction: among other eminent individuals, Addison had attended it when his father was Dean of Lichfield—Addison, another impecunious lad who had made his way to the heights of both the intellectual and the political worlds through brains, learning, and literary skill. His career must have often been in the young Johnson's mind. Among his schoolmates were boys who were to achieve high places in the legal and ecclesiastical professions; who, when they passed out of school, were sent to the university and then established in their careers by their relations and friends, good Whigs, as virtually everyone in public life in the eighteenth century was. Along with these boys, the poor bookseller's son followed the traditional course of study—the minute and precise study of Latin and Greek language and literature—and easily surpassed them all, even the future Lord Chief Justice of the Common Pleas and the future Lord Bishop of Bristol.

But, for Johnson, there was to be no such easy road to a career. When he was sixteen, for an unknown reason, he withdrew from the Lichfield school and went to spend almost a year at Stourbridge in Worcestershire, where many of his Ford relations lived. He spent a short time at the Stourbridge grammar school, but what seems to have made a much greater impression on him was the society of his cousin, the Reverend Cornelius Ford, a witty and somewhat licentious man in his early thirties, who had had a distinguished career at Cambridge and had been associated with Alexander Pope and Lord Chesterfield in London. The awkward lad was fascinated by the reflected brilliance from the intellectual *grand monde* and was always grateful to his cousin Neely for encouraging him to use his fine mind—"to study the principles of everything, that a general acquaintance with life might be the consequence of his inquiries."[9]

When Johnson was seventeen he returned to Lichfield—reluctantly, one must suppose—and spent two years helping in his father's bookshop before money became available to send him to Oxford. It must have been an unpleasant time, with his father's financial distress, his mother's querulousness, and the fact that his former schoolmates were already pursuing their university careers. And yet, as Johnson himself was to acknowledge, it was, educationally, perhaps the most profitable period in his life: "In my early years I read very hard. . . . I knew almost as much at eighteen as I do now [at fifty-four]."[10] He devoured the contents of the bookshop and made himself familiar with the Latin writers of both the classical age and the Renaissance: "I looked into a great many books which were not known at the universities, where they seldom read any books but what are put into their hands by their tutors."[11] It was in the bookshop that Johnson's interest in Renaissance literature was awakened. When he was twelve, looking for a supply of apples hidden by Nathanael, he took down a folio Petrarch from the top shelf, stopped to look into it, and forgot the apples as he pored over "the restorer of poetry." In his early twenties he was boldly to publish proposals for an edition of Politian's Latin poems, together with "a history of Latin poetry from the age of Petrarch to that of Politian, with a life of Politian fuller than in the past."

"What a man reads as a task will do him little good," was Johnson's verdict on formal education and when he finally got to Oxford the experience seems to have done him little good, however much reverence he later expressed for all that Oxford symbolized. On his first day he astonished his tutor by quoting Macrobius (not one of the books normally "put into the hands" of students), soon found the lectures useless, and instead of attending them went sliding on the ice in Christ Church meadows. "The pleasure he took in vexing the tutors and fellows has often been mentioned," his friend Bishop Percy later recorded. "I have heard from some of his contemporaries that he was generally seen lounging at the college gate, with a circle of young students round him, whom he was entertaining with wit and keeping from their studies, if not spiriting them up to rebellion against the College discipline." "Ah, Sir," Johnson said, "I was rude and violent. It was bitterness which they mistook for frolic. I was miserably poor, and I thought to fight my way by my literature and my wit: so I disregarded all power and all authority."[12] For all Johnson's "conservatism"—and one factor in that conservatism may be simply the fact that "liberalism," then as now, was the fashionable and accepted attitude in intellectual circles—the bitterness of the lonely rebel, the outsider, was never far from the surface of any period of his life; and, as with other artists, the alienation accounts for much of the emotional intensity in his writing.

Before London

The seven years between Johnson's leaving Oxford at the end of 1729 and his going to London early in 1737 are obscurely recorded, and the occasional glimpses one catches of him during this time, as he wandered about the Midlands looking for an occupation in which he could make some kind of living by the use of his brains, are on the whole depressing enough. Their combination of unemployment, squalor, and bitterness with intellectual and artistic pride and ambition is reminiscent of young Stephen Dedalus in Dublin. For the first two years Johnson, with reluctance, helped his father in his declining bookseller's business, squabbling with the old man about the degradation of Sam's attending the stall in the marketplace at Uttoxeter (many years later, himself an old man, Johnson did penance for this, standing bareheaded in the rain for an hour, exposing himself to the stares of the passersby).

Life in Lichfield had one compensation, however: as a cathedral town, it made some pretensions to having an intellectual life. One of the leaders of this was Gilbert Walmesley, a successful lawyer who in his youth had lived a busy and fashionable life in Oxford and London and who now held the post of Register of the diocese and occupied the Bishop's Palace. Walmesley "took up" the awkward bookseller's lad, talked literature with him, introduced him to friends who had similar interests, and encouraged him to write. Long afterward Johnson was to pay him public tribute—together with two other clever Lichfield boys whom Walmesley had befriended at the same time:

He was one of the first friends that literature procured me. . . . He was of an advanced age, and I was only not a boy; yet he never received my notions with contempt. . . . I honoured him, and he endured me. . . . At this man's table I enjoyed many cheerful and instructive hours, with companions such as are not often found; with one who has lengthened and one who has gladdened life; with Dr. James, whose skill in physic will be long remembered, and with David Garrick [whose recent death has] eclipsed the gayety of nations and impoverished the public stock of harmless pleasure.[13]

Old Michael Johnson died in great poverty in December 1731, a sad change from the proud sheriff who had "invited all the town now" to celebrate the birth of his son. Mrs. Johnson took over the bookshop and presumably proceeded to run it more efficiently than her husband had: for several decades it was to support her and later her step-granddaughter Lucy Porter (the eldest of Mrs. Samuel Johnson's three children). But one may guess that Samuel was informed that he need not expect it to support him, for soon afterward he was employed as a junior master in Market Bosworth Grammar School in Leicestershire, where he quarreled fiercely with the local tyrant, Sir Wolstan Dixie, at whose house he had to live and to whom he was supposed to act as "a kind of private chaplain." From this "life of complicated misery" Johnson resigned after a few months (he was later to remember Sir Wolstan in his vivid portrait of Squire Bluster in *Rambler* 142). In 1733 he went to Birmingham to live with his former schoolfellow, the surgeon Edmund Hector. He seems to have picked up some money writing for the Birmingham *Journal* (though the issues to which he may have contributed have not survived). Presently Johnson became engaged in what was to be his first published book, a "translation" (it is also a condensation and to some extent a rewriting) of a work of considerable contemporary interest—a version, in French, by the Oratorian Father Joachim Le Grand, of the Portuguese Jesuit Father Jeronymo Lobo's account of his part in the Jesuit missionary expedition to Abyssinia in the early seventeenth century. This incident was one of much historical significance and the source of vigorous politico-religious controversy for decades: half of the book consists of "dissertations" by Le Grand on the matters under dispute.

The neurotic inhibition ("indolence" or "slothfulness" he called it) that was to plague Johnson all his life was already well developed; Hector reported how he had to bring the book to Johnson as he lay groaning in bed in the morning, unable to rise, and take down his words as he persuaded him to dictate his translation. Johnson got five guineas for these labors. During these years there were other unsuccessful attempts to obtain teaching positions. In November 1734 he wrote a letter, under a pseudonym, to Edward Cave, proprietor of the newly established *Gentleman's Magazine* in London, offering his services. Nothing came of it.

In Birmingham, Hector had introduced Johnson to a prosperous woolen draper named Harry Porter. Porter died in September 1734, and the following July Johnson married his widow Elizabeth (whom Johnson, always fond of abbreviating names, referred to as "Tetty"). Many eyebrows have been raised at this marriage. Johnson was twenty-four; Tetty, forty-five. Much later David Garrick described her as "very fat, with a bosom of more than ordinary protuberance, with swelled cheeks, of a florid red, produced by thick painting, and increased by the liberal use of cordials [liquor], flaring and fantastic in her dress, and affected both in her speech and her general behaviour."[14] Garrick used to put on vicious imitations, for the delight of Johnson's friends, of her and Johnson's lovemaking. Perhaps this was the jealousy of a favorite pupil, for, with Tetty's small personal fortune, Johnson opened a boarding school at Edial, near Lichfield, of which young Davy, then eighteen, was one of the handful of inmates. It is true that, in her later life, Mrs. Johnson was in ill health and became addicted to alcohol and opium. But a portrait exists of Elizabeth Jervis as a young woman—a pretty, slender blonde with a vivacious and intelligent face. She seems to have been capable of appreciating Johnson's mind—and of coping with his temper—and Johnson no doubt appreciated a mind that could do so.

To London

The school was a dismal failure. On 2 March 1737 Johnson, without Tetty but with Davy Garrick, set out for London to make his fortune. They shared one horse between them on the hundred-and-twenty-mile trip, alternately "riding and tying," and arrived in London with only a few pence between them. With Johnson's arrival in London, a good deal of the ordinary "biographical" interest in him ceases, at least partly because only scanty materials have been so far discovered. What is known of his life for many years becomes, for the most part, merely the history of his various publications, which are dealt with in more detail in the following chapters. As Boswell, equally unable to find out much about the early years in London, stated, he is to be considered as "tugging at his oar"—and Johnson would not have demurred at the galley-slave metaphor.

Like other ambitious young writers of the time, though Johnson was now not so very young, he had arrived with a manuscript in his pocket: a blank-verse historical tragedy entitled *Irene,* the story of the love of the Sultan Mahomet for a beautiful Christian taken at the capture of Constantinople. Addison's *Cato* had begun the fashion of setting the world on fire with a blank-verse historical tragedy, as young writers from the backwoods would later arrive in Greenwich Village bearing the manuscript of the Great American Novel. Not until twelve years afterwards would *Irene* be produced and published, and then only by courtesy of Davy Garrick, now England's most famous actor and theatrical manager. Meanwhile, Johnson again made contact with Cave and persuaded him to let him try his hand at writing for the *Gentleman's*. Pieces identifiable as Johnson's began to appear in its pages early in 1738: an outrageously flattering Latin poem on Cave himself; short biographies; an allegory based on *Gulliver's Travels*, introducing the magazine's new way of getting around the parliamentary ban on reporting its debates by publishing the "Debates of the Senate of Magna Lilliputia," where Lilliputian statesmen by the names of Walelop and Ptit orated on matters of the day. Johnson is credited with having created this device.

These debates were highly popular. It was a period of frenetic political activity, with Sir Robert Walpole fighting a grim, last-ditch battle against the opposition which was finally to pull him down in 1742; the debates made the fortune of the *Gentleman's*—and of its hated rival and imitator, the *London Magazine,* which had also had the idea of running the parliamentary debates in disguised form. For several years Johnson was in sole charge of writing the debates; indeed, his forceful personality and talent for vivid writing seem to have made him Cave's right-hand man in the conduct of the *Gentleman's Magazine.* He was also engaged in much literary activity outside its pages. His poetic satire *London,* a witty, bitter, fast-moving account of the corruption at the heart of English life (all because of Walpole, naturally), was praised by the acknowledged king of satiric poetry, Alexander Pope. Two vicious anti-Walpolian pamphlets followed, which provoked the government into issuing a warrant for the author's arrest; and Johnson is said to have had to "go underground," hiding for a while in Lambeth under an assumed name.

Part of the bitterness of these early satires may be due to Johnson's resentment at finding himself, with his acute mind and superb learning, condemned at the age of thirty to scratch out a scanty living in the squalor of Grub Street ("SLOW RISES WORTH BY POVERTY DEPRESS'D," he wrote, in capital letters, in *London*). And part of it was surely due to the encouragement of his natural rebelliousness by his friendship with the brilliant, charismatic, half-mad Richard Savage, who, like his junior Johnson, was an erudite, poverty-stricken poet and "injustice collector."[15] There were nights when, without even enough money to buy a bed in the cheapest flophouse, they walked "round Grosvenor Square till four in the morning, dethroning princes, establishing new forms of government, and giving laws to the several states of Europe."[16] Not too long after his arrival in London, having seen what life in Grub Street was like, Johnson seems to have made a last desperate effort to find a teaching position back in the Midlands. When he failed, he returned with Tetty to London and apparently settled down to make the best of things. About the same time, Savage went to Bristol, where he died in a debtor's prison. Johnson presently wrote and published a superb life of his friend; and, in the brilliant psychologizing he put into it, he may have purged some of his own bitterness toward life.

After Walpole's disappearance from the political scene in 1742, interest in parliamentary debates languished, and the magazines discontinued reporting them. Johnson then engaged in other cooperative projects by writing biographical articles on great medical figures of the past, one of which he expanded for his friend Dr. Robert James's vast *Medicinal Dictionary*, and by helping to prepare the monumental catalog of the great Harleian Library and the eight-volume collection of early political and religious controversial pamphlets selected from it, the famous *Harleian Miscellany*. But soon a pattern begins to be detected in his plans for writing—an ambitious pattern to make himself the authoritative critic of English language and literature of his generation. "Always fly at the eagle," he once counseled young Fanny Burney, who had just published her first novel and was timorous about standing up to the great Mrs. Montagu, "Queen of the Bluestockings," at a reception.[17] Johnson's first flight at the eagle was to issue proposals in 1745, together with a specimen of his criticism of *Macbeth*, for a new edition of Shakespeare's plays, although an edition by Sir Thomas Hanmer, speaker of the House of Commons under Queen Anne, had appeared the previous year and, not long before that, one edited by Pope himself.

The Shakespeare edition proved abortive: Johnson was not to fulfill this particular ambition for another twenty years. Its place was taken by an even more formidable project, a *Dictionary of the English Language*. The plan for it, published in 1747, was addressed to the earl of Chesterfield, Secretary of State, and head of "the Establishment" in arts and letters. Chesterfield, who sent the unknown hack ten pounds and forgot about him, was to be punished for his neglect eight years later, when Johnson wrote his famous letter of reproach. What Johnson planned (and what he achieved) he accurately described in the opening sentence of his preface to his later abridgment of it: "Having been long employed in the study and cultivation of the English language, I lately published a dictionary like those compiled by the academies of Italy and France, for the use of such as aspire to exactness of criticism or elegance of style." It had taken forty French academicians (under governmental sponsorship) forty years to compile the definitive modern dictionary of the French language, Johnson later remarked, only half-humorously—it took him, a single private Englishman, only seven years to do the same, for such was the superiority of English free enterprise to French collectivism. To be sure, Johnson was loyally supported by the syndicate of London publishers who advanced him a total of fifteen hundred guineas and by his gallant band of six amanuenses (five of them Scottish, Boswell gleefully pointed out) who slaved away with him those seven years in the garret of the house in Gough Square. The work remains a landmark in the serious modern study of the English language.

While it was being composed, Johnson also found time to issue, each Tuesday and Saturday for two years (1750–52), the great series of periodical essays which he modestly called *The Rambler*. Their sale in London was not great, only about five hundred copies of each issue, far less than the spectacular sales of Addison and Steele's *Spectator* forty years before. Yet everyone seems to have read them. It has recently been pointed out that they were very widely reprinted as they were issued (without permission, in those days of loose copyright laws) in magazines and newspapers, provincial as well as metropolitan; and they were immediately reprinted in collected form. "The Author of the Rambler" became Johnson's usual designation. *The Idler*—lighter, more amusing, more easily read, but more easily forgotten—followed in 1758–60. Immediately after the publication of the *Dictionary* in 1755—and the world-famous snub to Chesterfield, who, hearing that the work was likely to succeed, had hastened to get on the Johnsonian bandwagon—Johnson published a new set of proposals for an edition of Shakespeare. Circumstances, however, prevented its publication for another decade.

The Pension

The most important of these circumstances was the award to Johnson in 1762 of an annual pension of three hundred pounds (equivalent today to perhaps fifteen thousand dollars) from the "secret-service fund" of the government. Perhaps no grant from a government to a literary man has ever caused such a furor. The official theory was that it had nothing to do with political services, past or future, that it was a token of the disinterested desire of the enlightened new regime of young King George III and his prime Minister Lord Bute—by contrast with the materialism, cynicism, and corruption of the Walpolian and post-Walpolian Whig ministries of old George II—to encourage the arts and assist a most distinguished and deserving ornament of British letters who was in financial need. Certainly, the *English Dictionary* was a worthy object of national pride, and Johnson was certainly in need. On the other hand, he was the worst possible object for an allegedly nonpolitical award, for he had long been stridently political in his public utterances, from the 1739 pamphlets that almost caused him to be arrested for sedition to the *Dictionary* itself, where, glancing at the alleged practices of the Walpolians, he had defined *pensioner* as "a slave of state hired by a stipend to obey his master."

The complete "inside story" of the award of Johnson's pension will probably never come to light. It is apparent that he did have many connections with political figures and participated in many political activities during the 1750s and 1760s, although little is known of the details. For instance, a short series of letters in 1766 shows him preparing to use his pen in connection with the then very controversial issue of the conduct of the East India Company, but what happened as a result of this involvement one has no idea. A correspondence that exists between Johnson and Charles Jenkinson, one of Bute's closest supporters, seems to show Jenkinson hinting strongly that Johnson ought to help earn his pension by aiding Jenkinson write a pamphlet on the controversial Peace of Paris, just concluded; but Johnson, with massive politeness, refused. On the other hand, in 1756, as editor of the short-lived *Literary Magazine*, and later, in the *Universal Chronicle*, Johnson had published an amazingly violent series of "pacifist" articles against the Seven Years' War, conducted by Walpole's political heir, the duke of Newcastle, and William Pitt, one of Bute's worst enemies, for the aggrandizement of the young British Empire. These attacks would have been remembered with gratitude by Bute and Jenkinson as they sought to bring that war to a close. Moreover, Johnson's four political pamphlets of the 1770s supported, without deviation, the political line of the governments that paid his pension— two, indeed, were "touched up" at the printer's by government officials (to Johnson's great disgust, for the effect of the changes was to soften the violence of his attack). It is hard, however, to believe that he was meekly writing what authority told him to write—as his political opponents naturally charged him with doing.

At any rate, the pension gave him, for the first time in his life, financial security and with it, as has been suggested, the cessation of the motive to write that had kept him so active—and relatively mentally healthy—during the past two decades. With his leisure came the onset of a pathologically severe mental depression. In the midst of it he turned to a new friend, the intelligent, vivacious, and sociable Hester Thrale, the charming young wife of the pompous and wealthy Henry, with whom she was not at all in love, although she bore him twelve children in the quickest possible succession while Henry amused himself with outside interests, contracting venereal disease from time to time in the process. It was perhaps natural that two individuals who both nursed feelings of rejection, together with a deservedly high estimate of their own abilities, should be drawn together. Besides that, Johnson was flattered at being fussed over by an attractive young woman; and Mrs. Thrale was triumphant at having captured the greatest lion of them all from a pack of competing bluestockings.

Shortly after they became acquainted, Johnson's neurosis seems to have developed into a thoroughgoing classic case of masochism, straight out of Krafft-Ebing, complete with suggestions of chains, padlocks, and whippings. Mrs. Thrale apparently nursed him through it with the utmost tact and good sense.[18] The intense tenderness of Johnson's many letters to her seems to indicate that he felt something very close to love for her; so too does the hysterical vindictiveness of the letter he wrote her when, after Henry Thrale had fallen victim to his gluttony, she announced her intention to wed the Italian musician Gabriel Piozzi, with whom she had fallen deeply in love and later made a happy marriage. Her spirited reply—she had learned from Johnson the art of writing memorable letters—and Johnson's dignified apology made a sad termination to this long friendship—or to something deeper than friendship. True, Mrs. Thrale, still a vigorous woman of forty and able for the first time in her life to indulge her capacity for normal sexual love, now had eyes only for Piozzi and had grown somewhat tired of Johnston's irritating habits and patronizing ways. Still, those who have come to care for Johnson may on the whole feel grateful to the woman who helped to give the last twenty years of his tumultuous emotional life some happy affection.

In Society

About the time Johnson got his pension, he apparently decided to give freer rein to his great capacity for human friendship and social intercourse than had been possible during the slavery of journalism and dictionary-making. To be sure, he had always relished society, as his tribute to Walmesley's "hospitable table" shows. An old associate of his in the early days on the *Gentleman's Magazine*, John Hawkins—whose own delightful and useful earlier *Life of Johnson* Boswell's animus has prevented too many people from reading—tells something of the conviviality among the young writers for the *Magazine* in the 1740s: the virtuous and erudite Elizabeth Carter ("who could make a pudding as well as translate Epictetus," Johnson once grumbled to Mrs. Thrale, who could only translate Epictetus, or at any rate Boethius); the lady novelist and translator, Charlotte Ramsay Lennox, of obscure American origin; the industrious Jacobite William Guthrie, who taught Johnson how to report parliamentary debates; John Hawkesworth, whom Johnson in turn taught; and Tom Birch, "brisk as a bee in conversation; but no sooner does he take a pen in hand than it becomes a torpedo to him, and benumbs all his faculties." Hawkins's account of Johnson's party to celebrate the publication of Mrs. Lennox's novel *Harriot Stuart* is as good as anything recorded by Boswell:

The place appointed was the Devil tavern. . . . Our supper was elegant, and Johnson had directed that a magnificent hot apple-pye should make a part of it, and this he would have stuck with bay-leaves, because, forsooth, Mrs. Lennox was an authoress, and had written verses; and further, he had prepared for her a crown of laurel, with which, but not till he had invoked the muses by some ceremonies of his own invention, he encircled her brows. . . . About five Johnson's face shone with meridian splendour, though his drink had been only lemonade; but the far greater part of us had deserted the colours of Bacchus, and were with difficulty rallied to partake of a second refreshment of coffee, which was scarcely ended when the day began to dawn.[19]

Much less is known about this earlier coterie than about the famous Club (the second of the three that Johnson helped to found) of Johnson's years of fame, which included Reynolds, Burke, Gibbon, and Goldsmith, whose conversations Boswell so brilliantly recorded. But Birch, Guthrie, Mrs. Carter, and the others were by no means contemptible writers, and it is a pity no more is recorded about Johnson's relations with them in his younger, formative years.

In his later life Johnson sought human society for the sake of his own mental health, as the schizophrenic astronomer in *Rasselas* is advised to do (he takes the advice and returns to normality) and as Johnson advises Boswell and his other correspondents to do ("Keep your friendships in repair"). He began to travel a great deal: to Scotland with Boswell, to Wales and France with the Thrales, to Northamptonshire to help Percy put his *Reliques* into shape for the press, to Portsmouth to spend a week on board a ship of the Royal Navy, to Lincolnshire to visit the Langtons, to Brighton to swim in the ocean, and many times to Oxford, Lichfield, and Derbyshire to see old friends. He had a room reserved for him at the Thrales' country home at Streatham and spent weeks at a time there. His friends suggested that this peripeteia was partly due to his desire to escape the squabbling of the queer assortment of inmates of his own home: Mrs. Desmoulins and blind Miss Williams, relics of the time when Tetty was alive; the ambiguous Poll Carmichael; old Dr. Levet, the unlicensed practitioner of medicine among the slum inhabitants of London; and Frank Barber, the Negro whom Dr.

Richard Bathurst had brought as a boy from slavery in Jamaica, and to whom Johnson tried to teach Latin—as a result of which Frank ran away to sea, and had to be brought back (through the help of John Wilkes, of all people)—and to whom he willed the residue of his estate, as though to an adopted son.

But there was more than Christian charity in Johnson's providing a home for these waifs, for Herman Liebert is undoubtedly right in suggesting that Johnson was sometimes glad to escape from the elegant periods of Gibbon and Burke and return to them: "Neither from such relations [as those with Burke and Reynolds], nor from the sly satisfaction he took in playing 'Dr. Johnson' could he draw the deeper strength he needed most. This he could only gain, Antaeus-like, in the world from which he sprang."[20] Another notable class of his friendships consisted in the fatherly ones he cultivated with younger men: he sometimes took part in a nocturnal "frisk" with the fashionable Beauclerk and the scholarly Langton, then just down from Oxford—"I love the acquaintance of young people. . . . Young men have more virtue than old men; they have more generous sentiments in every respect. I love the young dogs of this age."[21] And Johnson tried to supervise the education, moral and emotional as well as intellectual, of young George Strahan and especially young James Boswell, who needed a father even more than Johnson needed a son.

The Last Years

The last years of Johnson's life were complicated with disease, the loss of old friends, and depression; his letters and diary entries up to the spring of 1784 make gloomy reading. In February of that year, however, an incident took place that seemed to him of great importance and that caused his last months to take on something approaching such an unknown serenity of mind that not even Mrs. Thrale's defection disturbed it for too long. He referred to this event in the prayer he composed for his last Communion, eight days before his death, as his "late conversion." The story is recorded in full detail by Sir John Hawkins, like Johnson a serious Christian and Anglican. Hawkins was summoned to Johnson's home on Thursday, 19 February, and found him in great perturbation of spirit:"With a look that cut me to the heart, [he] told me that he had the prospect of death before him, and that he dreaded to meet his Saviour. 'Every man knows his own sins . . . and also what grace he has resisted. . . . Shall I, who have been a teacher of others, myself be a castaway?'" When Hawkins tried to comfort Johnson with "the services he had rendered to the cause of religion and virtue, as well by his example as his writings," he was not at all comforted—nor should he have been; for as a devout adherent to the Augustinian Christianity taught by the Book of Common Prayer, he could have had no belief in the doctrine that any man's works in themselves can contribute to the salvation of his soul.

On the following Saturday Hawkins called again, and "upon entering the room, observed in his countenance such a serenity as indicated that some remarkable crisis of his disorder had produced a change in his feelings." Johnson joyfully reported that during his devotions the previous day the dropsical condition from which he had suffered had spontaneously relieved itself. "It is wonderful, very wonderful!" cried Johnson. He and Hawkins agreed in thinking that this might be taken as a sign "that he had not in vain humbled himself before his Maker," a token of divine assurance that Johnson's sincere contrition and faith were acceptable. Boswell too agreed when he arrived from Scotland a few months afterward and Johnson eagerly told him what had happened.[22]

From this time on, Johnson's letters and prayers, despite occasional backslidings into melancholy, indicate a calm of mind previously absent. In a prayer on 5 September 1784 he thanked God for "the awakening of my mind"; and on his seventy-fifth birthday, 18 September he acknowledged "the great mercies of the last year." In the most solemn prayer he composed for his last Communion he asked God to "forgive and accept my late conversion," but the phrase was deleted from the version published by the Reverend George Strahan, who had administered the Communion, and later by Boswell in his *Life*, although Hawkins printed it in full. After some harrowing days (on one of which Johnson, thinking that his physicians had not lanced his dropsical tissues deeply enough, stabbed himself with a pair of scissors), he died. "I will not capitulate, I will be conquered," he had said. He was buried in Westminster Abbey, in the "Poets' Corner" near the foot of Shakespeare's monument. His old school friend, John Taylor, read the burial service, and the pallbearers included Edmund Burke, Bennet Langton, and other old friends and distinguished men of the era.

A Note on Johnson's Letters

No one should neglect Johnson's letters, which tell a great deal about him. Not that he went along with Pope's theory that people were more sincere in letters than in other forms of communication; indeed, he makes devastating fun of that theory in a letter to Mrs. Thrale:

In a man's letters, you know, Madam, his soul lies naked, his letters are only the mirror of his heart, whatever passes within him is now undisguised in its natural process. Nothing is inverted, nothing distorted. . . . Is not my soul laid open in these veracious pages? do you not see me reduced to my first principles?[23]

This deflation of cant could worthily be placed beside his reply to Goldsmith's complaint that he and his friends had traveled over one another's minds: "You have not travelled over my mind, I promise you," Johnson growled. All the same, one does learn a great deal about the fascinating variety of Johnson's interests, friends, and versatility of prose style by thumbing through the fine three-volume edition of his letters by R. W. Chapman.

Johnson's letters have been somewhat unjustly disparaged by critics, in favor of the great "self-conscious" letter writers of the century, Horace Walpole, Lord Chesterfield, Thomas Gray. Johnson's letters may be defended in the words Lady Louisa Stuart uses to defend those of her grandmother Lady Mary Wortley Montagu: "Lady Mary wrote admirable letters; *letters*—not dissertations, nor sentimental effusions, nor strings of witticisms, but real letters, such as any person of plain sense would be glad to receive."[24] Not that all of Johnson's were calculated to gladden their recipients. It must have been a traumatic experience to find on one's breakfast table such a bombshell as his famous letter to Chesterfield, which Thomas Carlyle called "the death-knell of patronage":

My Lord,
    I have been lately informed, by the proprietor of The World, that two papers, in which my Dictionary is recommended to the public, were written by your Lordship. To be so distinguished is an honour which, being very little accustomed to favours from the great, I know not well how to receive, or in what terms to acknowledge. . . . Seven years, my Lord, have now passed since I waited in your outward rooms, or was repulsed from your door; during which time I have been pushing on my work through difficulties of which it is useless to complain, and have brought it at last to the verge of completion without one act of assistance, one word of encouragement, or one smile of favour. Such treatment I did not expect, for I never had a Patron before. . . . Is not a Patron, my Lord, one who looks with unconcern on a man struggling for life in the water, and, when he has reached ground, encumbers him with help?[25]

Or there is the letter to James Macpherson, who had been uttering vague threats of violence because Johnson refused to believe his "Ossian" poems were genuine:

Mr. James Macpherson—

I received your foolish and impudent note. Whatever insult is offered me I will do my best to repel, and what I cannot do for myself the law will do for me. I will not desist from detecting what I think a cheat, from any fear of the menaces of a ruffian,

or the terrible one to Mrs. Thrale, when she announced her marriage to Piozzi:

Madam,

If I interpret your letter right, you are ignominiously married. If it is yet undone, let us once talk together. If you have abandoned your children and your religion, God forgive your wickedness; if you have forfeited your fame and your country, may your folly do no further mischief. . . .

At the other end of the scale are the charming and whimsical letters to "Queeney," the Thrales' eldest daughter:

Dear Sweeting,

Your pretty letter was too short. . . . I am glad to hear of the improvement and prosperity of my hen. Miss Porter has buried her fine black cat. So things come and go. Generations, as Homer says, are but like leaves; and you now see the faded leaves falling about you.

So too to Frank Barber, away at school:

Dear Francis,

I am at last sat down to write to you, and should very much blame myself for having neglected you so long. . . . Let me know what English books you read for your entertainment. You can never be wise unless you love reading. Do not imagine that I shall forget or forsake you, for if when I examine you, I find that you have not lost your time, you shall want no encouragement from

Yours affectionately
Sam: Johnson

and to Lucy Porter:

You frighted me, you little Gipsy, with your black wafer, for I had forgot you were in mourning [for an uncle] and was afraid your letter had brought me ill news of my mother. . . . Your poor Mamma is come home but very weak, yet I hope she will grow better, else she shall go into the country. She is now upstairs and knows not of my writing.

Johnson could write with the most intense and tender feeling, as to his mother on her deathbed, or to Hill Boothby, a pious and learned young lady with whom he was more than a little in love; it seems possible that, after Tetty's death, he may have wanted to marry her, but she was dying:

It is again midnight, and I am again alone. With what meditation shall I amuse this waste hour of darkness and vacuity? If I turn my thoughts upon myself, what do I perceive but a poor helpless being reduced by a blast of wind to weakness and misery? . . . Continue, my Dearest, your prayers for me, that no good resolution may be vain. You think, I believe, better of me than I deserve. I hope to be in time what I wish to be,

and later,

I beg of you to endeavour to live. I have returned your [William] Law, which however I earnestly entreat you to give me. I am in great trouble; if you can write three words to me, be pleased to do it. I am afraid to say much, and cannot say nothing when my dearest is in danger.
The All-merciful God have mercy on you.

He could write pompously to the dignified Mrs. Montagu:

Madam,
Goodness so conspicuous as yours will be often solicited and perhaps sometimes solicited by those who have little pretension to your favour. . . .

and to his friend Baretti sometimes intimately:

Last winter I went down to my native town, where I found the streets much narrower and shorter than I thought I had left them, inhabited by a new race of people, to whom I was very little known. My play-fellows were grown old, and forced me to suspect that I was no longer young. . . . My daughter-in-law [Lucy Porter], from whom I expected most, . . . has lost the beauty and gaiety of youth, without having gained much of the wisdom of age. I wandered about for five days, and took the first convenient opportunity of returning to a place [London], where, if there is not much happiness, there is at least such a diversity of good and evil that slight vexations do not fix upon the heart. . . .

and sometimes with vivid sententiousness:

I will not trouble you with speculations about peace and war. The good or ill success of battles and embassies extends itself to a very small part of domestic life: we all have good and evil which we feel more sensibly than our petty part of public miscarriage or prosperity.

Johnson took delight in abrupt and striking openings for his letters:

I received in the morning your magnificent Fish, and in the afternoon your apology for not sending it.

Sweet meat and sour sauce.—With your letter, which was kind, I received another from Miss [Langton], to let me know with what *frigidity* I have answered her.

I did not expect to hear that it could be, in an assembly convened for the propagation of Christian knowledge, a question whether any nation uninstructed in religion should receive instruction. . . .

and in ingenious closings:

I have been long wakened from that dream of hope, in which I once boasted myself with so much exultation, My Lord,
                              Your Lordship's Most Humble, Most Obedient servant.

I have now the full effect of your care, and benevolence, and am far from thinking it a slight honour or a small advantage, since it will put the enjoyment of your conversation more frequently in the power of, Dear Sir,
                              Your most obliged and affectionate.

If you cannot think I am good, pray think I am mending, and that in time I may deserve to be, Dear Madam,
                              Your most obedient and most humble servant.

Among the most important of the more or less continuous correspondences are those with his old school friend, the Reverend John Taylor, to whom he gives good advice about his relations with his powerful patrons, the family of the duke of Devonshire, and about his matrimonial troubles, and those with his young friends Bennet Langton and George Strahan, whose careers at school and university he follows closely and to whom he constantly sends good, and sometimes sharp, advice about their studies, morals, and mental health. The chief recipient of such advice was, of course, the unsatisfactory James Boswell. Johnson, who never wastes tact on the young Scot, uses his heaviest bludgeon in an effort to try to break through Boswell's thick wall of egocentricity. "You are not to think yourself forgotten or criminally neglected that you have had yet no letter from me," his first communication begins, in a no–nonsense fashion.

There lurks, perhaps, in every human heart a desire of distinction, which inclines every man first to hope, and then to believe, that Nature has given him something peculiar to himself [too true of Boswell].

As to your History of Corsica, you have no materials which others have not, or may not have. You have, somehow or other, warmed your imagination. . . . Mind your own affairs, and leave the Corsicans to theirs.

I have omitted a long time to write to you, without knowing very well why. I could now tell you why I should not write, for who would write to men who publish the letters of their friends without their leave [as Boswell had done with Johnson's]?

I write . . . lest in some of your freaks and humours you should fancy yourself neglected.

You are always complaining of melancholy, and I conclude from those complaints that you are fond of it. No man talks of that which he is desirous to conceal.

I hope you had got rid of all this hypocrisy of misery. What have you to do with Liberty and Necessity? Or what more than to hold your tongue about it?

The last letter continues, as so many do, in a vein of kindness: "Do not doubt but I shall be most heartily glad to see you here again, for I love every part about you but your affectation of distress. . . . Come to me, my dear Bozzy, and let us be as happy as we can. We will go again to the Mitre, and talk old times over." If any psychotherapist had been able to rescue Boswell from the mental torture he caused himself and those around him it would have been Johnson, who in these letters certainly tries his best.

But the preeminent correspondence is, of course, with Mrs. Thrale— charming, tender, concerned, wise, and—no doubt to the surprise of those who know only the Johnson of legend—gay. Johnson relaxes with her and indulges his capacity for sheer fun; they have a stock of private jokes, about John Taylor's pride in his prize bull and Mrs. Thrale's alleged unwillingness to provide Johnson with enough strawberries and cream in season; Johnson displays talent for parodying the kind of pomposity he himself has been accused of:

Wisely was it said by him who said it first, that this world is all ups and downs.

This little Dog [Johnson] does nothing, but I hope he will mend; he is now reading Jack the Giant Killer. Perhaps so noble a narrative may rouse in him the soul of enterprise.

Last Saturday I came to Ashbourn; the dangers or the pleasures of the journey I have at present no disposition to recount. Else might I paint the beauties of my native plain, might I tell of "the smile of Nature and the charms of Art," else might I relate how I crossed the Staffordshire Canal, one of the great efforts of human labour and human contrivance, which from the bridge on which I viewed it, passes away on either side, and loses itself in distant regions, uniting waters that Nature had divided, and dividing lands which Nature had united. I might tell how these reflections fermented in my mind till the chaise stopped at Ashbourne, at Ashbourne in the Peak. Let not the barren name of the Peak terrify you; I have never wanted strawberries and cream. The great Bull has no disease but age. I hope in time to be like the great Bull.

The inequalities of human life have always employed the meditation of deep thinkers, and I cannot forbear to reflect on the difference between your condition and my own. You live upon mock turtle and stewed rumps of beef; I dined yesterday upon crumpets. . . .

On Saturday I shewed myself again to the living world at the Exhibition; much and splendid was the company: but like the Doge of Genoa at Paris, I admired nothing but myself.

I went, as I took care to boast, on Tuesday, to the Club, and hear that I was thought to have performed as well as usual.

Mrs. Thrale writes to him in the same spirit. The correspondence gives a lively and valuable picture of English life at the time, together with much wise observation by Johnson on the basic problems of life—and much fun, for all its somber conclusion when Mrs. Thrale married Piozzi. It continues for twenty years, comprises five hundred letters, and deserves to be separately published.

Chapter Two
The Poet

The great English critics have often been great poets—Sidney, Ben Jonson, Dryden, Coleridge, Wordsworth, Shelley, Arnold, Eliot. Johnson is no exception. This statement would have surprised Arnold's generation. But it would not have surprised Johnson's own, which carved the word "POETA" on his statue in St. Paul's Cathedral. Nor does it surprise those modern critics who have freed themselves from the limitations of a narrowly romantic conception of poetry and are able once more to appreciate the poetic merit of the tradition in which Johnson wrote, the tradition of Dryden and Pope. "Of the strength of Johnson's imagination," Bertrand Bronson writes in his fine essay *Johnson Agonistes*,

all that need be said at present is that it was no faculty of a "harmless drudge," but the boiling, turbulent imagination of a poet capable of fine frenzy. All Johnson's most characteristic utterances, oral or written, display this fundamentally imaginative quality, this need for *poiesis*, seeking always the vivid metaphor or simile, the telling word. . . . In the deepest sense of the word—in his imaginative apprehension of the quality and texture of experience, in his dynamic attitude to life and its values, in his need of the shaping expression of his perceptions—he was a poet, a *maker.*[1]

But the classic study is by T. S. Eliot, who uses Johnson's poetry as the starting point to demolish Arnold's theory of an opposition between good poetry and good prose. This theory can be traced back at least to Joseph Warton's *Essay on Pope*, of which Johnson wrote a somewhat patronizing review. As Eliot puts it,

certain qualities are to be expected of any type of good verse at any time; we may say the qualities which good verse shares with good prose. Hardly any good poet in English has written *bad* prose; and some English poets have been among the greatest of English prose writers. The finest prose writer of Shakespeare's time was, I think, Shakespeare himself. . . . This is not a sign of versatility but of unity. Of Goldsmith and Johnson [as of Donne, Dryden, and Pope] we can say . . . their verse is poetry partly because it has the virtues of good prose.[2]

Eliot then praises the "precision" of Johnson's poetry; "the certainty, the ease with which he hits the bull's-eye every time"; and, with an echo of Johnson's own retort to Warton—"It is surely superfluous to answer the question that has once been asked, Whether Pope was a poet? otherwise than by asking, in return, If Pope be not a poet, where is poetry to be found?"[3]—Eliot concludes, "If lines 189–220 of *The Vanity of Human Wishes* [the passage about Charles XII] are not poetry, then I do not know what is."

Criteria of Excellence in Poetry

It will help to see the merits of Johnson's poetry if one glances briefly at some of his own criteria of excellence in poetry. Johnson would have concurred with Mallarmé (and Eliot) that poetry is made up not of "ideas" but of words, and that the poet's task is the skilled handling of words so as to produce vivid emotional effects in the reader. The great enemy of achieving those effects is the cliché, the literary reminiscence. "No man ever yet became great by imitation,"[4] Johnson set down in print on two separate occasions; he would have sympathized with Eliot's complaint how "the moment his attention is relaxed, or his mind fatigued"[5] the writer's ear fails to shut out the host of echoes from earlier writing that continually beats upon it.

Johnson agrees with Donne, Dryden, and Pope before him, and Wordsworth and Eliot after him, that poetry must be made out of *contemporary* language, because only through it is firsthand, direct contact with what the poet wants to communicate about things of *current* concern made possible. Like Wordsworth and Eliot, Johnson is deeply hostile to "artificial" language, to linguistic gimmicks—archaisms, inversions, "traditional imagery, hereditary similes" (Johnson's expressions)—that any pedant can quickly learn to use and put together into what *looks* like a poem. But such a work provides the reader, not with the vivid communication of present experience, but only with a woolly pleasure at vaguely recognizing something he has met before and knows is approved. Johnson dismisses most of Thomas Gray (not too unjustly) with "Gray thought his language more poetical as it was more remote from common use."[6] He is suspicious of Milton's peculiar language: although (like Eliot) he recognizes that behind it there is great and genuine poetic merit, he feels that Milton sets a very bad example; and, when one has struggled through some of the mass of pseudo-Miltonic blank verse that infested the eighteenth and nineteenth centuries, churned out by bright young writers who discovered that any literate person could easily produce line after line of unrhymed iambic pentameter and invert the normal order of the English sentence, one sympathizes with him.

The point is made clear by Johnson's numerous parodies of the gimmicks that were becoming popular in his later life. For example, Johnson's friend Thomas Percy had discovered the fine old English ballads; that Johnson did not despise them is evident from the fact that he spent two months in Percy's home helping to prepare the *Reliques* for the press and writing the dedication of the book. But when Percy, who had little poetic ability himself but saw that a "ballad" looked easy to write, began publishing ballads of his own composition, this was too much for Johnson; and he made exquisite fun of Percy (and Thomas Warton, another academic ballad- and sonnet-monger) with parodies that are much more memorable than the efforts they parody:

> I put my hat upon my head,
>   And walked into the Strand,
> And there I met another man
>   Whose hat was in his hand.

> Hermit hoar, in solemn cell,
>   Wearing out life's evening gray,
> Smite thy bosom, sage, and tell,
>   Where is bliss? and which the way?

> Thus I spoke; and speaking sigh'd,
>   Scarce repress'd the starting tear;
> When the smiling sage replied,
>   "Come, my lad, and drink some beer."[7]

Johnson's view of what the language of poetry should be is well illustrated by comparing his own serious translation of a chorus from Euripides' *Medea* (concerning traditional feasting) with his burlesque of how it would be done by one Robert Potter, who had been inspired by the "gimmickism" of Warton and Gray. The parody begins

> Err shall they not who resolute explore
>   Time's gloomy backward with judicious eyes;
> And scanning right the practices of yore
>   Shall deem our hoar progenitors unwise.

"Backward run the sentences till reels the mind," as used to be said of *Timestyle*. Johnson's own translation is not the greatest of poetry, but at least it is English:

> The rites derived from ancient days
> With thoughtless reverence we praise,
> The rites that taught us to combine
> The joys of music and of wine. . . .

Or, as Johnson summed up the situation in 1777,

> Wheresoe'er I turn my view,
> All is strange, yet nothing new;
> Endless labour all along,
> Endless labour to be wrong;
> Phrase that time has flung away,
> Uncouth words in disarray,
> Trick'd in antique ruff and bonnet,
> Ode and elegy and sonnet.

His "strange" dislike of Milton's *Lycidas*—"It is not to be considered as the effusion of real passion; for passion runs not after remote allusions and obscure opinions"[8]—becomes more comprehensible when one reads Johnson's own elegy on a dead friend, the humble "Doctor" Levet who practiced among the slum dwellers of London:

> Condemn'd to Hope's delusive mine,
>   As on we toil from day to day,
> By sudden blast, or slow decline,
>   Our social comforts drop away.

> Well tried through many a varying year,
>   See Levet to the grave descend,
> Officious, innocent, sincere,
>   Of every friendless name the friend.

> Yet still he fills Affection's eye,
>   Obscurely wise, and coarsely kind,
> Nor, letter'd Arrogance, deny
>   Thy praise to merit unrefin'd.

> When fainting Nature call'd for aid,
>   And hovering death prepared the blow,
> His vigorous remedy displayed
>   The power of art without the show.

In Misery's darkest caverns known
　　His useful care was ever nigh,
Where hopeless Anguish poured his groan,
　　And lonely Want retired to die.

No summons mock'd by chill delay,
　　No petty gain disdained by Pride,
The modest wants of every day
　　The toil of every day supplied.

His virtues walked their narrow round,
　　Nor made a pause, nor left a void;
And sure th' eternal Master found
　　The single talent well employed.

The busy day, the peaceful night,
　　Unfelt, uncounted, glided by;
His frame was firm, his powers were bright,
　　Though now his eightieth year was nigh.

Then, with no fiery throbbing pain,
　　No cold gradations of decay,
Death broke at once the vital chain
　　And freed his soul the nearest way.

This lacks the lushness of Milton's great poem; but after one has read it one has a much more vivid picture of Robert Levet than one ever gets of Edward King in *Lycidas*; and it could be maintained that this should be the first duty of an ostensibly commemorative poem. Not that Johnson's elegy—any more than *Lycidas*, or any other really good poem—is *easy* to read properly. To get its full effect one should be aware of such things as (1) the persistent image of the prisoner in the mine (criminals were actually so condemned on the Continent in Johnson's day) which appears not only in the opening stanza but also in the fifth ("Misery's darkest caverns") and the last ("Death broke at last the vital chain / And freed his soul the nearest way"); (2) the necessity of fully realizing—concretizing, visualizing—the personification, so important a form of imagery in eighteenth-century poetry;[9] (3) the precise meanings of words—"officious," for instance, means "full of good offices"; (4) such subtleties as, in the seventh stanza, the allusion to the technical expression of a physician "walking the rounds" of his patients. One should also sense, throughout the poem, that it is more than merely a lament of the passing of a friend: it is a comment on the whole human situation. Like so much of Johnson's writing, this poem is a fierce protest against the inhumanity of man to man, and it expresses the feeling that made him exempt from his general condemnation of Gray the *Elegy in a Country Churchyard*.

Also with Wordsworth and Eliot, Johnson believed that "the music of harmonious metrical language, the sense of difficulty overcome,"[10] is an indistinguishable part of "the complex feeling of delight" of poetry; that is, what the poet has to say should be said within the framework of a regular verse pattern. Like other critics after him, Johnson was properly suspicious of the seeming ease with which any one could ramble on in the blank verse authorized by Milton's example. "Blank verse left merely to its numbers," he remarked, "has little operation either on the ear or mind: it can hardly support itself without bold figures and striking images. A poem frigidly didactic without rhyme is so near to prose that the reader only scorns it for pretending to be verse."[11] Milton, with his "subjects of inconceivable grandeur" and sublimity of imagery, could handle it, and so could James Thomson and Edward Young. But, for most writers, "the shackles and circumspection of rhyme" were necessary; the metrical pattern of the ordinary English iambic line "strikes the ear so faintly that it is easily lost" unless the lines are kept distinct by "the artifice of rhyme."

Johnson's Lighter Verse

So Johnson concludes that distinguishable verse forms are needed, and it is interesting to note how much more successfully he handles stanzaic patterns, like that of the poem to Levet, than he does the conspicuously unhappy blank verse of *Irene*. It might be argued that, for all Johnson's appreciation of the virtues of the standard verse of his day, the heroic couplet, he was really more at home in shorter lines and longer verse-units than the couplet. There is an ease and competence about some of his "lighter" verse, where he felt free to use such forms that are missing in the usually excellent but sometimes labored couplets of *London* and *The Vanity of Human Wishes*, successful as those poems are. Such poems as the epitaph on Hogarth are very fine—

> The hand of him here torpid lies
> That drew th' essential form of grace;
> Here closed in death th'attentive eyes
> That saw the manners in the face—

and the epigram translated from Benserade—

> In bed we laugh, in bed we cry,
> And, born in bed, in bed we die.
> The near approach a bed may show
> Of human bliss to human woe—

or the impromptus to Queeney Thrale, on buying a new gown—

> Wear the gown and wear the hat,
>   Snatch thy pleasures while they last;
> Hadst thou nine lives like a cat,
>   Soon those nine lives would be past—

and to her mother, on her birthday—

> Oft in danger, yet alive,
> We are come to Thirty-five;
> Long may better years arrive,
> Better years than Thirty-five;
> Could philosophers contrive
> Life to stop at Thirty-five,
> Time his hours should never drive
> O'er the bounds of Thirty-five.
> . . . .
> For howe'er we boast and strive,
> Life declines from Thirty-five.

In the same vein is the recently discovered "An Extemporary Elegy," made half as a joke with Mrs. Thrale and Fanny Burney, yet surprisingly poignant as well as sardonic:

> Here's a woman of the town,
>   Lies as dead as any nail!
> She was once of high renown—
>   And so here begins my tale.
>
> She was once as cherry plump,
>   Red her cheek as Cath'rine pear,
> Toss'd her nose, and shook her rump,
>   Till she made the neighbours stare.

> But there came a country 'squire,
>   He was a seducing pug!
> Took her from her friends and sire,
>   To his own house her did lug.
>
> There she soon became a jilt,
>   Rambling often to and fro';
> All her life was naught but guilt,
>   Till purse and carcase both were low.
>
> Black her eye with many a blow,
>   Hot her breath with many a dram,
> Now she lies exceeding low,
>   And as quiet as a lamb.[12]

Johnson's best-known and most successful effort in this idiom, one almost peculiar to himself, is the set of verses he tossed off on the coming-of-age of Mrs. Thrale's scapegrace nephew:

> Long-expected one and twenty,
>   Ling'ring year, at last is flown;
> Pomp and pleasure, pride and plenty,
>   Great Sir John, are all your own.
>
> Loosen'd from the minor's tether,
>   Free to mortgage or to sell,
> Wild as wind, and light as feather,
>   Bid the slaves of thrift farewell.
>
> Call the Bettys, Kates, and Jennys,
>   Ev'ry name that laughs at care;
> Lavish of your grandsire's guineas,
>   Show the spirit of an heir.
>
> All that prey on vice and folly
>   Joy to see their quarry fly;
> Here the gamester, light and jolly,
>   There the lender, grave and sly.
>
> Wealth, Sir John, was made to wander,
>   Let it wander as it will;
> See the jockey, see the pander,
>   Bid them come and take their fill.

> When the bonny blade carouses,
>   Pockets full, and spirits high,
> What are acres? What are houses?
>   Only dirt, or wet or dry.
>
> If the guardian or the mother
>   Tell the woes of wilful waste,
> Scorn their counsel and their pother,
>   You can hang or drown at last.

Something about the combination of the grimness of the thought, the economy of the language, and the rollicking rhythm of the verse makes the poem curiously memorable. Clearly the "empathy" that Johnson insists on as an important ingredient in literature enables him to participate in the boy's feelings; there is, to use current jargon, something highly "existential" about it. It seems probable that this "short song of congratulation," as Johnson called it in the letter in which he sent it to Mrs. Thrale, had some influence on the formation of A. E. Housman's characteristic poetic idiom—especially since, in the form in which it was known until recently, Mrs. Thrale had substituted "my lad" for "Sir John."

Johnson's Major Poems

Johnson's two greatest poems are, of course, *London*, which he published in 1738, shortly after moving to the capital, and *The Vanity of Human Wishes*, published (with his name on the title page, a rare tribute by Johnson to one of his own pieces) in 1749. Both are major works and are seemingly alike in their use of the closed pentameter couplet and in their being "imitations" of satires of Juvenal, the third and the tenth. They make, however, very different impressions on the reader. A reminder is perhaps needed that the eighteenth-century "imitation" is by no means a translation or even a paraphrase of the original poem; it could be described as a set of variations on a theme by Juvenal or Horace, for it is a genuinely new composition, just as Brahms's "Variations on a Theme by Handel" is.

London purports to be a diatribe on the life of that city by one Thales, who it is hard not to suspect was modeled on Richard Savage, although there has been much controversy as to whether or not Johnson had actually met him at this time. Thales is about to exile himself to the "purer air" of primitive Wales—indeed, the whole poem is a curious expression of a Rousseauistic "primitivism" that consorts oddly with the Johnson who was later to insist that he who is tired of London is tired of life. Joseph Wood Krutch is inclined to dismiss the work as "more of an exercise than a poem" on the ground that "its opinions and attitudes are usually not really Johnson's."[13] But Johnson was young at the time and perhaps more given to facile enthusiasms than he later was. Krutch has fallen into the familiar error of supposing that the "Doctor Johnson" of Boswell, who first encountered him when he was in his fifties, could never have been anything else. Young Johnson was certainly disillusioned when he first arrived in London with the squalor of life in Grub Street (he had probably come with hopes for a quick success with *Irene*); and he was an easy prey, if not to Savage's "injustice-collecting" example, at least to his own marked tendencies in that direction. The poem is, moreover, an extremely political work. Its implied thesis, that Walpole's government was in the process of corrupting every aspect of English life, is one that Pope and Swift were making into great literature at precisely the same time.

But the poem is very much a young man's poem, and its charm comes from the youthful exuberance and violence with which the witty invective comes tumbling out, with little discernible attempt at organization:

> Here malice, rapine, accident conspire,
> And now a rabble rages, now a fire;
> Their ambush here relentless ruffians lay,
> And here the fell attorney prowls for prey;
> Here falling houses thunder on your head,
> And here a female atheist talks you dead.

So a brilliant but provincial young man might write after his first few months in New York. Then as now, gangs of juvenile delinquents prowled the streets, and emancipated young women attempted to shock intellectual gatherings with the freedom of their sentiments. Contrary to Krutch, the tumbling down of bricks from jerry-built houses *was* one of the dangers of walking the streets of London in the 1730s.

In rapid succession Johnson goes on to castigate masquerades, excise, flattery, unrewarded learning, pensioned politicians, *castrati* opera singers, the Stage Licensing Act, titled plagiarists, obsequious and pushing French immigrants, the builder of huge and tasteless mansions, poets laureate, the current crime wave, the parliamentary Committee of Ways and Means, George II's annual visits to his mistress in Hanover—"Much could I add, but see the boat at hand," Thales concludes, breathless. A curious effect of this exuberance is that the reader's final impression may not be that life in London in 1738 is very depressing, as the poem ostensibly portrays it, but that, although exasperating from time to time, it is, on the whole, great fun. Sometimes the epithets are so exaggerated as to react upon themselves with almost comic effect—for instance, the "fell attorney" who "prowls for prey." No doubt, ambulance-chasing lawyers and the like also infest the modern city, but "fell" and "prowl for prey" are a little too much. (To be sure, it might be argued that there is something of this quality of comic exaggeration in Juvenal too.) Johnson is very sorry for himself as he writes, but perhaps the general effect of the poem proves that, in the end, "cheerfulness breaks in." *London* is still a delightfully *live* and readable poem, especially for the young reader.

The Vanity of Human Wishes, Johnson's masterpiece, is a very different matter. *London* is easy to read; *The Vanity of Human Wishes* is not—it is so difficult, apparently, that a great many readers miss the point of it. One reason for this difficulty is that what Johnson is trying to convey in it—the central teaching of the Christian ethic—though a commonplace in his own time, seems very hard for modern readers and professional critics, even those who proclaim themselves Christian, to understand. This teaching is that material, self-seeking values—merely *human* wishes—are an unsatisfactory basis on which to build a life; for only the nonmaterial, un-self-seeking values result in enduring happiness. Critics have called the poem gloomy and pessimistic and have talked about Johnson's Stoicism in it (or his "Christian Stoicism," unaware that this is a contradiction in terms). Noting, what is perfectly true, that a great part of the poem is devoted to proving the inability of "human"—materialistic—wishes to guarantee happiness, they have assumed that the subject of the poem is "the vanity of human *life*"; some have even summed up Johnson's attitude with this very phrase.

But the poem says nothing of the kind. To rebut this interpretation, one need only turn to the last couplet of the poem (indeed, it might be better to begin by reading the end of the poem and work forward):

> With these ["goods," i.e., values] celestial wisdom calms the mind
> And *makes* the happiness she does not *find*.

Happiness, then, *is* possible; it *can* be "made" (though not "found"); the poem does *not* reach a pessimistic conclusion; human *life* (a precious gift of God), if properly conducted, is *not* vanity. The conclusion is an eminently cheerful, not a gloomy, one.

How does Johnson reach that conclusion? It is true that the first 342 of the 368 lines of the poem recount in depressing detail the failure to insure happiness of such values as wealth, fame, political ambition, scholarly ambition, military power, length of life, and physical beauty. The careers of Wolsey,

Charles XII, Swift, Marlborough, Lady Vane, Catherine Sedley, and many others are outlined or referred to, and dismissed. To be sure, the contemplation of these lines is not pleasant. But for critics to maunder on about Johnson's "tragic view of life" and "the great epic wind of sadness blowing through" the poem is utterly beside the point: Wolsey and Charles XII did not have to pursue the mistaken ends they did, nor need one imitate them. Even to argue, with a little more plausibility, that although the poem has a "happy ending," the amount of misery depicted in the first 342 lines is so great that it makes the ending unconvincing and leaves a net impression of pessimism on the reader cannot be justified. The "answer," to be sure, is short—only the last twenty-six lines of the poem. But that answer is given with convincing finality. Perhaps its shortness is even part of the strategy of the poem: the Christian answer is so simple and unarguable that only a few lines are needed to convey it; and the long, involved, tortuous struggles of the Wolseys and Charleses to reach the goal of happiness by taking the wrong path, by following erroneous guideposts, are made to seem the more absurd.

This last section is indeed a triumph of concision and precision of writing. After 342 lines describing individuals directing their hopes and fears to mistaken objects, Johnson finally asks, "Where then *shall* Hope and Fear their objects find?" He presents, as a possible alternative, the Stoic answer, "Direct them to nothing outside yourself; disengage yourself from life; repress all such emotions; commit yourself to nothing, let your judgment of values remain in suspense *(epoche)*." But Johnson puts forward this alternative in such a way that it must be at once rejected:

> Must dull Suspense corrupt the stagnant mind?
> Must helpless man, in ignorance sedate,
> Roll darkling down the torrent of his fate?
> Must no dislike alarm, no wishes rise,
> No cries attempt the mercies of the skies?

The Stoic answer is abandoned with almost pitying abruptness, and for it is substituted the Christian answer of full emotional commitment, but to the right values—the nonmaterial, the spiritual ones of faith, hope, and, above all, love:

> Enquirer, cease: petitions yet remain
> Which Heav'n *may* hear; nor deem religion vain.
> Still [continually] raise for good the supplicating voice.

....

> Pour forth thy fervours [emotion, not Stoic apathy is wanted]
>   for a healthful mind,
> Obedient passions and a will resign'd;
> For love, which scarce collective man can fill—

This last puzzling line, as it has been called, is perhaps an expression of the Miltonic view that God's love is so vast that even the whole of creation is not enough to exhaust it; but it is no less effective for not being easily paraphrasable in prose.

> For patience, sov'reign o'er transmuted ill [an image from alchemy];
> For faith, that panting for a happier seat,
> Counts death kind Nature's signal of retreat.

If there can still be any doubt about Johnson's position, it is explicitly stated in the last four lines:

> *These* goods [values] for man the laws of heav'n ordain;
> These goods He grants, Who grants the pow'r to gain—

how, in the face of this statement, can the poem be termed "pessimistic"?—

> With these, celestial wisdom calms the mind,
> And makes the happiness she does not find.

The student of psychiatry will not be surprised at Johnson's insistence on "mental health" and a "calm mind," or at his insight that happiness is not something one finds but something one makes. Johnson's recipe for happiness is, in fact, not only that of orthodox Christian morality, but also that of much modern psychotherapy; and it is anything but "gloomy" and "pessimistic" and "tragic" in distinctly asserting that happiness is within the reach of anyone who wants it and seeks it the right way. The poem has much in common with T. S. Eliot's *The Waste Land*, another work that has been much misinterpreted. Certainly, the opening picture of life lived according to mistaken values is a dreary one; but this picture is presented only to convince the reader that he should avoid such a life and that he can avoid it; and that the way to avoid it, to transform the sterile waste land of materialistic and ego-centered values into a fruitful one, is the old answer of love.

The second reason for the difficulty of *The Vanity of Human Wishes* is the great density of its texture—in particular, the richness of its imagery—which necessitates a closeness of reading that students have learned to give to the poetry of Donne, Shakespeare, and Yeats but not yet, on the whole, to that of Johnson and Pope. Two of Johnson's criteria of poetic excellence have been mentioned above, and to some extent illustrated from his own verse: contemporaneity of language and formality of structure. A third which must be insisted on is richness and freshness of imagery. In the critical parts of the first thirty *Lives of the Poets* the words "image," "imagery," and "imagination," in the sense of image-making, are used some seventy times. To assess the effectiveness of a poet's imagery is almost always one of Johnson's chief concerns; perhaps no English critic before the advent of the New Critics of the twentieth century was so interested in the use of imagery.

Imagery (in its various forms, simile, metaphor, personification, and the rest) is the making of an abstract idea concrete, or a vague notion vivid, by connecting it in the reader's mind with a picture that he can directly visualize. These connections, if they are fresh and apt, entail a certain degree of paradox, surprise, *discordia concors*, to use Johnson's own phrase. Although Johnson criticized some metaphysical poetry, it had been a powerful tradition in the preceding century; and it is not too surprising that one still finds a good deal of "metaphysical" quality in the poetry of Johnson, as of his masters Dryden and Pope. As Eliot pointed out,

A degree of heterogeneity of material compelled into unity by the operation of the poet's mind is omnipresent in poetry. . . . We may find it in some of the best lines of Johnson himself . . .

> His fall was destined to a barren strand,
> A petty fortress, and a dubious hand;
> He left the name at which the world grew pale
> To point a moral, or adorn a tale,

where the effect is due to a contrast of ideas, different in degree, but the same in principle, as that which Johnson mildly reprehended [in Cowley and others].[14]

Saintsbury once gave Coleridge (and others) a deserved lesson in how to read the first couplet of *The Vanity of Human Wishes*, which Coleridge was fond of denouncing as "bombast and tautology."[15] The couplet may or may not be a felicitous one; but to say that "Let Observation with extensive view / Survey mankind from China to Peru" is the same as "Let observation with extensive observation observe mankind extensively" is to ignore the meaning of

words. This "paraphrase" overlooks the fact that the picture, with the personification "Observation" and the particularization of "China" and "Peru," *is*
concretized, whether happily or not.

If one continues with the poem, bringing to it something of the willingness
to respond to imagery that one brings to Donne and Shakespeare, one can become dazzled by its richness, as one watches

> how Hope and Fear, Desire and Hate,
> O'erspread with snares the clouded maze of Fate,
> Where wav'ring man, betray'd by vent'rous Pride,
> To tread the dreary paths without a guide,
> As treach'rous phantoms in the mist delude,
> Shuns fancied ills, or chases airy good.

He must picture a "maze" (like that at Hampton Court); a mist has descended on it; in the semidarkness, a man staggers along the devious path,
unsuccessfully seeking his way out; there is no guide (as at Hampton Court);
on the contrary, it is "vent'rous Pride"—personified, of course— who urges
him on. In the mist, fleeting will-o'-the-wisps appear and vanish. He stum-
bles after them; or he suddenly imagines he is on the verge of a precipice
("fancied ill") and leaps back, his heart in his mouth. To make matters worse,
malignant beings have fastened snares (*Dictionary:* "Anything set to catch an
animal; a gin; a net; a noose") everywhere along the path. If there is a complaint to be made, it is that Johnson has been *too* extravagant with his imagery: the mind is taxed as it tries to take in all this condensed into the space
of six lines.

Or to take the passage dealing with the scholar (lines 134–156): "When
first the college rolls receive his name"—a highly concrete way of describing
the commencement of an academic career—

> The young enthusiast quits his ease for fame;
> Through all his veins the fever of renown
> Burns from the strong contagion of the gown.

The metaphor, from the shirt of Nessus, is audacious and memorable. "O'er
Bodley's dome his future labours spread"— he imagines the shelves of the
Bodleian library filling with the books he is going to write—"And Bacon's
mansion trembles o'er his head: . . ." Johnson provides the reader, who
might otherwise be lost, with a footnote explaining that "the study of Friar
Bacon, built on an arch over the bridge, will fall when a man greater than

Bacon shall pass under it." In order to say "the scholar becomes ambitious" Johnson has presented in rapid succession three vivid pictures—the burning gown, the "dome" with books spreading along its shelves, the trembling bridge house.

The principal metaphor is now introduced: the familiar one of a journey, a quest, like those of the Arthurian knights:

> Are these thy views? Proceed, illustrious youth,
> And Virtue guard thee to the throne of Truth!
> Yet should thy soul indulge the gen'rous heat—

a metaphor from the old physiology—

> Till captive Science yields her last retreat—

like a Spenserian hero, the questing youth has helpers—

> Should Reason guide thee with her brightest ray
> And pour on misty Doubt resistless day

(it is easy to visualize the sun of Reason dispelling the mist covering the path) —and would-be hinderers—

> Should no false Kindness lure to loose delight
> Nor Praise relax, nor Difficulty fright,
> Should tempting Novelty thy cell refrain—

these personifications easily expand into characters and situations like those in John Bunyan's *The Pilgrim's Progress*, which Johnson so loved.

Now the metaphor of the questing journey becomes almost surrealistic as one encounters opium pipes and Diana the huntress, with bow, quiver, and trophy bag:

> And Sloth effuse her opiate fumes in vain;
> Should Beauty blunt on fops her fatal dart
> Nor claim the triumph of a letter'd heart—

and is virtually abandoned as Disease is given an image from warfare, and the scholar is seen moping in a "shade" through which the phantoms of neurosis flit—

> Should no Disease thy torpid veins invade
> Nor Melancholy's phantoms haunt thy shade.

After an intervening line of perfectly literal meaning, a new image is introduced: the scholar is now (like Kafka's Josef K.) a prisoner before a tribunal from whose verdict of condemnation there is no appeal—

> Yet hope not life from grief or danger free,
> Nor think the doom of man revers'd for thee.

("Reverse," *Dictionary*, def. 4: "To contradict; to repeal," illustrated by Milton's "Death, his doom, which I / To mitigate thus plead, not to reverse.") Of the twenty-two lines of the passage, perhaps only one, the penultimate, is unequivocally free from imagery.

The Vanity of Human Wishes is undoubtedly Johnson's greatest poem, and it has genuine and unique poetic merit. It has not the miraculous and dazzling perfection of Pope, Keats, or Yeats at their best: Johnson's handling of the closed couplet lacks the brilliant versatility of Pope and (to a lesser extent) Dryden; there is a certain laboriousness in the texture of the poem—although this is, in itself, not really a blemish, but an intrinsic part of the peculiar effect Johnson achieves, as though to emphasize the laboriousness with which the average human being attains wisdom. In a sense the major English poet to whom Johnson is closest here is Donne. At any rate, throughout the poem one has the feeling that one is dealing with a writer who at least knows what fine poetry is and who will not be put off in his search for it by a willingness to accept something inferior. As Eliot says, "Goldsmith and Johnson deserve fame because they used the form of Pope beautifully, without ever being mere imitators. . . . There is much greater poetry than Johnson's; but after all, how little, how very little good poetry there is anyway."[16] *The Vanity of Human Wishes* is among that "little."

The Prologues and Latin Poetry

After *London* and *The Vanity of Human Wishes*, the best known of Johnson's poems are probably the group of five prologues that he wrote for theatrical occasions. There is the fine one for the reopening of Drury Lane Theatre in 1747 under the management of Garrick, which gives a delightful conspectus of the history of the English drama, beginning with Shakespeare—

> Each change of many-colour'd life he drew,
> Exhausted worlds, and then imagin'd new. . . .
> And panting Time toil'd after him in vain—

and going on through the "studious patience and laborious art" of Ben Jonson, "the wits of Charles," for whom "intrigue was plot, obscenity was wit," up to the drama of Johnson's time, of which he gives a not unjustifiedly gloomy picture, when

> crush'd by rules, and weaken'd as refin'd,
> For years the pow'r of tragedy declin'd;
> From bard to bard the frigid caution crept,
> Till Declamation roar'd, while Passion slept

and "the ghost of Wit" is laid by the farces and pantomimes that have replaced it. It will not be surprising, when Johnson comes to write the Preface to his Shakespeare, to find him sneering at "the Rules." He concludes by speculating on what the future may hold and laments the lot of the playwright when

> The Drama's laws the Drama's patrons give,
> For we that live to please, must please to live

and pleads with the audience to "bid the reign commence / Of rescu'd Nature, and reviving Sense."

The prologue to *Comus*, produced at Johnson's instigation as a benefit for Milton's granddaughter, who was discovered to be living in poverty, contains a glowing tribute to Milton and a slap at both the "Patriot crowds, who burn for England's fame" (but neglect that great patriot Milton) and the court of George II ("the mean pensions of Augustan times"). The other prologues, for plays by Goldsmith, Hugh Kelly, and Garrick, are less memorable; but, as with so much of Johnson's writing, pleasing through their simple competence.

Two other areas of Johnson's poetic production should be mentioned. One is his Latin poetry, of which he wrote a great deal throughout his life. Interestingly, his Latin poems are often more personal and "subjective" than anything he wrote in English. The "GNOTHI SEAUTON" ("Know Thyself"), composed in a fit of his habitual depression after he had completed the revision of the 1773 edition of the *Dictionary*, is an amazing piece of gloomy psychological introspection. He describes his mental state—his soul "shudders to behold its kingdom of night and silence, where empty forms, fleeting shadows, solitary shapes flit past in the void"—and ends by suggesting, with bitter irony, that he needs another dictionary to set to work on.

The Horatian odes from the Hebrides convey some fine "romantic" description of those lonely islands—

> Ponti profundis clausa recessibus,
> Strepens procellis, rupibus obsita
>   Quam grata defesso virentem
>   Skia sinum nebulosa pandis. . . .
>
> Permeo terras, ubi nuda rupes
> Saxeas miscet nebulis ruinas,
> Torva ubi rident steriles coloni
>   Rura labores.

Girt with deep inlets of the ocean, loud with storms, covered with rocks, how grateful to the weary one, misty Skye, do you spread out your green bay! . . .

I pass through lands where the naked rock mingles stony ruins with the clouds, where hostile fields mock the barren toil of the farmer. . . .

Late in life, hearing that the willow trees over the stream at Stowe Mill in Lichfield had been cut down, Johnson remembers how, when he was a boy, his father had taught him to swim there: *"Errat adhuc vitreus per prata virentia rivus* [and those who think Johnson has no ear should read this opening line aloud]. . . . Still wanders the glassy stream through the green meadows where I, a boy, so often bathed my little limbs. Here I threshed my arms about in vain while, with coaxing voice, my father taught me to swim. The boughs made secret places, the overhanging trees kept the water hidden. . . ."

Irene

The other sizable "set of verses" that needs to be mentioned is *Irene*. Amusing stories were told about Johnson's later disillusionment with this product of youthful ambition to achieve quick fame (like Addison with *Cato*): how, hearing it read aloud at a house where he was visiting, "he left the room; and, somebody having asked him the reason of this, he replied, 'Sir, I thought it had been better,'" and how, when a gentleman named Pot was reported as admiring *Irene* "as the finest tragedy of modern times," he growled, "If Pot says so, Pot lies."[17] Johnson may have been right about Pot's judgment (though it may be hard to say which of the English verse-tragedies of the eighteenth century is any better; for the genre, though prestigious, was unsatisfactory). Nevertheless, the student would be wrong to dismiss *Irene* as negligible. When Garrick did finally produce it, it had the respectable, if not overwhelming, run of nine nights; and it brought Johnson three hundred pounds, the equivalent later of a year's income from his pension.

And *Irene* by no means fails to repay reading today. The story has great possibilities for dramatic treatment: it is the kind of story that Racine could have made a great play of, and one can see why it fascinated Johnson (earlier English playwrights had used it). It is the story of the beautiful Greek Christian, Irene, with whom the Turkish Sultan Mahomet, after he has captured Constantinople, falls passionately in love. He offers her a crown and the glories of his realm—if, of course, we will embrace his religion. Conflicts immediately arise: Mahomet's lieutenants, shocked at their master's weakness, plan to overthrow him; other captive Greeks ally with them for their own ends; among them, the lovely Aspasia seeks to dissuade Irene from yielding to the temptation of worldly power and apostatizing. Considerable suspense is created in the play, and the representation of the struggle that goes on in Irene's mind before she succumbs to the temptation (and then falls a victim to slander and Mahomet's wrath) shows a mature grasp of psychological complexity. Even if one cannot go along with Bronson's thesis that the virtuous Aspasia is supposed to be a picture of the virtuous Tetty, the play adds to one's knowledge of Johnson's mind and art, and should not be ignored.[18]

At the same time it has one great defect that cannot be overlooked or excused—its versification. As Eliot accurately comments, "The phrasing is admirable, the style elevated and correct, but each line cries out for a companion to rhyme with it."[19] Such a passage as the following (in which Irene, alone, reflects on Aspasia and her lover Demetrius, now escaping to safety) *ought* to be very fine; but the reader's ear soon rebels against the sledgehammer monotony of the stop at the end of every ten syllables:

> Against the head which Innocence secures,
> Insidious Malice aims her darts in vain;
> Turn'd backward by the powerful breath of Heaven.
> Perhaps ev'n now the lovers unpursued
> Bound o'er the sparkling waves. Go, happy bark,
> Thy sacred freight shall still the raging main.
> To guide thy passage shall th' aerial spirits
> Fill all the starry lamps with double blaze;
> Th' applauding sky shall pour forth all its beams

> To grace the triumph of victorious virtue;
> While I, not yet familiar to my crimes,
> Recoil from thought, and shudder at myself.

The heroic couplet is masquerading as blank verse, and Johnson's experience at this time may well be responsible for his later judgment regarding blank verse as a form that should be used only by the very rare poet. It is a pity, but the blank verse of *Irene* remains a barrier between the modern reader and what Johnson was trying to do in the play, which was well worth doing.

These, then, are his major poetic accomplishments, and they seem small beside those of a Dryden, a Pope, or a Wordsworth. Nevertheless, poetry was much more than merely an occasional diversion for Johnson, as the large volume of his collected verse testifies. Much of that volume consists of scraps, fragments, jeux d'esprit; but the quantity of it shows how close poetry always was to him. He began experimenting with it when he was very young, and his considerable juvenilia are worth studying: translations from Horace, Virgil, and Homer into English verse; and from Dryden and Pope into Latin verse (his first publication, while at college, was a version in Latin hexameters of Pope's *Messiah*); an epilogue to Ambrose Philips's popular play *The Distrest Mother* (based on Racine's *Andromaque*); and mild love poems to various ladies. His earliest surviving English poem, written when he was fourteen or fifteen, is entitled (Wordsworth would have been surprised to learn) "On a Daffodil." One of his more ambitious ones, "Upon the Feast of St. Simon and St. Jude," is in the six-line stanza of Smart's "A Song to David," which it curiously resembles in its "extatick fury," to quote a phrase from the poem itself.

In his old age Johnson turned again to verse as his main literary activity, occupying his sleepless nights by turning the poignant epigrams of the Greek Anthology into Latin elegiacs, adapting the collects of the Prayer Book as private prayers in Latin verse, and composing in English his fine elegy to his old friend Levet. Poetry was an integral part of his life and his work as a writer; a way in which he continually exercised his talent for handling words; an occupation that always gave him pleasure and comfort; the medium by which, on infrequent but sometimes important occasions, he gave memorable form to the essentially poetic imagination that more often used prose as its means of expression.[20]

Chapter Three

The Journalist and Occasional Writer

Johnson's writings are so varied that it is sometimes a puzzle to know just how to designate him—a poet? a critic? an essayist? a moralist? A good case could be made for thinking of Johnson primarily as a journalist, in the sense that Macaulay, John Henry Newman, John Stuart Mill, and Bertrand Russell are journalists—that is, educators of the general reading public. Given this definition, the term *journalist* merits more respect than some more pretentious labels.

During a great deal of his lifetime Johnson made his living by writing for newspapers and magazines.[1] He displayed the characteristics of the born journalist—a nose for curious, "newsworthy" information in almost every branch of human activity, and a desire to make that information generally available. In his association with one periodical, at least, it seems possible to credit him with a significant part in the development of an important modern journalistic medium: the serious general magazine.

Edward Cave's monthly, which was first published in 1731 and whose staff Johnson joined when he came to London in 1737, was, as most students know, the first periodical publication to bear the designation of *magazine*. A glance at the early numbers shows that Cave at first took the term quite literally: to begin with, the *Gentleman's Magazine* was merely a "magazine," a storehouse of items collected and reprinted (without permission, of course) from other publications. For several decades its title page bore, surrounding the cut of the old gatehouse of the Knights of the Hospital of St. John in Clerkenwell where it was edited, the titles of the several dozen newspapers, London and provincial, that Cave rifled for his material. It was to begin with, a kind of *Reader's Digest* of the early eighteenth century. In its early volumes it did not maintain a very impressive level of taste or interest for the educated reader. Cave, as Johnson makes clear in his obituary "life" of him in 1754, was no intellectual. But he was a shrewd businessman and came to know the value of hiring intellectuals to carry on the magazine.

Too little detailed evidence is available to say precisely how it happened but a study of the issues between the early 1730s and the 1740s reveals an important change in the *Gentleman's Magazine*. It began to publish original material; it added new regular features; its interests branched out to include domestic politics, foreign affairs, history, science, antiquarianism, theology, and the current state of literature. The magazine began to be directed to educated, though nonspecialist, readers, and more and more one senses a feeling of responsibility to inform this audience and to interpret what was of most significance in the intellectual and public life of the time. Exactly what Johnson's part was in this development one has no way of telling exactly; but, from what one knows of the force of his personality and his ideas of the function of serious journalism, it seems safe to say that his influence was considerable. But, at the same time, it should not be forgotten that other very well qualified "staff writers" were working for the *Gentleman's Magazine*, notably William Guthrie and John Hawkesworth.

Addison and Steele are usually credited with having done much, through *The Tatler* and *The Spectator*, to "educate" the "rising middle class" of the time. If his part in the development of the *Gentleman's Magazine* was as formative as has been suggested, Johnson deserves at least as much credit. The rise of the "magazine" was the beginning of the journalistic tradition that was to be continued in the following century in *Blackwood's* and *Cornhill*, and on the other side of the ocean in the *Atlantic Monthly* and *Harper's*. This tradition can plausibly be argued to have been a more potent force than that somewhat whimsical genre, the periodical essay of *The Spectator*, in the creation of a well- informed, thoughtful, and intellectually responsible class of educated citizens. The *Gentleman's Magazine* itself (which flourished until 1907) was soon joined by a number of competitors, notably the *London Magazine*, its hated rival.

Concepts of Journalism

Whatever Johnson's share in creating "the first magazine," his philosophy of journalism can be established from his statements published at various times during his life. Indeed, in his mature years he seems to have been almost regarded as an official theorist of journalism, for he was called on to supply the opening manifesto of several newspapers: the *London Chronicle*, 1757; the *Universal Chronicle*, 1758; possibly the *Public Ledger*, 1760; and of course his own *Literary Magazine*, 1756. In addition, he wrote the introductions to other collections of popularized information—*The Preceptor*, 1748, and *The Publisher*, 1744. In these manifestos he insists on the importance, and the difficulty, of accurate reporting. He announces, for the *London*

Chronicle, policy not too often followed by its successors: "We shall always be conscious that our mistakes are involuntary, we shall watch the gradual discoveries of time, and retract whatever we have hastily and erroneously advanced."

He apologizes in advance for the deficiencies of newspaper style: "It must be considered that those passages must be written in haste . . . as life is very uniform, the affairs of one week are so like those of another that by any attempt after variety of expression, invention would soon be wearied, and language exhausted." He reprobates partisanship: "We shall repress that elation of malignity which wantons in the cruelties of criticism . . . whenever we feel ourselves ignorant, we shall at least be modest. Our intention is not to preoccupy judgment by praise or censure, but to gratify curiosity by early intelligence." This last passage refers particularly to the book review section, which is to be a feature of the *London Chronicle*—"the literary journal, or account of the labours and products of the learned. This was for a long time among the deficiencies of English literature; but . . . we have now, among other disturbers of human quiet, a numerous body of reviewers and remarkers."

Much of what is said in these manifestos, if fairly obvious today, was perhaps not so much so in Johnson's time; but it is always finely expressed. The article entitled "Of the Duty of a Journalist," prefixed to the first issue of the *Universal Chronicle*, contains some more striking notions; for instance, the paper would refuse to publish "the advertisements of apprentices who have left their masters, and who are often driven away by cruelty or hunger"; and there would be explanations of unfamiliar place names, military terms, and names of foreign currency appearing in the news items:

A journalist, above most other men, ought to be acquainted with the lower orders of mankind, that he may be able to judge what will be plain and what will be obscure; what will require a comment, and what will be apprehended without explanation. He is to consider himself not as writing to students or statesmen alone, but to women, shopkeepers, and artisans, who have little time to bestow upon mental attainment, but desire, upon easy terms, to know how the world goes; who rises, and who falls; who triumphs and who is defeated.

Among numerous other pronouncements by Johnson on the journalist's trade are those in *Rambler* 145, where he calls the journalist "a liberal dispenser of beneficial knowledge," and suggests that it is "necessary for every man to be more acquainted with his contemporaries than with past generations, and to rather know the events which may immediately affect his fortune or quiet than the revolutions of ancient kingdoms"; in *Idler* 7, "The knowledge of the common people of England is greater than that of any other vulgar. This superiority we undoubtedly owe to the rivulets of intelligence which are continually trickling among us, which every one may catch, and of which every one partakes"; though he cautions, in *Idler* 30 (where he laments the propagandist distortion of news in wartime), "To write news in its perfection requires such a combination of qualities that a man completely fitted for the task is not always to be found."

Democratic Government and Publicity

Johnson is peculiarly aware of the dependence of the British democratic conception of government on a well-informed public, a dependence which first became of real importance in political history during Johnson's lifetime. Those who have been taught the myth that Johnson's political views were those of a mossbacked authoritarian reactionary will be surprised by this statement from the Preface to the *Gentleman's Magazine* for 1743: "Under a form of government like ours, which makes almost every man a secondary legislator, politics may justly claim a more general attention than where the people have no other duty to practise than obedience and where to examine the conduct of their superiors would be to disturb their own quiet." And in the Preface to the *Harleian Miscellany*, 1744, Johnson asserts,

The form of our government, which gives every man that has leisure, or curiosity, or vanity, the right of enquiring into the propriety of public measures, and by consequence obliges those who are intrusted with the administration of national affairs to give an account of their conduct to almost every man who demands it, may be reasonably imagined to have occasioned innumerable pamphlets, which would never have appeared under arbitrary governments, where every man lulls himself in indolence under calamities of which he cannot promote the redress, or thinks it prudent to conceal the uneasiness of which he cannot complain without danger.

Throughout his career as a writer, a great deal of Johnson's energy was directed not merely to providing the intelligent reader with information about what was going on in the world of affairs, but to trying to persuade that reader to think and judge independently about them. His massive contribution to this end in the early *Gentleman's Magazine* in the form of reports of the parliamentary debates for at least three years will be discussed in a later chapter. But there is much more in Johnson's writings for the *Gentleman's Magazine* (the full extent of which is yet far from determined) that is designed with this objective in view. His hand has been tentatively identified in many installments of its "Foreign History" section, a monthly summary of international news. Boswell speculated that Johnson wrote one or two of these, but in many others the reader encounters, in the midst of a dry factual account of a military campaign, such a paragraph of incisive comment as the following, in the November 1742, issue—printed, moreover, in a smaller type than the rest of the article, and thus marked as a later insertion, probably by a different hand: "Upon these marches and counter-marches, it has been observed that the maxims of war have been much changed by the refinements of the present times. In the ruder and more heroic ages it was the standing practice to take at all events the first opportunity of fighting; the great rule of conduct at present is never to fight without a visible advantage, which rule, if it be observed on both sides, will for ever prevent a battle."

To Johnson also has been attributed, with much plausibility, the "Foreign Books" section of *Gentleman's Magazine*, which runs from November 1741 to September 1743, and reappears occasionally in later issues. This section consists of notes on important scholarly works published on the Continent and contains an invitation in dignified Latin to foreign scholars to communicate news of their activities. Johnson may also have been responsible for such contributions as the long-drawn-out series of abstracts and comments on a pamphlet controversy concerning governmental policy with regard to the export of wool—a most dry subject today, except for the trained economist, but one which someone on the staff of the *Gentleman's Magazine* thought the intelligent reader should know something about. Johnson, as his Preface to the *Preceptor* (1747) and such other works as *Further Thoughts on Agriculture* (1756), *Considerations on Corn* (1766?), and *A Journey to the Western Islands of Scotland* (1775) make clear, decidedly felt that a liberal education for a responsible citizen should include some knowledge of economics.

A sample of the quality of Johnson's journalism is provided by two of the numerous book reviews he contributed, not only to the *Gentleman's Magazine*, but throughout his life to many other journals. One is the review, in 1742, of *The Conduct of the Duchess of Marlborough*— memoirs by old Sarah Churchill, widow of the great Duke John, of the years in which she had governed Queen Anne and, through her, England. The Marlboroughs were no favorites of Johnson, who adhered to the view of Swift and the Tories that they had prolonged the War of the Spanish Succession with an eye to their own aggrandizement and enrichment, and that of the Whigs generally. Nevertheless, Johnson's treatment of the book is remarkably open-minded. He begins with several paragraphs discussing the historical value of such memoirs, and then he takes up the important question of whether true history is possible. Clearly, the duchess, in narrating what went on behind the scenes, is bound, consciously or unconsciously, to distort the facts to the advantage of her own reputation. But who else except such biased "insiders" knows what really went on? "The man who knows not the truth cannot, and he who knows it will not, tell it; what then remains [but] to distrust every relation, and live in perpetual negligence of past events, or, what is still more disagreeable, in perpetual suspense?" In the end, Johnson rejects this Pyrrhonist, or Marxist, view: one should be skeptical, certainly, of the motives of such writers as the duchess; but "Distrust quickens [the student's] discernment of different degrees of probability, animates his search after evidence, and perhaps heightens his pleasure at the discovery of truth, for truth, though not always obvious, is generally discoverable."

This is book reviewing, or journalism, of a very high order; it is directed not at persuading the reader of the truth or falsity of a certain thesis, but at educating him to judge for himself of truth and falsity generally. Of the same order is his review, in 1759, of William Tytler's *Historical and Critical Inquiry*, which was concerned with the problem of the famous "casket letters" attributed to Mary, Queen of Scots—a controversy still going on. If, writes Johnson, the letters are genuine, they convict Mary of complicity in the murder of her husband Darnley by his successor Bothwell; but this question of authenticity is not what primarily concerns Johnson. Instead, it is the question of unthinking public prejudice, especially among "intellectuals." "The writers of the present time," he begins, "are not always candidates for preferment, nor often the hirelings of a patron. They profess to serve no interest, and speak with loud contempt of sycophants and slaves." (Johnson, in his letter to Chesterfield, was himself a conspicuous case in point.) But "There is, however, a power from whose influence neither they nor their predecessors have ever been free. Those who have set greatness at defiance have yet been the slaves of fashion. When an opinion has once become popular, very few are willing to oppose it. Idleness is more willing to credit than enquire; cowardice is afraid of controversy, and vanity of answer; and he that writes merely for sale is tempted to court purchasers by flattering the prejudices of the public."

It is now fashionable, as Johnson says, to vilify the house of Stuart: "Yet there remains still among us, not wholly extinguished, a zeal for truth, a desire of establishing right, in opposition to fashion." He defends the Stuarts because it has become fashionable to express an unthinking contempt for them and because he resisted all his life the abdication of reason and observation to the power of intellectual fashion, as to any other form of authoritarianism. It is interesting to find Johnson anticipating John Stuart Mill's warning that in the modern world the great tyrant over the human mind will no longer be rulers, governments, or patrons, but majority opinion.

Even more striking instances of Johnson's passion to persuade the intelligent reader not to take for granted the "received" line on a matter of public concern, but to try to think out an answer for himself, are found in the history of his short-lived connection with the *Literary Magazine*, of which he seems to have been the first editor and almost the sole writer for some five months in 1756.[2] (He had just completed the huge task of the *Dictionary*, but found himself as impoverished as before.) The date of the first issue of the *Literary Magazine* coincides with that of the declaration of the Seven Years' War between France and Britain (and Prussia), the war that was to add Canada and India to Britain's possessions, to establish the British Empire of the nineteenth century, to make Britain for a time the greatest imperial and commercial nation in the world, to make North America north of the Rio Grande English- rather than French-speaking, and so to lay the foundation for the United States. It was a popular war, and its chief architect, William Pitt, was widely acclaimed, then and later, for the breadth of his vision.

But Johnson desperately tries to get his readers to see that the imperial vision is a shortsighted one. In long articles that sketch the history of European colonial and commercial expansion since the days of Columbus and trace the progress of French and British economic rivalry, he says, again and again, in the most emphatic way, that one cannot build enduring national happiness on the basis of competitive exploitation. He is violently "anti-patriotic"; he sees no reason to wish his own country well in what is "only the quarrel of two robbers for the spoils of a passenger."[3] His sympathies are all with the American Indians, from whom the English and French have stolen the land over which they now fight with such high-minded battle cries. (Later, his sympathy for the exploited Indians—and Negroes— keeps him from taking very seriously the lofty talk about "liberty" and "human rights" of the patriots of the American Revolution.) Between the warring parties, he feels that, on the whole, the French are the more deserving because they have at least attempted to treat the Indians with a little more respect. Their "great security is the friendship of the natives, and to this advantage they have certainly an indubitable right; because it is the consequence of their virtue. It is ridiculous to imagine that the friendship of nations, whether civil or barbarous, can be gained or kept but by kind treatment; and surely they who intrude, uncalled, upon the country of a distant people, ought to consider the natives as worthy of common kindness, and content themselves to rob without insulting them."[4] These marvelous words are pertinent in the twentieth as well as in the eighteenth century.

Johnson's direction of the *Literary Magazine* seems to have ceased after five or six months. After this period the number of his contributions drops

sharply, and the editorial policy of the periodical shifts overnight to the popular, patriotic, "anti-Gallican" one. A similar fate met a weekly column he
began to write for the *Universal Chronicle* two years later. In the fourth number he makes bitter fun of the popular rejoicing at the capture of the French
fortress of Louisbourg in Cape Breton. A shocked patriot is moved to reply
and denounce his defeatism. In the next issue Johnson is given a chance to
defend himself, which he does, not by softening or apologizing for his position, but by launching an even more vigorous assault on the "patriotic" one.
Then the weekly "Observations" are no more seen.[5] It may at least be said in
defense of eighteenth-century rationality that nothing worse happened to
Johnson as a result of his opposition to a great "national" war than the loss of
his job. Though deprived of these two outlets, Johnson was not yet silenced;
and, from time to time, under the innocuous mask of the Idler, he published
scathing comments on wartime propaganda and the alleged glorious exploits
of the not very glorious British army of the time. In his distrust of imperial
and commercial aggrandizement, of course, Johnson was perfectly right; but
this was journalism at far too high a level—to try to educate the British public to a point of view that only two centuries of subsequent history has reluctantly persuaded it to accept.

Some "Minor" Writings

The immense range of Johnson's "minor" writings has never been ade-
quately explored; indeed, it is far from even being fully determined. Very little of Johnson's published writings bears his signature. This anonymity is
partly, of course, in the older tradition of journalism, one recently adhered to
in a few periodicals such as the *Times Literary Supplement*. It is also partly because of Johnson's willingness to do ghostwriting, supplying prefaces, dedications, introductory paragraphs, "improvements" to verses, and public
statements of one kind or another for a host of acquaintances who appreciated the effectiveness of his lapidary style.[6] And, to some extent, perhaps, his
anonymity may be due to his curious, perhaps neurotic, reluctance to attach
his name to anything in print. He comments, for example, in the covering letter with which he transmits the manuscript of *Rasselas* to the publisher, "I
will not print my name, but expect it to be known."[7] No doubt it gave a small
fillip of gratification to his deep inner insecurity to think that he no longer
had to rely on the ordinary methods of publicity for his authorship of a work
to become known.

This anonymity has, of course, posed difficult problems for the student of
the canon of his writings and from Boswell's time onward a great deal of am-

ateur detective work has gone on in trying to identify Johnsonian contributions to eighteenth-century periodicals and books. Sometimes clues to his authorship turn up in letters and other private records; often attributions have been made only on the basis of what seems like a striking similarity to Johnson's known styles and patterns of thought. This last method is, naturally, very uncertain and attributions made on the basis of "internal evidence" alone are very hard to prove or disprove. Advances being made in mathematical methods of stylistic analysis, with the aid of computers, may eventually help to solve such problems.[8]

But no student of Johnson should remain satisfied with a knowledge merely of his major works—*The Rambler, Rasselas, The Lives of the Poets*— which represent, after all, not an overwhelming percentage of his total output. The student should at least browse in the bewildering and delightful variety of Johnson's contributions to contemporary periodicals and to books and pamphlets ostensibly by others. What follows is only a small sampling from works long established as Johnson's, but it gives some indication of the range of his interests and abilities.

In his early twenties, back at Lichfield after translating while in Birmingham the Lobo-Le Grand book on Abyssinia, Johnson borrowed from Pembroke College library the works of the Renaissance poet Angelo Poliziano; and he issued proposals and invitations to subscribe, in advance of publication, to an edition of "Politian's Latin poems, with notes, a history of Latin poetry from the time of Petrarch to that of Politian, and a life of Politian." It was to be a book of about five hundred pages, to sell for five shillings. The project was never completed, if any work was done on it at all; but it is a significant indication of Johnson's deep interest in the Renaissance and his familiarity with its writers and critics. No really satisfactory study of the background of Johnson's thought or of his criticism will be possible until someone has investigated the extent of his indebtedness to Petrarch, Politian, George Buchanan, Sannazaro, Lipsius, and the Scaligers, to mention no others. In particular the life of Politian, a turbulent, vigorous-minded, unconventional, highly learned individual, with the temperament of a scholar, an artist, and a Bohemian, seems a fitting subject for the young Johnson's pen.[9]

Another ambitious project which advanced somewhat further than the Politian was a translation, begun in 1738, shortly after the move to London, of Paolo (Father Paul) Sarpi's *History of the Council of Trent* (not from the original Italian but from the French of Le Courayer). This great historical classic—an account of the famous ecumenical council that heralded the Counter-Reformation, written by a Venetian priest bitterly hostile to the counter-reform movement—has affinities both with Johnson's interest in the

Renaissance and with his earlier work on the politico-religious controversy involving Jesuit missionary activity in Abyssinia. Cave, who was sponsoring the translation, paid Johnson a total of forty-seven guineas for his work on it, a sum which represents a good deal of writing; but the announcement of a rival translation in progress caused it to be abandoned, and none of Johnson's work has survived except the first two pages, reprinted in the *Proposals* for the book,[10] and a short *Life of Sarpi* in the *Gentleman's Magazine* for November 1738. Another large project in which Johnson was involved in these early years was the compilation of a detailed *History of Parliament* that was to cover the reign of at least George I. Johnson had written at least eighty pages of this work before it was abandoned (if it *was* abandoned); but what became of it is not known.

After his work on the parliamentary debates terminated in the early 1740s Johnson was occupied for a year or two with the Harleian library—the great collection of books assembled by the first earl of Oxford, Queen Anne's Tory prime minister, a favorite with both Johnson and Pope, and his son the second earl. On the latter's death, the bookseller Thomas Osborne purchased the collection and planned to dispose of the books at a profit. (This should not be confused with the Harleian collection of manuscripts, one of the glories of the British Museum.) Johnson and William Oldys were engaged to compile a monumental annotated catalog running to four large volumes. Its preface, *An Account of the Harleian Library*, is one that librarians and students who use catalogs should know. As usual, Johnson is not content merely to talk about the work immediately at hand; he insists on discussing the rationale of cataloging books in words every student should hang over his desk:

By means of catalogues only can it be known what has been written on every part of learning, and the hazard avoided of encountering difficulties which have already been cleared, discussing questions which have already been decided, and digging in mines of literature which former ages have exhausted. How often this has been the fate of students, every man of letters can declare; and, perhaps, there are very few who have not sometimes valued as new discoveries, made by themselves, those observations which have long since been published, and of which the world therefore will refuse them the praise; nor can the refusal be censured as any enormous violation of justice; for why should they not forfeit by their ignorance what they might claim by their sagacity?

Johnson was at the same time engaged in the task of extracting from the collection the eight-volume anthology of pamphlets on the religious and political controversies of the sixteenth and seventeenth centuries in Britain known as the *Harleian Miscellany*, still an invaluable source book for historians of that period. To it Johnson prefaced his brilliant *Essay on the Origin and Importance of Small Tracts and Fugitive Pieces*, a stirring plea for the study of documents which "preserve a multitude of particular incidents, which are forgotten in a short time, or omitted in formal relations, and which are yet to be considered as sparks of truth which, when united, may afford light in some of the darkest scenes of state . . . which it is, therefore, the interest of the public to preserve unextinguished." Johnson, as so often, was in advance of his time in distrusting the large, generalizing histories, but in treasuring the small, firsthand historical documentation the *Miscellany* provides.

A curious involvement of Johnson's in the late 1740s was in the "Miltonian controversy" initiated by the crackpot Scotsman William Lauder. Lauder, who may have been motivated by Jacobite leanings, sought to prove that parts of *Paradise Lost* had been plagiarized by Milton from a Latin poem on the Fall, *Adamus Exsul*, by Hugo Grotius, and other similar works. He proved this by triumphantly producing line after line from Grotius and the rest which, when translated into English, proved identical with lines from Milton's poem. Johnson and others were taken in, and Johnson contributed a commendatory preface to the book in which Lauder announced his great discovery. Others, however, who were not so easily convinced, were soon able to point out that Lauder's alleged parallels did not occur in Grotius and the rest at all: they had in fact been taken by Lauder out of a translation of *Paradise Lost* into Latin verse by one William Hogg, so that there was little wonder that, when translated into English, they resembled Milton. The controversy raged through the columns of the *Gentleman's Magazine* for some time, and Johnson for a while loyally supported Lauder. But the evidence proved overwhelming. At last Johnson printed an abject apology on his own behalf in the columns of the *Gentleman's Magazine*;[11] and he also dictated a most ignominious, detailed retraction to Lauder and forced him to publish it.

After Johnson's *Life of Milton* appeared many years later, critics of a Whiggish turn of mind referred sarcastically to the Lauder incident as early proof of Johnson's vindictive prejudice against Milton. In fact, however, Johnson's preface to Lauder's book is most respectful to Milton; the retraction is most damning to Lauder; and, at the same time, Johnson was organizing a benefit performance of *Comus*, for which he wrote the Prologue for Milton's granddaughter. Indeed, he incorporated as a postscript to Lauder's book a plea for subscriptions to a fund for the relief of the granddaughter which contains high praise of Milton: "It is yet in the power of a great people to reward the poet whose name they boast, and from their alliance to whose genius they claim, some kind of superiority to every other nation of the earth;

that poet whose works may possibly be read when every other monument of British greatness shall be obliterated . . . with tokens of gratitude which he, perhaps, may even now consider as not unworthy the regard of an immortal spirit."

Perhaps the experience with Lauder made Johnson suspicious of brilliant discoveries, like Macpherson's of the "Ossian" poems in the oral tradition of the Highland bards. At any rate, in a century in which there were a great many such ingenious attempts at public fraud (it was the century of Chatterton and Ireland) Johnson was generally to be found on the side of the detectors rather than the duped. The best known of these incidents was the Cock Lane ghost in 1762, when a servant girl pretended to have been possessed by the spirit of a murdered woman, which would communicate, by mysterious scratches and knocks, the facts relative to her murder. The scene of these manifestations was near St. John's Gate, and Johnson organized a party of trustworthy individuals to investigate and report on this mischievous rubbish. They had no trouble in demolishing it, and Johnson's report of the incident, in the *Gentleman's Magazine*, is a model of straightforward, no-nonsense reporting. Macaulay makes fun of Johnson for having taken the incident seriously enough to organize the investigation and he suggests that it is testimony to Johnson's superstition. But the tone of the report makes it clear that Johnson was properly concerned to demolish, once for all, the kind of rumor that, when circulating among the illiterates of a London given to frequent rioting, was potentially dangerous. It is, in fact, highly responsible journalism.

Other interesting evidence of Johnson's involvement with the public life of his time is afforded by the series of letters he published in 1759 in the *Daily Gazetteer* on behalf of his friend the architect John Gwynn, arguing that the projected Blackfriars Bridge over the Thames River should be built with circular arches (as Gwynn advocated) instead of elliptical arches (as in the design of the rival architect Mylne). In these letters Johnson writes learnedly about the engineering theory of stresses. In the *Gentleman's Magazine* of January 1749 Johnson published an amusing diatribe against the extravagant, governmentally sponsored display of fireworks planned to celebrate the Peace of Aix-la-Chapelle. They were the same fireworks for which Handel wrote his lovely "Royal Fireworks" music and which, readers of Horace Walpole's letters may recall, were in fact such a lamentable failure. At first, they refused to go off at all; but, when they did, they set fire to the spectators' stands and incidentally created a traffic jam that caused the loss of several lives.

Johnson, as a member of the opposition, views the whole project with unrelieved gloom: "In this will consist the only propriety of this transient show, that it will resemble the war of which it celebrates the period. The powers of this part of the world, after long preparations, deep intrigues, and subtle schemes, have set Europe in a flame, and, after having gazed a while at their fireworks, have laid themselves down where they rose, to inquire for what they had been contending." Moreover, he does not see why the display should be paid for out of public funds: "Many cannot forbear observing how many lasting advantages might be purchased, how many acres might be drained, how many ways repaired, how many debtors might be released, how many widows and orphans, whom the war has ruined, might be relieved by the expense which is about to evaporate in smoke. . . ." So much emotion over so trivial a matter seems perhaps a little silly, but it is first-rate professional editorial writing.

Johnson also has a good deal to say about the principles of publicly financed spectacles in the pamphlet *Thoughts on the Coronation* (of George III), in which he again assisted his friend Gwynn. It has one of Johnson's most spectacular opening paragraphs: "All pomp is instituted for the sake of the public. A show without spectators can no longer be a show. Magnificence in obscurity is equally vain with *a sundial in the grave.*" The quotation, so unexpected, is from Donne, who might well have been delighted by its use on such an occasion. Starting from this general principle, Johnson goes on to deduce, with great lucidity and force, that the route planned for the coronation procession is ineffective, and a longer one should be adopted.

The finest example, however, of Johnson's "occasional" writing is undoubtedly the short introduction he was commissioned (by that dogmatic Whig and republican, Thomas Hollis) to provide in 1760 for a pamphlet in which the "Committee for Cloathing French Prisoners of War" published an accounting of their expenditure of funds collected from the public. The committee was a group of volunteers who, shocked at the distress in which enemy prisoners were kept during the Seven Years' War, arranged to provide them with the necessities of life. The project had been attacked by noisy "patriots"—why spend money to give comfort to the hated French?—but it appealed to Johnson, who had opposed the war from the beginning. Johnson made, therefore, a moving appeal for humanity:

It has been urged that charity, like other virtues, may be improperly and unseasonably exerted; that while we are relieving Frenchmen, there remain many Englishmen unrelieved; that while we lavish pity on our enemies, we forget the misery of our friends.

Grant this argument all it can prove, and what is the conclusion? That to relieve the French is a good action, but that a better may be conceived. This is all the result, and this all is very little. To do the best can seldom be the lot of man; it is sufficient if, when opportunities are presented, he is ready to do good. . . . That charity is best of which the consequences are most extensive: the relief of enemies has a tendency to unite mankind in fraternal affection; to soften the acrimony of adverse nations, and dispose them to peace and amity: in the mean time, it alleviates captivity and takes away something from the miseries of war. The rage of war, however mitigated, will always fill the world with calamity and horror; let it not then be unnecessarily extended; let animosity and hostility cease together; and no man be longer deemed an enemy than while his sword is drawn against us.

Johnson's argument is so much in advance of its time that the International Red Cross, having rediscovered the piece a few years ago and been impressed by its anticipation of the principles on which Henri Dunant was to organize the Red Cross a century later, reprinted it in French translation in its bulletin, under the caption "Un Siècle avant Solférino."[12]

Variety of Interests

The range of Johnson's interests and involvements is, by modern standards, fantastically great. His major works alone are sufficiently varied, establishing him as a pioneer in lexicography, in biography, in criticism; as a skilled and original poet; as a periodical essayist; and as a writer of the *conte philosophique*. But, when one dips into his ostensibly minor writings, one is even more forcibly struck by the exuberance of his mind—and some of these are "minor" only by virtue of their being insufficiently known by the majority of students, even Johnsonian students. One cannot really call the law lectures he helped to compose for the Vinerian Professor of Law at Oxford, to deliver as a sequel to Blackstone's *Commentaries*, a minor work; nor the collection of nearly thirty sermons of his that have survived; nor the half-million or so words recording the parliamentary debating of the three hectic years surrounding the fall of Walpole.

If space permitted, many more quotations might be included here showing Johnson contributing to a medical encyclopedia; settling the principles of import taxation ("Further Thoughts on Agriculture" and "Considerations on Corn"); instructing his readers in a method of ascertaining the longitude at sea (for Anna Williams's father, Zachariah); contributing an excellent chapter to his friend Mrs. Lennox's novel *The Female Quixote;* writing election addresses for his friend Henry Thrale; introducing books on the design of Chinese buildings and how to play checkers; reviewing books on the involved controversy about whether or not it was right to shoot Admiral Byng (Johnson, as might be surmised, thought—along with Voltaire—that it was very far from right); and writing about the latest experiments, including Benjamin Franklin's, with electricity (about which Johnson predicted that a great deal more was going to be learned).

About the dangerous prevalence of the new-fangled custom of drinking tea, Johnson commented, "[The author] is to expect little justice from the author of this extract, a hardened and shameless tea-drinker, who has for twenty years diluted his meals with only the infusion of this fascinating plant, whose kettle has scarcely time to cool, who with tea amuses the evening, with tea solaces the midnight, and with tea welcomes the morning." Johnson also provided elegant dedications for Percy's *Reliques*, Reynolds's *Discourses*, Burney's *History of Music*, and for Burney's later account of the first great Handel festival, in Westminster Abbey in 1784 (Johnson's last piece of prose written for publication). When one finds him as well, in his more private moments, riding to hounds, swimming on Brighton beach, clambering among the Hebridean hills, charring his wig over the retorts in his private chemical laboratory, and, in the last months of his life, following with interest the first balloon ascents in London (had he not, in *Rasselas*, made a gloomily accurate prediction of the future use of military aircraft?), one sees how the tradition of the Renaissance man lived on, in one individual at least, into the eighteenth century. Or, if one does not want to hazard so grandiose an observation, at least it can be argued with justice that Johnson possessed the material out of which great journalists are made.

Chapter Four
The Biographer

"To write the Life of him who excelled all mankind in writing the lives of others . . . is an arduous, and may be reckoned in me a presumptuous task"—so Boswell begins his *Life of Johnson*. Certainly Johnson made great contributions to both the theory and the practice of biography, and this noble tribute to his pioneering achievement is well justified. The nature of Johnson's achievements was, in essence, to change the concept of the purpose of biography from a crudely didactic to a genuinely artistic one.

Before Johnson, biography may be said to have been dominated by the example of Plutarch, who wrote "parallel lives" of great Greeks and Romans in order to demonstrate to his readers the right or the wrong way to conduct a public life and to illustrate for them the consequences of virtue or folly. In practice, of course, the didactic purpose of Plutarch and his successors frequently fell victim to their delight in the variety of human life merely for its own sake. Still, in theory, the chief justification Plutarch and most other biographers before Johnson could find for writing biography was that of teaching by good or bad example; anything or everything else may be subordinated to that purpose, Plutarch proclaims:

As it is hard, or rather impossible, to find a man whose life is entirely free from blame, it becomes our duty to relate their noble actions with minute exactitude, regarding them as illustrative of true character, whilst, whenever either a man's personal feelings or political exigencies may have led him to commit mistakes and crimes, we must regard his conduct more as a temporary lapse from virtue than as disclosing any innate wickedness or disposition, and we must not dwell with needless emphasis on his failings, if only to save our common human nature from the reproach of being unable to produce a man of unalloyed goodness.[1]

If this intention now seems amusingly naive, one has Johnson largely to thank for the change in outlook. To be sure, the biographer's care for the reputation of "our common human nature" persisted long after Johnson; it gave rise, in Victorian times, to "those two fat volumes with which it is our custom to commemorate the dead . . . with their ill-digested masses of material, their slipshod style, their tone of tedious panegyric" of which Lytton Strachey complained. But, in challenging that custom, Strachey is merely Johnson's successor; his rebuttal is one that Johnson would surely have endorsed: "Human beings are too important to be treated as mere symptoms of the past. They have a value which is independent of any temporal process—which is eternal, and must be felt for its own sake. . . . It is not [the biographer's] business to be complimentary; it is his business to lay bare the facts of the case, as he understands them. . . . [His motto must be] 'Je n'impose rien; je ne propose rien; j'expose.'"[2]

The Theory of Biography

Johnson's concern for the "independent value" of human lives and the need of the biographer to "expose" without "imposing" was frequently expressed. When, in his *Lives of the Poets,* he came to the life of Addison and found himself treating of a time when persons who still lived might be hurt by his relation, he lamented that "The necessity of complying with the times and of sparing persons is the great impediment of biography"; he felt himself "walking upon ashes under which the fire is not extinguished." Charged with "mentioning ridiculous anecdotes in the lives of the poets, he said, he should not have been an exact biographer if he had omitted them. The business of such a one, said he, is to give a complete account of the person whose life he is writing, and to discriminate him from all other persons by any peculiarities of character or sentiment he may happen to have." Defending his life of Lyttelton, he observed that "it was the *duty* of the biographer to state *all* the failings of a respectable character. . . . 'Sir, I considered myself entrusted with a certain portion of truth.'" What he wants is "the little things which distinguish domestic characters"; he reprehends "the disposition generally found in writers of lives, to exalt every common occurrence and action into wonders." "If a man is to write a panegyric, he may keep vices out of sight; but if he professes to write a life, he must represent it really as it was." And Johnson said much more to the same effect.[3]

Johnson was acute enough to sense *why* some people are disturbed by honest biography, and to put his finger squarely on the fundamental mistake in their thinking. When told, in connection with his report that Addison had reclaimed a loan to his friend Steele by a legal execution, that "some people thought that Mr. Addison's character was so pure that the fact, though true, ought to have been suppressed," Johnson replied: "If nothing but the bright side of characters should be shewn, we should sit down in despondency and think it utterly impossible to imitate them in anything. The sacred writers [of the Bible] . . . related the vicious as well as the virtuous actions of men, which

had this moral effect, that it kept mankind from *despair,* into which otherwise they would naturally fall, were they not supported by the recollection
that others had offended like themselves, and by penitence and amendment
of life had been restored to the favour of Heaven."

This answer is the proper one of Augustinian Christianity—well aware
that "our common human nature" was corrupted at the time of the Fall and
can never be something to be proud of—to Plutarch's overly high Greek estimate of its claims. As Johnson suggests, there is a good deal of comfort in the
doctrine of original sin since, forgiveness being possible, the Christian need
not distress himself to preserve the reputation of the human race by distorting
the cold facts about it. Or, as Johnson put it on another occasion, when
Boswell expressed fear that he had put too many "little" incidents into his
journals: "Nothing is too little for so little a creature as man."[4]

Johnson's classic statement of the theory of biography, in *Rambler 60,* is a
remarkably brilliant piece of criticism. He begins by exploring the basic
sources of literary pleasure: "All joy or sorrow for the happiness or calamities
of others is produced by an act of the imagination that realizes [makes real]
the event, however fictitious, or approximates [brings close] it, however remote, by placing us, for a time, in the condition of him whose fortune we
contemplate; so that we feel, while the deception lasts, whatever motions
[emotions] would be excited by the same good or evil happening to ourselves" (the anticipation of Coleridge's "willing suspension of disbelief" will
be noted). Empathy, then, or identification, as one might call it, is the basis of
most literary experience. For such empathy to be possible, he continues, there
must be a basis of common experience: "Our passions are therefore more
strongly moved, in proportion as we can more readily adopt the pains or
pleasure proposed to our minds, by recognizing them as once our own. . . . It
is not easy for the most artful writer to give us an interest in happiness or misery which we think ourselves never likely to feel, and with which we have
never yet been made acquainted."

Johnson has, therefore, no love for "the general and rapid narratives of
history, which involve a thousand fortunes in the business of a day" and "afford few lessons applicable to private life, which derives its comforts and its
wretchedness from the right or wrong management of things which nothing
but their frequency makes considerable." On another occasion, when Lord
Monboddo declared, "I never set a high value on any other history [than the
history of manners]," Johnson agreed: "Nor I; and therefore I esteem biography, as giving us what comes near to ourselves, which we can turn to use."[5]
Johnson presumably would have approved of the modern "Namierian"

school of historiography, which regards history as essentially a collection of biography.

From these premises, it follows, first, that it is not necessarily those individuals who have made the greatest noise in the world, the Charles XIIs or the Napoleons, who are the most suitable or rewarding subjects for biography; second, that it is not the "large" but the "small" events of human lives that may be really the most significant. The passage in which Johnson formulates this idea is one of his most moving and memorable pieces of writing:

I have often thought that there has rarely passed a life of which a judicious and faithful narrative would not be useful. . . . There is such an uniformity in the state of man, considered apart from adventitious and separable decorations and disguises, that there is scarce any possibility of good or ill but is common to human kind. . . . We are all prompted by the same motives, all deceived by the same fallacies, all animated by hope, obstructed by dangers, entangled by desire, and seduced by pleasure. . . . The scholar who passed his life among his books, the merchant who conducted only his own affairs, the priest whose sphere of action was not extended beyond his duty, are considered as no proper objects of public regard, however they might have excelled in their several stations, whatever might have been their learning, integrity, and piety. *But this notion arises from false measures of excellence and dignity, and must be eradicated by considering that, in the esteem of uncorrupted reason, what is of most use is of most value.*

Johnson's set of biographical values agrees with Wordsworth's, when he speaks of "That best portion of a good man's life, / His little, nameless, unremembered acts / Of kindness and of love."

It is not too hard to see how what might be called Johnson's "existential" view of biography is related to his religion and, through it, to his social and political thinking. Johnson is always a Protestant—more precisely, a Christian of the Augustinian tradition—in that the fundamental unit in his thinking is never "society," or any sort of group postulated on the basis of some sociological theory, but always the lone individual, who in the sight of God is as important as any other individual. In light of this fact the petty social distinctions of this world become trivial; the value judgments of the historian become unimportant; in the end, the relationship that primarily matters is that between the individual and his God, and everything else reduces to terms of that relationship. Those biographies are therefore best—he remarks profoundly in his other essay devoted to the subject, *Idler 84*—"which are levelled with the general surface of life, which tell not how any man became great, but how he was made happy; not how he lost the favour of his prince, but how he became discontented with himself."

At first, it seems harder to understand how Johnson can reconcile an existential view of biography, an insistence on telling how things actually happened, and the rejection of Plutarchian didacticism, with his contention that the function of Plutarchian didacticism, with his contention that the function of biography, as of all other literature, is to "instruct." In fact, he begins *Rambler 60* by saying that biography is potentially the most instructive form of literature. This question of instruction appears frequently in any discussion of Johnson's literary theory, and it may as well be dealt with now. To attribute to Johnson so primitive a notion as that overt didacticism ("giving precepts," as his *Dictionary* defines the word)—the author's saying to the reader, "This is good, that is bad: do this, do not do that"—is the only, or the best, way that literature "instructs" is to make Johnson a far less acute and experienced observer of human psychology than he clearly was. He is as well aware as any modern aesthetic theorist that the instruction conveyed by art takes place on a much deeper neural level.

Johnson insists at the beginning of *Rambler 60* that the aesthetic pleasure inherent in successful literature comes from the deep emotional involvement of the reader in the work itself. As he says of Shakespeare, he "has perhaps excelled all but Homer in securing the first purpose of a writer, by exciting restless and unquenchable curiosity and compelling him that reads his work to read it through." Poetry must "instruct *by pleasing*," Johnson says time and again; one may venture to paraphrase this expression in modern psychological terms: "by involving the reader emotionally, literature effects desirable changes in the patterns in his nervous system." One learns from experiencing, not from listening to precepts; and the best way the writer can help the reader to learn is by extending his experience and involving him vicariously in more and deeper life—life as it has actually been lived.

"The most effective psychotherapy is that provided by life itself," a psychiatrist has remarked; and Johnson would have seen no reason to disagree: "Let us endeavour to see things as they are," he wrote to his friend Langton. "Whether to see life as it is will give us much consolation, I know not; but the consolation which is drawn from truth, if any there be, is solid and durable; that which may be derived from error must be, like its original, fallacious and fugitive."[6] Or, as his contemporary, the great Bishop Joseph Butler, put it, "Things and actions are what they are, and the consequences of them will be what they will be: why then should we desire to be deceived?" "If we owe regard to the memory of the dead," *Rambler 60* concludes, "there is yet more respect to be paid to knowledge, to virtue, and to truth."

The Practice; Early Lives

Johnson's theory of biography is one that not too many biographers since his time, and among them only the greatest, have succeeded in following. When one turns to his own practice, one finds that the impressionistic technique that such a theory entails is in fact used and with excellent artistic results. Johnson's selection of subjects for biography is highly various, including small as well as great names. Some of his finest touches come indeed in the biographies of "small" men. If the name of Edmund Smith, for instance, is at all remembered today, it is through Johnson's recording of his Oxford nickname, "Rag," given him for his carelessness of dress, and because Smith's friendship with Gilbert Walmesley gives Johnson an opportunity to include in his life memorable and moving tributes to Walmesley and Garrick. About all that is known of John Pomfret is Johnson's story that he got into trouble with the Bishop of London because of the implication in his poem "The Choice" that a mistress is preferable to a wife. Of Lord Lyttelton as an author (he was a prominent Whig politician, and he and Johnson may have known each other as boys), little is remembered except Johnson's amusing account of the vanity with which he wrote and published his *History of Henry II*—how he hired a self-proclaimed expert to punctuate the work for him, and appended to its third edition a list of errata nineteen pages long—and of how "poor Lyttelton," as Johnson deflatingly termed him, wrote a letter of humble gratitude to the *Critical Review* for a favorable notice of another of his books.

Johnson's insistence on the importance of the "trivial," concrete detail is well illustrated in his lives, especially the later ones. The following, describing Pope in later life, shows how effective it can be; after reading it, one feels that one has never really known Pope before:

He was then so weak as to stand in perpetual need of female attendance; extremely sensible of cold, so that he wore a kind of fur doublet, under a shirt of a very coarse warm linen with fine sleeves. When he rose, he was invested in a bodice made of stiff canvas, being scarcely able to hold himself erect, till [it was] laced, and he then put on a flannel waistcoat. One side was contracted. His legs were so slender that he enlarged their bulk with three pair of stockings, which were drawn on and off by the maid; for he was not able to dress or undress himself, and neither went to bed nor rose without help. His weakness made it very difficult for him to be clean.

Johnson's career as a biographer falls fairly neatly into three periods: the early lives, written chiefly for the *Gentleman's Magazine,* 1738 to 1744; a middle group in the 1750s and early 1760s; and finally the *Lives of the Poets,* 1777 to 1781. Johnson's introduction to biography came as something incidental to other activities. He planned to write a life of Politian in connection with his edition of Politian's poems in 1734 and one feels that the somewhat Bohemian career of this Renaissance poet would have been a congenial subject. The short sketch of Father Paul Sarpi, published in the *Gentleman's Magazine* in 1738, was, Sir John Hawkins says in his *Life of Johnson,* "an abridgement, as it seems, of that life of him which Johnson intended to have prefixed to his translation of the History of the Council of Trent." In this twenty-five-hundred-word sketch one already finds Johnson's characteristic way of proceeding: it contains a certain amount of factual information, quite baldly presented, interspersed with "editorial comment" by the compiler. For example, Johnson relates that Sarpi took the vows of the Servite order in his fourteenth year, and then he remarks: "a time of life in most persons very improper for such engagements, but in him attended with such maturity of thought, and such a settled temper, that he never seemed to regret the choice he then made." After Johnson lists in detail the doctrines regarding the authority and infallibility of the Pope that were maintained by the ultramontane side in the controversy between Rome and Venice at the time of the Council of Trent, he comments: "Maxims equally shocking, weak, pernicious, and absurd."

"The Life of Dr. Herman Boerhaave, late Professor of Physic [medicine] in the University of Leyden in Holland," which appeared in the *Gentleman's Magazine* in 1739, was reprinted three years later in revised form in Robert James's *Medicinal Dictionary,* together with a dozen other biographical articles perhaps by Johnson, mostly about ancient Greek, Roman, and Arabian writers on medicine (articles which have been very little studied by Johnsonian scholars).[7] In the life of Boerhaave, Johnson begins to develop his talent of relating the incidents he describes to broad questions of general interest. He does full justice to the very important place of Boerhaave in the history of medicine and scientific research, but he is clearly more interested in the working of the mind and sensibility of Boerhaave as a human being, and in the implications of his life for other human beings. After listing the honors bestowed on Boerhaave, Johnson adds: "Boerhaave was not one of those learned men of whom the world has seen too many, that disgrace their studies by their vices, and by their unaccountable weaknesses make themselves ridiculous at home while their writings procure them the veneration of distant countries, where their learning is known but not their follies."

After a harrowing account of Boerhaave's illnesses and his habit of diverting his mind from his sufferings by concentrating on his studies, Johnson adds: "This is perhaps an instance of fortitude and steady composure of mind, which would have been for ever the boast of the Stoic schools, and increased the reputation of Seneca or Cato. The patience of Boerhaave, as it was more rational, was more lasting than theirs; it was that *patientia Christiana* which Lipsius, the great master of the Stoical philosophy, begged of God in his last hours; it was founded on religion, not vanity." Again, summarizing an oration in which Boerhaave strongly criticized scholastic methods of inquiry, Johnson permits himself a short lecture on the subject of the superiority of Baconian and Lockean empiricism—the "scientific method": "The emptiness and uncertainty of all those systems, whether venerable for their antiquity, or agreeable for their novelty, he has evidently shown; and not only declared, but proved, that we are entirely ignorant of the principles of things, and that all the knowledge we have is of such qualities alone as are discoverable by experience, or such as may be deduced from them by mathematical demonstration."

With the life of Boerhaave may be joined that of another physician, the seventeenth-century Englishman Thomas Sydenham, which Johnson prefixed to an edition of Sydenham's works in 1742. One of Johnson's slightest productions, it deals principally with the questions of whether or not Syndeham's prowess in medicine was due to his following the regular laborious course of study (Johnson decides that it was, and that the theory of Sydenham's "spontaneous" genius appeals only to the lazy); whether he wrote the Latin in which his works appeared or his friends translated them for him (Johnson is sure he wrote the Latin); and what he could have meant, when Sir Richard Blackmore asked him what books he should read to qualify himself as a physician, by recommending *Don Quixote*.

Johnson's next two lives (1740), those of Oliver Cromwell's victorious admiral, Robert Blake, and Queen Elizabeth's Sir Francis Drake, seem curious excursions into naval history; but they are readily explained in terms of Johnson's political associations at the time. Since coming to London, he had been writing violent diatribes against the regime of Sir Robert Walpole, which was soon to fall. Badgered by the opposition clamor for a more aggressive foreign policy, Walpole had reluctantly declared war on Spain, Britain's chief naval and commercial rival; it had, indeed, been an incident involving an English merchant seaman, Captain Jenkins, that had precipitated the declaration. Walpole pursued the war halfheartedly and with little success; it was now obviously good tactics for the opposition to remind the public of the "glorious" triumphs of English naval might in the past—indeed, over Spain itself.

As with many of these early lives, much of the material in the Blake and

Drake pieces is "lifted" with little change from other sources.[8] Both are lucid and readable pieces of reporting; but, as usual, Johnson's editorial additions are of most interest. There are not too many in the life of Blake: a dry observation, "Of his earliest years we have no account, and therefore can amuse the reader with none of those prognostics of his future actions so often met with in memoirs"; a not very flattering reference to "Bishop Laud's violence and severity"; and a stern rebuke of the treatment of Blake's body after the Restoration when, with those of some other Puritan leaders, it was exhumed and treated with contempt: "Had he been guilty of the murder of Charles I," Johnson says, "to insult his body was a mean revenge; but as he was innocent, it was, at least, inhumanity, and, perhaps, ingratitude. 'Let no man,' says the Oriental proverb, 'pull a dead lion by the beard.'"

The life of Drake, the most ambitious biographical narrative Johnson had yet attempted, ran for five issues of the *Gentleman's Magazine*. A vivid and appreciative recital of exciting adventure, it is full of Johnsonian philosophizing. Speaking of Drake's opponents at court, he observes:

There are some men, of narrow views and grovelling conceptions, who without the instigation of personal malice treat every new attempt as wild and chimerical, and look upon every endeavour to depart from the beaten track as the rash effort of a warm imagination, or the glittering speculation of an exalted mind, that may please and dazzle for a time, but can produce no real or lasting advantage. These men value themselves upon a perpetual skepticism . . . upon inventing arguments against the success of any new undertaking, and, where arguments cannot be found, upon treating it with contempt and ridicule. Such have been the most formidable enemies of the great benefactors to mankind . . . for their notions and discourse are so agreeable to the lazy, the envious, and the timorous, that they seldom fail of becoming popular, and directing the opinions of mankind.

It is clear that Johnson's temperament, at this period at least, was hardly that of a mossbacked conservative. He brings to bear on the story of Drake's exploits two ideas that often recur in his later writing. One is his distrust of the notion of "the noble savage": "Whether more enlightened nations ought to look upon them [primitive races] with pity, as less happy than themselves, some skeptics have made, very unnecessarily, a difficulty of determining. More, they say, is lost by the perplexities than gained by the instruction of science. . . . The question is not, Whether a good Indian or bad Englishman be most happy? but, Which state is most desirable, supposing virtue and reason the same in both? . . . He that never saw, or heard, or thought, of strong liquors, cannot be proposed as a pattern of sobriety. . . ."

The second is his detestation of the oppression of indigenous populations by European invaders. Drake made a policy of "treating the inhabitants with kindness and generosity; a conduct at once just and politic, to the neglect of which may be attributed many of the injuries suffered by our sailors in distant countries, which are generally ascribed rather to the effects of the wickedness and folly of our own commanders, than the barbarity of the natives, who seldom fall upon any unless they have been first plundered or insulted."

The life of John Philip Barretier sprang from an incident in which Johnson was directly involved. Barretier had been a child prodigy of European scholarship: the German boy was supposed to have been the master of five languages at the age of nineteen, in 1740. Elizabeth Carter, who was only three years older than Barretier, and whom Johnson knew as a fellow contributor to the *Gentleman's Magazine,* had a similar reputation for precocious scholarship; and the parents of the two had entered into a correspondence, apparently with a view to a possible marriage between them.[9] After this romantic project was ended by the boy's death, the Reverend Mr. Carter turned the correspondence over to Johnson, who did what he could with it in an article in the *Gentleman's Magazine* in 1740, subsequently added to it, and published it as a separate pamphlet in 1742.

As might be expected, Barretier's is the most personal and in some ways the most interesting of these early biographical essays. Johnson declines to join in the uncritical acclaim of young Barretier's accomplishments and scrutinizes the evidence for them minutely (though, on the whole, he agrees that they were extraordinary). He often suggests the possibility of Barretier's father having exaggerated them. The life contains the amusingly cynical observation that, when Barretier's fame became known, "Princes, who are commonly the last by whom merit is distinguished, began to interest themselves in his success"—this is still the Johnson of "SLOW RISES WORTH BY POVERTY DEPRESS'D."

The life of Peter Burman, published in the *Gentleman's Magazine* in 1742, is less "Johnsonian." A fairly straightforward obituary of the noted Dutch jurist, historian, philologist, and rector of the University of Utrecht, who had died the year before, this account includes more than most about the subject's personal qualities:

He was a man of moderate stature, of great strength and activity, which he preserved by temperate diet without medical exactness. . . . In his hours of relaxation he was gay, and sometimes gave way so far to his temper, naturally satirical, that he drew upon himself the ill-will of those who had been unfortunately the subjects of his mirth; but enemies so provoked he thought it beneath him to regard or to pacify; for he was fiery, but not malicious, disdained dissimulation, and in his gay or serious hours preserved a settled detestation of falsehood. So that he was an open and undisguised friend or enemy, entirely unacquainted with the artifices of flattery, but so judicious in his choice of friends, and so constant in his affection to them, that those with whom he had contracted familiarity in his youth had for the greatest part his confidence in his old age.

Burman seems rather like the later Samuel Johnson; and, indeed, in these early lives of dedicated, ambitious, and venturesome scholars and public men, one can perhaps detect a kind of pattern of what Johnson wished to be himself. After this early group of lives Johnson wrote his masterpiece, the life of Richard Savage, published in 1744, and later included it in the *Lives of the Poets.* This work is important enough to deserve separate treatment later in this chapter.

The Middle Group

The middle group of lives is characterized, on the whole, by more interesting subjects—presumably Johnson was now in a better position to pick and choose—and by fuller and more interesting treatment. These biographies contain some of his most rewarding writing and have been unjustifiably neglected by students. The first of them—which, indeed, might be more suitably put in the first group, since like most of those it appeared in the *Gentleman's Magazine,* and is treated at about the same length and with the same amount of detail—is a rather perfunctory life (1748) of Lord Roscommon, a very minor Restoration poet noted chiefly for his verse translation of Horace's *Art of Poetry.* Johnson later reprinted the life among his *Lives of the Poets,* which are as much criticism as biography; indeed, the critical part of the Roscommon article is longer and better than the biographical section.

But the next in the group is a much more impressive performance—the life of Dr. Francis Cheynel (1751). Cheynel was the parliamentary "reformer" of Oxford University during the Civil War, a dogmatic and humorless Puritan scholar and divine. Johnson's detailed account of his career is a masterpiece of dry and deadly irony under a surface of seemingly objectivity:

As he appears to have held it as a first principle that all great and noble spirits abhor neutrality, there is no doubt but that he exerted himself to gain proselytes.

He then retired into Sussex, to exercise his ministry among his friends, in a place where, as he observes, there had been little of the power of religion either known or practised. As no reason can be given why the inhabitants of Sussex should have less knowledge or virtue than those of other places, it may be suspected that he means nothing more than a place where the Presbyterian discipline or principles had never been received.

Nor does [Cheynel] appear to have been cruel to [Chillingworth], otherwise than by that incessant importunity of disputation, to which he was doubtless inclined by a sincere belief of the danger of his soul, if he should die without renouncing some of his opinions.

Johnson makes skillful use of quotations from Cheynel's acrimonious prose, and the work adds up to a most delightful deadpan damning of a man who, to Johnson's mind, exemplified the dangers of the Puritan temperament; it is a kind of trial run for his later similar treatment of Milton's Puritanism.

Johnson's obituary in the *Gentleman's Magazine* of 1754 of his friend and employer, Edward Cave, is short (it was, of course, written quickly) and perhaps surprisingly—or perhaps not—free from extravagant encomium. Johnson bends over backward in order not to flatter the deceased. His "constancy was calm," one is told, "and to those who did not know him appeared faint and languid; but he always went forward, though he moved slowly. . . . He was a friend rather easy and constant than zealous and active. . . . His mental faculties were slow. He saw little at a time, but that little he saw with great exactness." Johnson cannot resist telling at least one amusing anecdote about Cave's intellectual pretensions:

Cave now began to aspire to popularity; and being a greater lover of poetry than any other art, he sometimes offered subjects for poems, and proposed prizes for the best performers. The first prize was £50, for which, being but newly acquainted with wealth, and thinking the influence of £50 extremely great, he expected the first authors of the kingdom to appear as competitors, and offered the allotment of the prize to the universities. But when the time came, no name was seen among the writers that had ever been seen before; the universities and several private men rejected the province of assigning the prize. At all this Mr. Cave wondered for a while; but his natural judgment, and a wider acquaintance with the world, soon cured him of his astonishment. . . .

The long memoir of the King of Prussia, written when he had just begun the career that was to win him the title of Frederick the Great, is more an exercise in historiography than in biography. Published in three installments in the *Literary Magazine* (1756–57), it was part of Johnson's ambitious project to provide the readers of that journal with "coverage in depth" of the Seven Years' War, which was just beginning. The English background of the conflict had been dealt with in a brilliant series of articles, and much of this memoir narrates the Continental background.

The first few pages of the article are an admirable sketch of the early life of the great Frederick, a subject that later engaged the talents of Macaulay and Carlyle. But whether their detailed pictures of Frederick's astonishing upbringing—his father's penchant for seven-foot grenadiers, the brutal discipline, Frederick's attempt to run away, the execution of his friend Katt before his eyes, and his forced marriage—are any more memorable than Johnson's terse one is hard to say. What interests Johnson most is Frederick's concern with learning and the arts. He describes this interest at some length, but is extremely skeptical: "The acquisitions of kings are always magnified. His skill in poetry and in the French language has been loudly praised by Voltaire, a judge without exception, if his honesty were equal to his knowledge."

The long life of Sir Thomas Browne, prefixed to an edition (largely done by Johnson) of Browne's *Christian Morals* in 1756, has always been somewhat of a disappointment to students of Johnson. One expects, perhaps, a tone of more enthusiasm for the Norwich physician who, like Johnson, cultivated poetic prose and an interest in scientific, moral, and psychological matters. Johnson's treatment of Browne is so detached that it gives the impression almost of coolness, if not hostility, toward his subject. The reader, however, should be cautioned that this impression may be largely the product of Johnson's "objective" idiom of biographical writing. Even the lives of those whom he most admired—Pope, for instance—contain a fair amount of adverse criticism of aspects of his subject, and, in such lives as those of Milton, Gray, Swift, and Lyttelton, the estimate of what has been called his "prejudice" against his subjects may be exaggerated because the reader does not sufficiently take this idiom into account.[10]

At the same time Johnson permits himself a good deal of real censure of Browne's life and works, and, in view of the tradition of somewhat uncritical encomium of the *Religio Medici,* one might do well to take more seriously Johnson's strictures, or rather faintness of praise: "It, indeed, contains many passages which, relating merely to his own person, can be of no great importance to the public; but when it was written, it happened to him as to others, he was too much pleased with his performance not to think that it might please others as much; he therefore communicated it to his friends, and receiving, I suppose, that exuberant applause with which every man repays the grant of perusing a manuscript, he was not very diligent to obstruct his own praise by recalling his papers."

Johnson then discusses at some length the matter of an author's slyly making it feasible for his work to be published "without his permission." He also mentions, rather perfunctorily, the book's "novelty of paradoxes, the dignity of sentiment, the quick succession of images, the multitude of abstruse allusions, the subtlety of disquisition, and the strength of language"; but he spends more time over the complimentary correspondence about the book between Browne and Sir Kenelm Digby, which he sums up in the memorable aphorism, "The reciprocal civility of authors is one of the most risible scenes in the farce of life." Johnson wonders whether the book is not too self-centered. He takes exception to Browne's remark that "his life has been a miracle of thirty years." What, after all, is so miraculous about Browne's life? For "The wonders probably were transacted in his own mind: self-love, cooperating with an imagination vigorous and fertile as that of Browne, will find or make objects of astonishment in every man's life; and, perhaps, there is no human being, however hid in the crowd from the observation of his fellow mortals, who if he has leisure and disposition to recollect his own thoughts and actions, will not conclude his life is in some sort of a miracle." This statement is, of course, little more than a paraphrase of what Johnson has already said in *Rambler 60*: "I have often thought that there has rarely passed a life of which a judicious and faithful narrative would not be useful." Johnson, however, seems to miss the point here: if Browne insists that his life is a miracle, surely it is only to imply that any other man's, viewed in the same way, would likewise appear one.

In connection with the *Vulgar Errors*, Johnson comments: "Notwithstanding his zeal to detect old errors, he seems not very easy to admit new positions, for he never mentions the motion of the earth but with contempt and ridicule." And of the *Urn Burial*, he writes: "Of the uselessness of these inquiries, Browne seems not to have been ignorant"; but he goes on to praise the concluding paragraphs in which Browne discourses on the doctrine of the immortality of the soul. Johnson makes mild fun of *The Garden of Cyrus*, with its obsession about quincunxes—"so that a reader, not watchful against the power of his infusions, would imagine that decussation was the great business of the world, and that nature and art had no other purposes than to exemplify and imitate a quincunx." (Interestingly, Johnson himself was sufficiently influenced by Browne's infusions to incorporate the vocabulary of the quincuncial treatise into his notorious definition of *network* in the *Dictionary*: "Anything reticulated or decussated, with interstices between the intersections.") He defends Browne against the charge of being an infidel but is no admirer of his prose style: "It is vigorous, but rugged; it is learned, but pedantic; it is deep, but obscure; it strikes, but does not please." All this, of course, is far too judicious to please the full-fledged Browne enthusiast.

The life of Roger Ascham was prefixed to an edition of Ascham's works in 1761, Johnson apparently having done the work of editing for the nominal editor, James Bennet. It is one of Johnson's most felicitous lives, perhaps because he finds himself back in his favorite period, the Renaissance, the time when, as he says in the *Life,* "Learning . . . was prosecuted with that eagerness and perseverance which in this age of indifference and dissipation it is not easy to conceive." Johnson follows Ascham's career as a scholar and teacher with loving care, digressing to discuss such matters as the supersession of the longbow by the musket (apropos of *Toxophilus*), the variation in the value of money from one era to another (apropos of Ascham's pension of ten pounds), the reason Ascham should have obtained preferment under Queen Mary Tudor and Bishop Gardiner, although his Protestantism was well known (Johnson is inclined to attribute it to caprice, which he feels plays a larger part in history than it is generally given credit for).

The Lives of the Poets

The third group of Johnson's biographies is the *Lives of the Poets,* begun in 1777 and published in two installments, the first in 1779 and the second in 1781. The title by which they are generally known is somewhat of a misnomer, and it has perhaps misled students who expect to find them full-fledged "lives" and discover they are not. The story of how the lives came to be written is well known. A syndicate of the leading London booksellers, in order to preserve what they considered their copyright against "invasion" by a similar scheme of an Edinburgh publisher, decided to issue a collection of the works of the English poets of the past hundred years or so in sixty or seventy volumes, and engaged Johnson to write a short biographical and critical prefatory note to the work of each of the fifty-two poets to be included. Many of Johnson's prefaces remained just that, but for many of the major poets he expanded the piece far beyond the length the publishers had contemplated (in the end they generously paid him double what they had contracted).

Johnson's prefaces were first published together with the volumes containing the poetry, and designated *Prefaces, Biographical and Critical, to the Works of the English Poets.* And this title expresses precisely what they are. Johnson usually devotes the first half of each preface to biography, often concluding this part with a "character," a summing up of the personality of the poet; the second half is a critique of his writings. In later editions, where they were published separately from the poems, they were entitled *The Lives of the Most Eminent English Poets; with Critical Observations on their Works;* in time, the second phrase came to be dropped, with resulting bafflement to the novice.

The critical sections of the *Lives of the Poets* add up to the most substantial body of literary criticism yet produced in English (with the possible exception of Johnson's own preface and annotations to Shakespeare's plays). As biography, they are perhaps not quite so impressive. Certainly, as everyone has complained, the biographical sections give the impression of having been written in a desultory manner: Johnson is often frank in saying that he found little material available, and Boswell leaves the impression that his indolence was so great that he could hardly bestir himself to make use of anything except what was immediately at hand—an impression that should be corrected, however, by reading F. W. Hilles's study of the making of the *Life of Pope*.[11]

It is clear, of course, that Johnson took some lives much more seriously than others. The biographical part of the *Life of Pope* runs to around thirty-seven thousand words; those of Milton and Dryden to around twenty-two thousand (though a great deal of the Dryden is "critical" rather than biographical, including short summaries of Dryden's works as the "life" proceeds); of Swift, to sixteen thousand; of Addison, to thirteen thousand; of Waller, to twelve thousand. The remaining forty-six are much shorter, only a few (Cowley, Prior, Blackmore—the *biographical* parts) running to as much as five thousand words. The great bulk of the long Cowley essay is criticism; the biographical part of the *Life of Young* was written by Herbert Croft; the long *Life of Savage,* written thirty-five years before, will be discussed separately.

There seems to be general agreement that the *Life of Pope* is, as biography, the masterpiece of the group. Its "texture" is close: Pope led (outwardly) an uneventful life, and the space Johnson allots to it permits him to treat it with an amount of detail not available for the others. That detail is often brilliant, as in the description of Pope's physical weakness, quoted earlier, or in the account of his upbringing and education—a part of his subjects' lives to which Johnson gave particular care: as he says, in connection with Addison, "Not to name the school or the masters of men illustrious for literature is a kind of historical fraud"—or the account of the famous grotto at Twickenham:

Here in his garden he planted the vines and the quincunx which his verses mention; and being under the necessity of making a subterraneous passage to a garden on the other side of the road, he adorned it with fossil bodies, and dignified it with the title of a grotto, a place of silence and retreat, from which he endeavoured to persuade his friends and himself that cares and passions could be excluded. A grotto is not often the wish or pleasure of an Englishman, who has more frequent need to solicit than to exclude the sun; but Pope's excavation was requisite as an entrance to his garden, and as some men try to be proud of their defects, he extracted an ornament from an inconvenience, and vanity produced a grotto where necessity enforced a passage.

If the *Life of Pope* is outstandingly successful, it is because it is close to Johnson's own life (Johnson was thirty-five when Pope died, and they had many acquaintances in common), because Johnson had the greatest admiration of Pope as a writer, and because the highly "literary" life of Pope, in circles and under circumstances that Johnson knew very well, was exactly the kind of thing Johnson was best qualified to write and best liked writing. On the other hand, of Dryden's life, too little was known to Johnson to make a really satisfying biography possible. The *Life of Addison*, though on a smaller scale, is also excellent; perhaps for the same reason the *Life of Pope* is. The *Life of Milton* belongs to a very different class from that of Pope. Milton's was an eventful life, closely connected with the highest affairs of state; and it belonged to a bygone generation, of which Johnson could have no direct knowledge and which had passed into history—history more controversial in Johnson's day than it is now, even though Eliot once remarked that the Civil War is not yet ended.

The *Life of Milton* is unquestionably a work with a thesis—what might be called a politico-psychological thesis. Whether or not one is convinced by that thesis, it must be granted that it is carefully worked out and that such a thesis is a rather remarkable anticipation of the kind of thing such recent sociologists as David Riesman and Harold Lasswell have done in attempting to work out correlations between certain types of personality and certain patterns of political thinking and behavior. Although Johnson throughout the work pays the highest tribute to Milton's intellectual and artistic genius, he points at the same time, whenever the opportunity arises, to what he sees as Milton's egocentricity and the querulousness (and sometimes self-contradiction) that arose from it. After quoting Milton's denunciation of university theatricals ("the antic and dishonest gestures of Trincalos, buffoons, and bawds"), Johnson remarks: "This is sufficiently peevish in a man who, when he mentions his exile from the college, relates, with great luxuriance, the compensation which the pleasures of the theatre afford him." Of Milton's refusal to become a clergyman, who must "subscribe slave, and take an oath withal," Johnson's comment is that "The thoughts of obedience, whether canonical or civil, raised his indignation." He cites Milton's exalted opinion of his own talents, which, however, Johnson does not entirely disapprove, committed as he is to the principle he enunciates in the *Life of Pope*, "Self-confidence is the first requisite to great undertakings." (Johnson is remarkably close to modern psychiatry in recognizing how much the inner security of most people—like his own—has been damaged and how much it needs support.)

From self-importance, however, arises unjustified resentment and hostility. Johnson quotes the full title of Milton's *Of Prelatical Episcopacy,* in which the generally popular Archbishop Ussher is contemptuously referred to, "to show . . . that he [Milton] had now adopted the puritanical savageness of manners" ("savageness," to be sure, in the sense of barbarousness, lack of cultivation, rather than of violence). Quoting a long diatribe against the university, Johnson remarks: "This is surely the language of a man who thinks that he has been injured"—though how Cambridge had injured Milton would be hard to determine. Milton's psychology is the target of some of Johnson's driest wit:

Such is his malignity that hell grows darker at his frown.

[Milton's first wife, who deserted him] seems not much to have delighted in the pleasures of spare diet and hard study. . . . Milton was too busy to much miss his wife.

[Apropos of Milton's turning against the Presbyterians, whimsically, as Johnson thinks.] He that changes his party by his humour is not more virtuous than he that changes it by his interest; he loves himself rather than truth.

[On Milton's continuing in the post of Latin secretary after Cromwell abolished Parliament and ruled as Protector.] Milton, having tasted the honey of public employment, would not return to hunger and philosophy; but, continuing to exercise his office under a manifest usurpation, betrayed to his power that liberty which he had defended. Nothing can be more just than that rebellion should end in slavery.

Next year, having defended all that wanted defense, he found leisure to defend himself.

[After the Restoration] Proportioning his sense of danger to his opinion of the importance of his writings, he thought it convenient to seek some shelter, and hid himself for a time in Bartholomew close.

To Johnson, "His political notions were those of an acrimonious and surly republican. . . . Milton's republicanism was, I am afraid, founded in an envious hatred of greatness, and a sullen desire of independence; in petulance impatient of control, and pride disdainful of superiority. . . . It is to be suspected that his predominant desire was to destroy rather than establish, and that he felt not so much the love of liberty as repugnance to authority. It has been observed that they who most loudly clamour for liberty do not most liberally grant it." The "observer" here was probably Johnson himself, who, a few years before in *Taxation No Tyranny* had inquired of southern American patriots like Thomas Jefferson and Patrick Henry, "How is it that we hear the loudest yelps for liberty from the drivers of Negroes?" There were not wanting those in Johnson's own time or later who raised their hands in shocked horror at such treatment of the sainted Milton (or, for that matter, the sainted Jefferson). Yet the charges are not easy to rebut; and to condemn Johnson for giving them publicity, if they do have weight, one must have recourse to Plutarch's principle that it is desirable for the reputation of human nature to have good men made to seem better than they actually are.

In the still uncertain state of studies of Swift's psychology one cannot quickly pass judgment on Johnson's *Life of Swift*. Johnson, it is clear, thought considerably less of Swift, both as man and as writer, than most people now do (though much more highly of him than such Victorians as Thackeray and Macaulay did). Certainly, some of his barbed shafts were sharpened for certain attitudes of Swift's; in particular, an attitude Swift shared with Pope and Gay, alluded to at the end of this summing-up paragraph of the *Life*:

> Of Swift's general habits of thinking . . . he was not a man to be either loved or envied. He seems to have wasted life in discontent, by the rage of neglected pride and the languishment of unsatisfied desire. He is querulous and fastidious, arrogant and malignant; he scarcely speaks of himself but with indignant lamentations, or of others but with insolent superiority when he is gay, and with angry contempt when he is gloomy. From the letters that passed between him and Pope it might be inferred that they, with Arbuthnot and Gay, had engrossed all the understanding and virtue of mankind; that their merits filled the world, or that there was no hope of more.

Perhaps the explanation of the something less than idolatry of the *Life of Pope* and the straightforward disparagement of Swift (though allowance must always be made for the normal "objectivity" of Johnson's biographical idiom) is that, when Johnson was a young, struggling, unknown writer in London in the 1730s and 1740s, Pope and Swift were the recognized masters of their craft, the literary Establishment of their time. Johnson, as always, was one to "fly at the eagle," as he advised Fanny Burney to do; and, even forty years later, he could not forget that they had been the Establishment. But

Johnson's attitude toward Swift is a matter that should some day be made the subject of close analysis.

A great many of the lesser lives are, of course, only the barest summaries in a few paragraphs of what was generally known about their subjects. But the delight the lives hold for the modern reader comes not from these bare facts so much as from their operation on Johnson's mind. He reminisces freely, as when the mention of "Rag" Smith leads him to his memories of Walmesley and Garrick. Speaking of the reception of *Absalom and Achitophel,* he is reminded that "the sale was so large that my father, an old bookseller, told me he had not known it equalled but by Sacheverel's trial." He dwells on Addison's schooldays at Lichfield and tells the story of Addison's organizing a "barring-out" of a schoolmaster—a tale "told me when I was a boy, by Andrew Corbet of Shropshire, who had heard it from Mr. Pigot, his uncle."

He editorializes in the most casual and open way. When he comes to Dryden's career as a playwright, he (like other students, perhaps) is bored by the prospect and is quite frank in telling the reader so: "I wish that there were no necessity of following the progress of his theatrical fame or tracing the meanders of his mind through the whole series of his dramatic performances." In the life of Watts, the great Nonconformist hymn-writer, Johnson lets it be known that "The poems of Dr. Watts were by my recommendation inserted in the late collection: the readers of which are to impute to me whatever pleasure or weariness they may find in the perusal of Blackmore, Watts, Pomfret, and Yalden" (it is wily of Johnson to insert the statement here, for Watts is a fine poet). After giving copious extracts from Pope's translation of Homer: "Of these specimens every man who has cultivated poetry . . . will naturally desire a greater number; but most other readers are already tired, and I am not writing only to poets and philosophers." The short *Life of Collins* (an expansion of an earlier journalistic piece) is very personal; Johnson knew the unhappy young poet well: "By degrees I gained his confidence; and one day was admitted to him when he was immured by a bailiff that was prowling in the street"—Johnson had had some experience with prowling bailiffs himself. He helped Collins to get an advance from a bookseller and did not leave him until "He showed me the guineas safe in his hand."

Even when Johnson does not use the first-person pronoun, he never hesitates to make known his own opinions and feelings about what he reports; and he is sometimes delightfully witty. Speaking of Collins's poverty, he observes: "A man doubtful of his dinner, or trembling at a creditor, is not much disposed to abstracted meditations or remote inquiries"—as no doubt Johnson knew from experience. He makes devastating fun of Shenstone's landscape gardening on a shoestring: "In time his expenses brought clamours about him that overpowered the lamb's bleat and the linnet's song; and his groves were haunted by beings very different from fawns and fairies"— insistent creditors and bailiffs, no doubt. He shocked "liberal" readers by observing of Akenside (much as he had of Milton): "He certainly retained an unnecessary and outrageous zeal for what he called and thought liberty; a zeal which sometimes disguises from the world, and not rarely from the mind which it possesses, an envious desire of plundering wealth and degrading greatness." And Johnson concludes the life of "poor" Lord Lyttelton with an outrageously ambiguous observation: "Of his death a very affecting and instructive account has been given by his physician, which will spare me the task of his moral character." The *Lives* are casual, opinionated, vivid, impressionistic, intensely personal, and about as far away as one can get from "academic." They are very "modern" in the sense of being tremendously alive.

Life of Savage

But Johnson's masterpiece of biography was his *Account of the Life of Richard Savage,* which, as has been already noted, was written shortly after Savage's death in 1743 and reprinted several times before being included in the *Lives of the Poets* in 1781. It was written with great speed—one account says in thirty-six hours—and obviously with great emotion, which informs the whole work. The critic Cyril Connolly some years ago included it as the first item in a collection entitled *Great English Short Novels,* and it is not hard to see why: quite apart from the obvious comment, that Savage's story of his birth and upbringing was fictitious, the power and feeling with which Johnson tells the story are closer to the novelist's art than to that of most biographers.

The themes of the story are archetypal: the child persecuted by the wicked stepmother (in this case, the real mother); the individual of great gifts, the tragic hero, doomed to destruction; the misery of the artist in a hostile society. Savage (according to his own story, which no one yet has been able either to prove or disprove) was the child of the Countess of Macclesfield by the Earl Rivers. On her public confession of adultery Lord Macclesfield divorced her and had an act of parliament passed declaring the child illegitimate (otherwise, it would have been the legal heir to his earldom). As Savage and Johnson tell the story, Lady Macclesfield, who had an intense hatred for the child, neglected and disowned him. Johnson recounts all this in a heightened, even melodramatic, manner. Savage had been brought up to believe himself the son of his nurse and only discovered he was Lady Macclesfield's by going through some letters after the nurse's death: "Savage was . . . so touched with the discovery of his real mother that it was his frequent practice to walk in the dark evenings for several hours before her door, in hopes of seeing her as she might come by accident to the window, or cross her apartment with a candle in her hand. But all his assiduity and tenderness were without effect, for he could neither soften her heart nor open her hand." One wonders what bearing this reveling of Johnson's in the theme of maternal rejection has on his own personal problems.

Johnson then narrates Savage's career as a poverty-stricken Grub Street writer, and gives a wonderfully vivid picture of the Bohemia of the time that he himself knew so well. He tells the story of Savage's conviction for murder after a brawl in a coffeehouse; how Lady Macclesfield attempted to persuade Queen Caroline not to pardon him (according to Savage)— "Thus had Savage perished by the evidence of a bawd, a strumpet, and a mother"—and how the gentle countess of Hertford interceded for him and secured his freedom. He recounts how Savage, who must have had an amazingly attractive personality, was taken up by one patron after another, and succeeded in alienating them all; and at last was persuaded to live in Wales on a small stipend raised by the charity of friends: "He left London in July, 1739, having . . . parted from the author of this narrative with tears in his eyes." In Swansea, and later Bristol, Savage continued his improvident way and finally was put in debtors' prison, where he died. Johnson paints the scene of his death vividly: "The last time that the keeper saw him was on July 31st, 1743; when Savage, seeing him at his bedside, said, with an uncommon earnestness, 'I have something to say to you, sir'; but, after a pause, moved his hand in a melancholy manner; and, finding himself unable to recollect what he was going to communicate, said, ' 'Tis gone!'"

The greatness of the work lies in the amount of himself that Johnson put into it. Like many others he was obviously fascinated by Savage and greatly influenced by him. Much of the bitterness and violence found in Johnson's writings during 1738 and 1739 may be the result of his association with Savage: both Savage and the young Johnson had decided masochistic ("injustice collecting") tendencies. It is clear that Johnson identifies himself to some extent with Savage, and that the indignation he expresses so dramatically for Savage's apparent wrongs is also indignation for Samuel Johnson's— "SLOW RISES WORTH BY POVERTY DEPRESS'D."

At the same time Johnson is a shrewd enough psychologist to see how much of Savage's misery was self-inflicted, and along with the indignation and sympathy goes much devastatingly acid comment on Savage's own folly and self-deception. Indeed, Johnson states this theme clearly at the beginning of the life:

That affluence and power . . . should very often flatter the mind with expectations of felicity which they cannot give raises no astonishment; but it seems rational to hope that intellectual greatness should produce better effect . . . that they who are most able to teach others the way to happiness should with most certainty follow it themselves. But this expectation, however plausible, has been frequently disappointed.

As in the case of Samuel Johnson himself, one is compelled to add:

It was his peculiar happiness that he scarcely ever found a stranger whom he did not leave a friend; but it must likewise be added that he had not often a friend long without obliging him to become a stranger.

By imputing none of his miseries to himself, he continued to act upon the same principles and to follow the same path; was never made wiser by his suffering, nor preserved by one misfortune from falling into another. He preceded throughout his life to tread the same step on the same circle; always applauding his past conduct, or at least forgetting it, to amuse himself with phantoms of happiness which were dancing before him.

Johnson tells the story of how, when Savage was in dire poverty, some friends decided to furnish him charitably with a much-needed suit of clothes: "Instead of consulting him and allowing him to send a tailor his orders for what they thought proper to allow him, they proposed to send for a tailor to take his measure and then to consult how they should equip him. . . . Upon hearing the design that was formed, he came to the lodging of a friend with the most violent agonies of rage; and, being asked what it could be that gave him such disturbance, he replied, with the utmost vehemence of indignation, 'That they had sent for a tailor to measure him.'" One is uncomfortably reminded of the pair of boots left by some kind friends at the door of Johnson's room in Oxford, when he was unable to attend lectures for want of footwear; as the friends stole away, the boots came flying after them, hurled down the stairs by the indignant Johnson.[12]

  At the end of the *Life,* Johnson prints a moving justification for Savage, which is also one for Johnson:

The insolence and resentment of which he is accused were not easily to be avoided by a great mind, irritated by perpetual hardships, and constrained hourly to return the spurns of contempt, and repress the insolence of prosperity; and vanity may surely be readily pardoned in him to whom life afforded no other comforts than barren praises, and the consciousness of deserving them.

  Those are no proper judges of his conduct who have slumbered away their time on the down of plenty; nor will any wise man presume to say, "Had I been in Savage's condition, I should have lived or written better than Savage."

It may well be that the *Life of Savage* is a kind of self-psychoanalysis of the resentful young Johnson, and that the act of writing it effected some kind of purgation of his resentment against the world: although flashes of violence were to recur throughout the rest of his life, he never again repeated in his writing the sustained bitterness of *London, Marmor Norfolciense,* and the *Complete Vindication of the Licensers.* But, whatever the cause, the *Life of Savage* is an extremely moving and effective work; and it is also an important pioneering application of psychological analysis to biography.

Johnson as Autobiographer and Diarist

In *Idler 84* Johnson recommends autobiography as of "most value," since the writer of it has no motive to distort the facts except "self-love, by which all have so often been betrayed that all are on the watch against its artifices." His encouragement of Boswell's diary-keeping is well known. Johnson's own practice was much more sporadic than Boswell's; nevertheless, there seem to have been few periods in his life, from the time he reached manhood, when he was not in the habit of jotting down records of his own activities and thoughts. Some days before he died he burned a large quantity of his private papers, including presumably "two quarto volumes, containing a full, fair, and most particular account of his own life, from his earliest recollection." Frank Barber rescued a few pages of an autobiography from the flames; the extracts given at the beginning of chapter 1 give some idea of its quality, and make us deeply regret the loss of the rest. Boswell's *Life of Johnson* is often praised for the amount of vivid and concrete detail that he uses, following Johnson's own precepts for biography, but Johnson's own *Life of Johnson* would clearly have been even finer.

In spite of the holocaust, enough fragments of private jottings have survived to fill a fairly large volume, the first of the Yale Edition of Johnson's *Works* (1958). Its most important contents, apart from the fragment of autobiography, are (a) his journals of his trips in 1774 and 1775 to Wales and France with the Thrales; (b) religious meditations, prayers, and self-examinations, usually at New Year's Day, at Easter, and on his birthday; (c) in his later years, a detailed medical diary. As reviewers pointed out when the volume appeared, it does not, on the whole, make very interesting or revealing reading. But there is no evidence that Johnson ever intended its contents to be read; and, in any case, his most revealing memoranda were presumably burned.

There has been a good deal of criticism of Johnson's diary entries. When his "Prayers and Meditations" were published shortly after his death, they were thought to exhibit "morbidity," in that Johnson examines his failings minutely and continually asks God for forgiveness of them. When the medical diary was added to these in the 1958 edition, the charge of "morbidity" was intensified; but this criticism is surely misconceived. The medical jottings are intended merely as a case history, for the assistance of Johnson's physicians and of himself in treating his numerous ailments; today these records are kept on charts at the foot of the patient's hospital bed. As for the prayers and meditations, the practice of frequent religious self-examination and periodical confession of one's sins (to God and oneself, if not to a priest) has been recommended for serious Christians for many centuries. The self-condemnations recorded in Johnson's prayers are no more "morbid" than those of the General Confession said at every morning and evening service in the Anglican Church: "We have left undone those things which we ought to have done, and we have done those things which we ought not to have done; and there is no health in us."

Users of older editions of the "Prayers and Meditations" should be warned that their first editor, the Reverend George Strahan (whom Johnson befriended as a boy), took outrageous liberties with them, deleting entries like this, from a paragraph written on the anniversary of Tetty's death, "On what we did amiss, and our faults were great, I have thought of late with more regret than at any former time. She was I think very penitent." He also omitted from Johnson's last prayer the important petition "Forgive and accept my late conversion." The editors of the 1958 edition, by use of infrared ray photography, were able to restore some, though not all, of Strahan's deletions.[13]

Chapter Five

The Moralist

Of the various epithets that have been applied to Johnson, that of "the great moralist" is certainly the most apt. But the term must not be misunderstood: Johnson's morality is not that of rigidly insisting on a predetermined and authorized pattern of "good behavior." True, he may, after consideration, come to the conclusion that certain traditionally approved ways of conduct are, in the end, the best; and he often expresses the opinion that, other things being equal, the preservation of tradition has the virtue of convenience: "All change is of itself an evil, which ought not to be hazarded but for evident advantage." But, when the "advantage" of change is "evident," the antiquity of a custom never deters him (as it might Burke) from condemning it. Boswell, who fulminated at Johnson's "prejudice" against Negro slavery, argued that "To abolish a status which in all ages GOD has sanctioned and man has continued would . . . be robbery to an innumerable class of our fellow-subjects [i.e., the slave-owners]." But this argument impressed Johnson not a whit; he had no intention of identifying God with the practice, however historic, of fallible human beings; and "In company with some very grave men at Oxford, his toast was 'Here's to the next insurrection of the Negroes in the West Indies.'"[1]

Morality for Johnson (as for other great writers on morality) is something that must rest on observation and information, on constant self-awareness and self-criticism. Johnson's practice as a moral writer can be described in the words Lionel Trilling uses to describe the modern novel, "the most effective agent of the moral imagination in our time": "Its greatness and its practical usefulness [lie] in its unremitting work of involving the reader himself in the moral life, inviting him to put his own motives under examination, suggesting that reality is not as his conventional education has led him to see it."[2] It is, of course, not merely in the works that, for convenience, are discussed in this chapter, but in his biographical work, his poetry, his journalism, and his criticism that one finds Johnson seeking to stimulate the reader's moral imagination, arouse his self-awareness, and inspire him to examine his motives, and question the teaching of his conventional education.

Morality and Religion

Johnson's morality is, of course, a part of his general religious position. A thorough study of Johnson's religion has yet to be undertaken. Students have been in the habit of dwelling on and magnifying trivial comments he made in the heat of conversation (often when baited by Boswell) so as to make his religious views seem much narrower and more prejudiced than they really were, and of neglecting the basic and important beliefs he held in common with thoughtful Christians of all denominations. It is true that Johnson was a "High Church" Anglican, in the eighteenth-century sense of "High Church" —the sense in which the Wesleys and William Law were "High Church": they took their religion very seriously and insisted on a high and respected status for the Church of England as the official vehicle of the religion in the general polity of the nation.

But one finds many expressions in Johnson's writings of a broad ecumenism, to use a modern term. If a person shows signs of a genuine adherence to the fundamentals of Christianity, Johnson does not worry a great deal about the denominational label to be attached to him. He gives unstinted praise to such "Dissenters" as Richard Baxter and Isaac Watts and to John Wesley, father of Methodism. Where T. S. Eliot, for instance, finds Milton a "Christadelphian," and other modern students have thought it necessary to explore at length Milton's deviation from strict orthodoxy in subtle points of doctrine, Johnson, despite his dislike of Milton's personality and political views, says flatly that he "appears . . . to have been untainted by any heretical peculiarity of opinion," and he makes copious use of quotations from his works in illustrating theological terms in the *Dictionary*. Of the Congregationalist Watts, he remarks: "It was not only in his books but in his mind that orthodoxy was united with charity."[3]

He devotes much space to defending Sir Thomas Browne from the charge of infidelity; and perhaps one fine paragraph from the *Life of Browne* may serve as a general statement of Johnson's feelings on the matter of denominational differences: "Men may differ from each other in many religious opinions, and yet all may retain the essentials of Christianity; men may sometimes eagerly dispute, and yet not differ much from one another: the rigorous persecutors of error should, therefore, enlighten their zeal with knowledge, and temper their orthodoxy with charity; that charity without which orthodoxy is vain." The point is made again in his preface to Lobo's *Abyssinia,* where, after describing the controversy between seventeenth-century Protestant and Catholic scholars over the orthodoxy of the Abyssinian church, he dismisses it with, "Upon the whole, the controversy seems of no great importance to those who believe the Holy Scriptures sufficient to teach the way of salvation."

When Johnson from time to time censures members of other Christian bodies, both Catholics and Protestants, it is generally for betraying Christianity by uncharitable violence and persecution: John Knox's activities in Scotland, for instance—"I hope [he is buried] in the highway. I have been looking at his 'reformations'"—or the Catholic missionaries in South America and Abyssinia—

Let us suppose an inhabitant of some remote and superior region, yet unskilled in the ways of men, having read and considered the precepts of the Gospel and the example of our Saviour, to come down in search of the "true church." If he would not inquire after it among the cruel, the insolent, and the oppressive; among those who are continually grasping at dominion over souls as well as bodies . . . if he would not expect to meet benevolence engaged in massacres, or to find mercy in a court of inquisition, he would not look for the "true church" in the church of Rome.

Nor does Johnson spare the Anglican archbishop who later came to symbolize "High Churchmanship" for many people, William Laud. Johnson pairs him with the acrimonious Puritan Cheynel: "It had not been easy to have found either a more proper opposite; for they were both, to the last degree, zealous, active, and pertinacious."[4] It is true that Boswell also records Johnson's dropping adverse comments on doctrinal and disciplinary aspects of Nonconformity and Roman Catholicism. "In everything in which they differ from us they are wrong," he once said of the Roman Catholics; but Boswell could also lead him into defending certain Roman Catholic practices.[5] These differences were in the end unimportant to Johnson in comparison with the essential principles.

What *was* "orthodox" Christianity for Johnson? It was that which is defined in the Book of Common Prayer, the Thirty-Nine Articles, the Book of Homilies, and the writings of the great seventeenth-century Anglican divines which he read—men like Henry Hammond, John Pearson, and Robert South. His Christianity is well summarized in the translation of Boerhaave's statement of his creed with which Johnson concluded his life of the great Dutch scientist:

He asserted on all occasions the divine authority and sacred efficacy of the Holy Scriptures; and maintained that they alone taught the way of salvation, and that they only could give peace of mind. . . . A strict obedience to the doctrine, and a diligent imitation of the example of our blessed Saviour, he often declared to be the foundation of true tranquillity. He recommended to his friends a careful observation of the precept of Moses concerning the love of God and man. He worshipped God as he is in himself, without attempting to inquire into his nature. He desired only to think of God what God knows of himself. There he stopped, lest, by indulging his own ideas, he should form a Deity from his own imagination, and sin by falling down before him. To the will of God he paid an absolute submission, without endeavouring to discover the reason of his determinations; and this he accounted the first and most inviolable duty of a Christian. When he heard of a criminal condemned to die, he used to think, who can tell whether this man is not better then I? or, if I am better, it is not to be ascribed to myself, but to the goodness of God.

Perhaps the best word to describe the posture described here is "Evangelical"—a word that came in the nineteenth century to connote bitter religious controversy, but that Johnson himself had no hesitation in using. He praises Watts because "Under his direction, it may be truly said, *theologiae philosophia ancillatur,* philosophy is subservient to evangelical instruction"; "Nothing can be more repugnant to the general tenor of the evangelical revelation," he says in his *Sermon* XIII, "than an opinion that pardon may be bought, and guilt effaced, by a stipulated expiation." Johnson is, of course, using the word in the sense defined in his *Dictionary:* "Agreeable to gospel; consonant to the Christian law contained in the holy gospel." It would certainly seem a grave mistake, in view of these very serious statements of Johnson (and other similar ones), if one thought that the teachings of Christ in the Gospels were not the supremely important aspect of Johnson's religion. Other matters—church discipline, minute points of doctrine, the role of the church in the state—were important only as they influenced the propagation of that teaching. It is surely only on the basis of such a position that Johnson can resolutely affirm the orthodoxy of men so seemingly different from him as Milton, Watts, and Browne. If the reader, however, objects to the word "Evangelical," he may substitute for it "Augustinian."

For the benefit of some readers, it may be desirable to go into some detail about what the teachings of the Gospels implied in terms of individual morality for the sixteenth- to eighteenth-century English Christian; the same doctrine will be found in, say, Spenser, Milton, Donne, Herbert, Bunyan (whom Johnson greatly praised), and Swift, as well as Johnson. It insists, to begin with, that morality is an inward, not an outward, affair. In his *Sermon* XIII, on the text "Having a form of godliness, but denying the power thereof," Johnson tells us, "To give the heart to God, and to give the whole heart, is very difficult . . . but we may be zealously religious at little expense. . . . Thus some please themselves with a constant regularity of life, and decency of behaviour. . . . Their religion is sincere; what is reprehensible is that it is partial, that the heart is not yet purified."

When the heart is turned toward good and away from self-seeking, the outward behavior will follow. Going mechanically through the outward forms of "moral" behavior in the hope of propitiating a tyrannical God—the heresy of Pelagianism—is not virtue but sin. This simple meaning of the doctrine of justification by faith alone, often misunderstood by modern students, is clearly stated in the eleventh and thirteenth Articles of Religion of Johnson's church:

We are accounted righteous before God only for the merit of our Lord and Saviour Jesus Christ by Faith, and not for our own works or deservings. . . . Albeit that Good Works, which are the fruits of Faith, and follow after justification, cannot put away our sins . . . yet are they pleasing and acceptable to God in Christ, and do spring out necessarily of a true and lively faith. . . . Works done before the grace of Christ, and the inspiration of his spirit are not pleasant to God . . . yea rather, for that they are not done as God hath willed and commanded them to be done, we doubt not but they have the nature of sin.

What keeps the heart from turning toward good is self-will, egocentricity, *superbia*—pride, the first of the sins and the father of the rest. One has too high an opinion of one's importance in the scheme of things, and always feels that one's status is being threatened—"pride, simply considered," Johnson says, "is an immoderate degree of self-esteem, or an over-value set upon a man by himself. . . . He that overvalues himself will undervalue others, and he that undervalues others will oppress them." From pride stem envy, resentment, hatred, cruelty, inner discontent: "it mingles with all our other vices, and without the most constant and anxious care, will mingle also with our virtues."[6] It is therefore necessary to fight a constant war against it: to remind oneself continually that, measured with God's omnipotence and perfection, a human being can have little reason to feel complacent about his power, intellect, or virtue.

The converse of pride is love: only by cultivating genuine humility can one become capable of love—of God and of one's neighbor—and this perfect humility is something no sinful human being ever fully or permanently achieves; it must always be fought for anew. Johnson's private prayers must be read, therefore, in the light of this great tradition of morality: of Swift's conclusion about the Yahoos, "When I behold a lump of deformity and diseases both in body and mind smitten with *pride*, it immediately breaks all the measures of my patience"; Herbert's "Thou hast a garden for us where to bide; / Who would be more, / Swelling through store, / Forfeit their Paradise by their Pride"; Milton's "God doth not need / Either man's work or His own gifts"; Bunyan's Vanity Fair. Or, to cite later examples, there are Gerard Manley Hopkins's "dark sonnets" and Carlyle's "Reduce your denominator," up to such contemporary moralists as W. H. Auden ("You shall love your crooked neighbor / With your crooked heart") and T. S. Eliot (in *The Cocktail Party*):

> Half the harm that is done in this world
> Is due to people who want to feel important.
> They don't mean to do harm—but the harm does not interest them,
> Or they do not see it, or they justify it
> Because they are absorbed in the endless struggle
> To think well of themselves.

An excellent modern study of Johnson begins with the striking sentence, "Johnson was a pessimist with a great zest for living."[7] But the insistence on the necessity of reducing one's denominator, which informs so much moral teaching, from the Pentateuch up through the Gospels, St. Paul, and St. Augustine to the present time, is not pessimism. It is a message of hope; it tells how things can be improved, how happiness can be increased. The message may be comfortless to human complacency, but that is because it maintains that such complacency is itself the main thing that prevents genuine human happiness.

The Sermons

The most concise statement of the core of Johnson's moral position is *The Vanity of Human Wishes,* which, as has been noted in chapter 2, concludes that the mind *can* "make" the happiness it does not "find" by adopting as its values the nonmaterial ones of love, hope, patience instead of the worldly, self-seeking ones of fame, wealth, and power (all of which are servants of pride, means of ego-bolstering, of helping oneself to feel important). After reading the poem, the student does well who then explores Johnson's *Sermons,* a neglected but important and rewarding section of his writings. Not too much is known about the circumstances in which they were composed. They were all ghostwritten for others. Hawkins says in his *Life:* "About this time [before 1760], as it is supposed, he for sundry beneficed clergymen that requested him, composed pulpit discourses. . . . He reckoned that he had written about forty sermons; but, except as to some, knew not in what hands they were." And Hawkins adds in a footnote, "Myself have heard in the church of St. Margaret's, Westminster, sundry sermons; one in particular, Johnson being present"; and, when Hawkins charged him with its authorship, Johnson did not deny it. It was perhaps delivered by Johnson's friend from grammar school days, the Reverend John Taylor, rector of Ashbourne, Derbyshire, who was also a prebendary of Westminster from 1746 and eventually became rector of St. Margaret's. Johnson charged two guineas a sermon and could write one after dinner and send it off by post that night.

After Johnson's death, twenty-fine *Sermons on Different Subjects, Left for Publication by John Taylor* were published. All but two of them (*Sermon* XXI and the conclusion of *Sermon* XVIII), J. H. Hagstrum thinks, were by Johnson.[8] The last, *Sermon* XXV, was composed by Johnson for his wife's funeral. Taylor, so it is said, refused to deliver it on the grounds that it was too flattering to Tetty, but this late story is discredited by an examination of the sermon, which reveals nothing that might be termed exaggerated praise. Other sermons have been identified as Johnson's: a charity sermon preached at St. Paul's in 1745 by his friend Henry Hervey Aston; one delivered by the Reverend William Dodd at Newgate in 1777 before his execution for forgery; and one in manuscript in Taylor's hand with corrections by Johnson. The number identified still does not add up to forty (which, in any case, is likely to be an underestimate); and one hopes that in time others may be identified—for instance, one said to have been preached in a London church on the fifth of November and "afterwards published by command of the Archbishop." To read Johnson's thoughts about the religious significance of the Gunpowder Plot would be interesting. Yet even twenty-five published sermons is a fair number, when one recalls that only twelve by Swift, an ordained clergyman, seem to have survived.

The student who comes to Johnson's sermons from, say, Donne's, or even from *The Rambler,* may be surprised by the relatively dry, bare, formal quality of their style and organization. If so, he should remember that in the late seventeenth century there was a strong reaction against the emotionality and the elaborately ornamented prose of the great "metaphysical" preachers such as Donne and Lancelot Andrewes. It was felt by their successors, Tillotson and Barrow, that the pulpit was not the place for theatrical displays of baroque rhetoric, and that the preacher should address himself lucidly and directly to the minds of the members of the congregation. Hence even Johnson has to subdue some of the fairly large amount of early seventeenth-century baroque exuberance in his *Rambler* style, and confine himself to a straightforward "Firstly, secondly, thirdly." Less ornate though the prose is, however, it still has Johnson's basic strength, and his sermon style tends to grow on the reader, once he gets accustomed to its unfamiliarity.

The strength of such a passage as the following (the conclusion of *Sermon* XII, on the text "All is vanity"—a sermon which should be read as an explicatory footnote to *The Vanity of Human Wishes* by those who feel that the poem is "gloomy" and "morbid") is very satisfying:

When the present state of man is considered, when an estimate is made of his hopes, his pleasures, and his possessions; when his hopes appear to be deceitful, his labours ineffectual, his pleasures unsatisfactory, and his possessions fugitive, it is natural to wish for an abiding city, for a state more constant and permanent, of which the objects may be more proportioned to our wishes, and the enjoyments to our capacities; and from this wish it is reasonable to infer that such a state is designed for us by that infinite Wisdom which, as it does nothing in vain, has not created minds with comprehensions never to be filled. When revelation is consulted, it appears that such a state is really promised; and that, by the contempt of worldly pleasure, it is to be obtained. We then find, that instead of lamenting the imperfection of earthly things, we have reason to pour out thanks to Him who orders all for our good; that he has made the world such as often deceives, and often afflicts us; that the charms of interest are not such as our frailty is unable to resist; but that we have such interruptions of our pursuits, and such languor in our enjoyments, such pains of body and anxiety of mind, as repress desire and weaken temptation; and happy will it be if we follow the gracious directions of providence, and determine that no degree of earthly felicity shall be purchased with a crime; if we resolve no longer to bear the chains of sin, to employ all our endeavours upon transitory and imperfect pleasures, or to divide our thoughts between the world and heaven; but to bid farewell to sublunary vanities, to endure no longer an unprofitable vexation of spirit; but with pure heart and steady faith to "fear God and to keep his commandments"; and remember that "this is the whole duty of man."

The sermons deal, for the most part, with the basic commonplaces of Christian religion and Christian ethics: if one is uncertain about what these are, there could be no better way of beginning their study than by reading the sermons through carefully. There are sermons on marriage ("Though obediences may be justly required, servility is not to be exacted"); on repentance ("Not he that only bewails and confesses, but he that forsakes his sins, repents acceptably to God, that God . . . who will only accept a pure heart and real virtue, not outward forms of grief, or pompous solemnities of devotion"); on "hardness of heart" ("That which frequently occurs, though very dangerous, is not desperate; since it consists, not in the perversion of the will, but in the alienation of the thoughts; by such hearts God is not defied, he is only forgotten. Of this forgetfulness, the general causes are worldly cares and sensual pleasures"). There are also several on charity ("No method of charity is more efficacious than that which at once enlightens ignorance and relieves poverty. . . . Poverty for the greatest part produces ignorance; and ignorance facilitates the attack of temptation"); on pride ("To this fancied superiority it is owing that tyrants have squandered the lives of millions and looked unconcerned on the miseries of war. . . . Pride has been able to harden the heart against compassion, and stop the ears against the cries of misery"). There are sermons on not being "wise in your own conceits" ("Knowledge is to be attained by slow and gradual acquisitions . . . and is, therefore, the reward only of diligence and patience. But patience is the effect of modesty; pride grasps at the whole, and what it cannot hold, it affects to despise"); on "compassion of one another" ("To feel sincere and honest joy at the success of another, though it is necessary to true friendship, is perhaps neither very common nor very easy. There is in every mind, implanted by nature, a desire of superiority. . . . As cruelty looks upon misery without partaking pain, so envy beholds increase of happiness without partaking joy"). On the text "Man that is born of a woman is of few days, and full of trouble," Johnson prepared a sermon that concludes in a very different spirit: "In the multifarious afflictions with which every state of human life is acquainted, there is place for a thousand offices of tenderness; so that he, whose desire it is to do good, can never be long without an opportunity." There are sermons on the Communion, against calumny, and on the ignorance of man of the attributes of God. There are two very interesting sermons, XXIII and XXIV, on morality in questions of government, which will be referred to in the following chapter on Johnson's political attitudes.

This is only the briefest of samplings from this important record of Johnson's beliefs, forming a total of perhaps sixty thousand close-textured words of some of his most serious and effective writing. No one unfamiliar with them should think himself qualified to pronounce on the nature of Johnson's thought, for the positions discussed in them, resting on his lifetime acquaintance with the Bible, the Book of Common Prayer, and other Christian teachings, are very basic to his thinking. And they are rewarding to read, merely for the competence of the style.

Review of *A Free Enquiry into the Nature and Origin of Evil*

Another important work, somewhat better known than the sermons, though still not well enough, is Johnson's long review of Soame Jenyns's *A Free Enquiry into the Nature and Origin of Evil,* which ran in three issues of the *Literary Magazine,* April to June, 1757. It is a testimonial to the quality of Johnson's intellect that the book is now remembered only through Johnson's review of it. Jenyns was one of those pleasant, well-to-do, dilettantish gentlemen that eighteenth-century England seemed to abound in. Five years older than Johnson, he was an obedient Whig member of Parliament and a copious publisher of light verse and political pamphlets. For some reason he began to fancy himself as a theologian, and casually set himself the task of explaining to the world the age-old problem: how it happens, given a God who is both omnipotent and benevolent, that suffering exists in the world.

Jenyns, like Pope before him (Johnson's critique of the *Essay on Man,* in his *Life of Pope,* should be read along with the review of Jenyns) and to some extent Milton in *Paradise Lost,* opts for the old explanation that rests on the doctrine of "great chain of being." This doctrine, which derives from early Greek philosophy, sees the whole of existence in the universe as a hierarchal continuum that stretches without a break from infinity (perfection) at the top (God), down through the nine gradations of angels, through man (somewhere in the middle) and the animal creation, to zero. "Good," then, is to be defined as what is good for the "chain" as a whole. From this point of view, there is no evil: the lamb (to use one of Pope's examples) no doubt *thinks* his being butchered is an evil, but this is shortsighted reasoning on the lamb's part. From the point of view of his superiors in the chain of being, who are going to dine on him, it is a good thing (fortunately, Pope explains, Providence keeps the lamb in ignorance of his fate, so that on the whole he lives a happy life). So, if one takes the enlightened view, "Whatever is, is right," as Pope expressed it, or in the words of Dr. Pangloss in *Candide,* "Everything is for the best in the best of possible worlds."

It is interesting to find Voltaire, the avowed enemy of organized religion, and Johnson, the devout "High Churchman," joining forces against the Roman Catholic Alexander Pope and the moderately orthodox Anglican Jenyns (at least, he later became so, apparently after a flirtation with deism) —interesting if only to show how little such labels may tell about an individual's fundamental beliefs. Voltaire and Johnson are so hostile to this view because in the first place, as humanitarians, they are appalled by what seems a justification for cruelty and a recommendation to view it with complacency. In a passage of magnificent invective Johnson charges Pope and Jenyns with callousness: "Life must be seen before it can be known. This author and Pope perhaps never saw the miseries they imagine thus easy to be borne. The poor indeed are insensible of many little vexations which sometimes embitter the possessions and pollute the enjoyments of the rich [Jenyns had been using such arguments to minimize the alleged miseries of poverty]. They are not pained by casual incivility, or mortified by the mutilation of a compliment; but this happiness is like that of a malefactor who ceases to feel the cords that bind him when the pincers are tearing his flesh."

Later, with a brutality of satire never surpassed in Johnson, or perhaps in any other writer, even Swift, he takes up Jenyns's cool theory that, as human beings hunt animals for sport, so some invisible higher beings "may deceive, torment, or destroy us for the ends only of their own pleasure or utility":

I cannot resist the temptation of contemplating this analogy, which I think he might have carried further very much to the advantage of his argument. He might have shewn that these "hunters whose game is man" have many sports analogous to our own. As we drown whelps and kittens, they amuse themselves now and then with sinking a ship, and stand round the fields of Blenheim or the walls of Prague, as we encircle a cock-pit. As we shoot a bird flying, they take a man in the midst of his business or pleasure, and knock him down with an apoplexy. Some of them, perhaps, are virtuosi, and delight in the operations of an asthma, as a human philosopher [scientist] in the effects of the air pump. To swell a man with a tympany is as good sport as to blow a frog. Many a merry bout have these frolic beings at the vicissitudes of an ague, and good sport it is to see a man tumble with an epilepsy, and revive and tumble again, and all this he knows not why.

In the second place, Johnson, as a rationalist like Voltaire, cannot stomach the recommendation of ignorance as a good. Jenyns has argued that those "born to poverty and drudgery" should not be deprived by an "improper education" of the "opiate of ignorance." Johnson replies that even to concede this view "will not be of much use to direct our practice, unless it be determined who are those that are 'born to poverty.' To entail irreversible poverty upon generation after generation only because the ancestor happened to be poor is in itself cruel, if not unjust."

Jenyns has also argued that madness is one of kind Providence's ways of keeping the underprivileged happy; but Johnson knows better: "On the happiness of madmen, as the case is not very frequent, it is not necessary to raise a disquisition, but I cannot forbear to observe that I never yet knew disorders of mind increase felicity; every madman is either arrogant and irascible, or gloomy and suspicious, or possessed by some passion or notion destructive to his quiet. He has always discontent in his look, and malignity in his bosom. And, if we had the power of choice, he would soon repent who should resign his reason to secure his peace."

And then, in a superb passage, Johnson hurls at Jenyns and Pope the charge that their argument involves the dangerous immorality of making the end justify the means: "I am always afraid of determining on the side of envy or cruelty. The privileges of education may sometimes be improperly bestowed, but I shall always fear to withhold them lest I should be yielding to the suggestions of pride, while I persuade myself that I am following the maxims of policy; and under the appearance of salutary restraints, should be indulging the lust of dominion, and that malevolence which delights in seeing others depressed."

It might be added—what Johnson does not explicitly state but what is surely strongly implied in his comments on the well-to-do Pope's and Jenyns's willingness to administer opiates to the poor—that their view is a politically conservative one in the worst sense of the word, a view which ensures that the "haves" will conserve what they have and the sufferings of the "have-nots" can be safely ignored. Johnson, as a "have-not" for most of his life, was in a better position than Pope to know that "whatever is" very often is *not* right, and he had much more motive than Pope or Jenyns to rectify social wrong.

But Johnson's antipathy to the Pope-Jenyns thesis has still deeper roots. Many varieties of "Whatever is, is right" theorizing became popular in the eighteenth century—the vague Deistic benevolism of the third Lord Shaftesbury, with its notion that human nature has a built-in sense of what is virtuous; the primitivism of Rousseau, with the "noble savage" and the return to nature; the "self-evident natural rights of man" of the British "patriots" and the American revolutionists; laissez-faire economics as expounded by Adam Smith and adumbrated by Bernard Mandeville. And that of Jenyns rests on what is essentially the Stoic concept of "nature": the idea of the universe, things as they are, as an absolute, a norm, a legislator of moral law. How far this conception could go may be seen in the statements of seventeenth-century expounders of "natural law": "natural law" would exist even if God did not; God Himself cannot contravene its dictates.

As Lovejoy has suggested, the "great chain of being" concept so closely related to such theories has its roots in a Manichean, or dualist, theology. In it, one has no longer a single omnipotent Deity, but two equal and rival ones; and the other is matter, "nature," things as they are, over which God apparently has no control, or has surrendered it. Any hint of such a view must be anathema to the Augustinian Christian, who holds that, at the time of the Fall, nature too was corrupted, along with man, and that no norm can be taken from it. The implications, theological, moral, and political, of this fundamental difference are vast.

Johnson was not a professional theologian or philosopher, but in the

Jenyns review he seems to be well aware that it all goes back to the theological question: he speaks contemptuously of Jenyns's "revival of Chrysippus's untractableness of matter" (Chrysippus was one of the most noted Stoic writers); and he charges Jenyns and Pope with "dogmatical limitations of Omnipotence." Johnson is appalled by Jenyns's effrontery, as Voltaire is by Pangloss's. This kind of grandiose and futile theorizing is only another of the innumerable manifestations of spiritual pride. Jenyns would do better to examine his own limitations instead of God's, and like Candide, cultivate his garden: that is, write books that will "enable the readers better to enjoy life, or better to endure it."

Rasselas

Two years after the Soame Jenyns review Johnson wrote *Rasselas* "in the evenings of a week" in order to pay the expenses of his mother's last illness. Voltaire's *Candide, or Optimism,* another *conte philosophique* of about the same length, appeared at almost the same time; its hero, like Johnson's, is a naïve young man who wanders about the world and sees one illusion after another perish. One of the most remarkable coincidences in literary history is that the best-known living writers in both France and England should have had the same idea at the same time. Still, the "optimistic" nonsense both were attacking was widespread throughout Europe at the time (and later). There are, of course, some obvious contrasts in their works: Johnson, to be sure, introduces supernatural considerations that Voltaire avoids—but Johnson does so only very briefly and almost at the end of the story in the discussion of the immortality of the soul. The tone of *Candide* is one of grim, sardonic, deadpan satire, whereas that of *Rasselas* is mellower. G. B. Hill illustrates the difference by suggesting that, when the deluded aeronaut in *Rasselas* jumps from the cliff, Voltaire would have had him plunge instantly to the bottom of the lake and be drowned. Johnson allows his wings to bear him up in the water so that he can be hauled to shore. But the points of view of the two books are really astonishingly close.

Nothing is known about the actual genesis of *Rasselas.* It is, however, in the genre of the "Oriental tale," so popular in the eighteenth century: by shifting the scene from Europe to an idealized country in the East, greater scope for generalized teaching is achieved. The exotic "Eastern" country with which Johnson was of course most familiar was Abyssinia because of his early work in translating Father Lobo's account of his experiences there. It has been recently established, however, that most of the background material in *Rasselas* derives not from Lobo but from other books about travel in

Abyssinia that were available to Johnson.[9] That background material, by the way, is quite concrete and authentic: princes of the royal family of Ethiopia were, historically, exiled to a place similar to "the happy valley," the location of which is known—it is in the northern province of Amhara, as Johnson says. The name Rasselas ("Ras Selah" or "Ras Selach") is taken from the historical lists of members of the royal family, and the name Imlac (an Old Testament name) also appears in Ethiopian history.

As in the case of Candide, Rasselas, an inexperienced and good-hearted young man, wanders in search of an education, which turns out to consist chiefly of the destruction of various comforting illusions. Johnson's original title for the work was "The Choice of Life" (it was actually published as "The Prince of Abissinia" and was retitled Rasselas only in later editions), and the ostensible theme is that of finding the best way to live one's life. But it takes Rasselas some time even to get started on his quest, for the first of the four sections into which the book may for convenience be divided (the first fourteen of its forty-nine chapters) shows Rasselas still in the ironically named "Happy Valley," where every inhabitant's material and sensual wants are fully catered to. This state does not make the imaginative young man happy. The title of the third chapter, "the wants of him that wants nothing," indicates that man's mind and emotional apparatus cannot live by bread alone. He must have something to seek—later in the book Johnson speaks in a memorable phrase of "that hunger of imagination which preys incessantly upon life, and must be always appeased by some employment." This statement is, for one thing, a rebuttal of Stoicism—"Where then shall Hope and Fear their objects find? / Must dull Suspense corrupt the stagnant mind," as the Stoics recommend? Johnson makes it clear that he thinks man's capacity for thought and feeling was given to him by God to be used, not repressed, as in Stoic ethics; for life is to be involvement, not detachment. This point of view is consistent with the Gospel teaching of loving one's neighbor; and it also has overtones of Goethe's Faust, of Arnold's and Browning's divine discontent, even perhaps of Schopenhauer; for there is no guarantee that that involvement automatically produces happiness on earth.

The prince determines to get out of the "happy valley" and see the world, and the activity of planning and effecting the escape makes him happy for a while. The episode of the aeronaut is amusing: the enthusiastic theorist works out the aerodynamics of a pair of wings and proves mathematically that they will fly—only to plunge into the lake. It includes the already mentioned grim forecast, too accurately realized, of the development of military aircraft: "A flight of northern savages might hover in the wind, and light at once with irresistible violence upon the capital of a fruitful region that was rolling under them." (Johnson, as has been noted, lived to see the first flights of lighter-than-air craft in London the year before he died, and his letters show considerable interest in them.)

The second section, chapters 15 to 29, shows Rasselas, accompanied by his mentor Imlac and (unexpectedly) his sister Nekayah and her companion Pekuah, emerging from the tunnel they have driven through a mountain, travelling to Cairo, and proceeding to carry out their survey of the various schemes of life thought to make men happy. None of them turn out to be as advertised. The café society of "young men of spirit and gaiety" soon palls on the prince: "their mirth was without images, their laughter without motive." The simple life of the country dwellers, so praised by Rousseau and his disciples, turns out to be full of discontent. Men of wealth and high position cannot sleep for fear of the malice of those who envy them, or of losing the favor of the potentates upon whom they depend. They question a hermit as to the advantages of solitude; he is so upset by his inability to answer the question that he returns to Cairo with them. When Nekayah examines the theory that marriage and family life provide the deepest of satisfactions for women, she discovers that family life generates much rivalry and hostility; and she concludes, in a memorable remark, that "Marriage has many pains, but celibacy has no pleasures."

In two chapters Rasselas encounters lecturers who preach philosophic systems of happiness. In chapter 18 a Stoic, who advocates detachment, is unable to go on lecturing because of his grief over the death of his daughter (an old tale that Voltaire also made use of about the same time in his *Les Deux Consolés*). In chapter 22 another philosopher preaches impatiently that no one is unhappy but by his own fault. "The way to be happy," he proclaims, "is to live according to nature, in obedience to that universal and unalterable law with which every heart is originally impressed. . . . Let them observe the hind of the forest and the linnet of the grove; let them consider the life of animals, whose motions are regulated by instinct." Rasselas, much impressed, asks the philosopher just how to go about living according to nature. The philosopher obligingly explains: "To live according to nature is to act always with due regard to the fitness arising from the relations and qualities of causes and effects; to concur with the great and unchangeable scheme of universal felicity; to cooperate with the general disposition and tendency of the present system of things."

So Rasselas leaves in bafflement, and the philosopher "rose up and departed with the air of a man that had cooperated with the present system." One of the funniest passages in Johnson, its satire on philosophies resting on "following nature," is devastating. Shaftesbury, Samuel Clarke, perhaps

Rousseau, seem to be some of the individuals touched on in the passage; the "eternal fitness of things" is an old Stoic phrase. Perhaps the finest touch of satire comes when, after delivering his oration, that philosopher "looked round him with a placid air, and enjoyed the consciousness of his own beneficence."

In the third section, chapters 30 to 38, the story unexpectedly develops a hint of plot. The group visits the pyramids, which give Imlac an opportunity to discourse on the "hunger of imagination" that impels man to expend his effort on these useless objects. As the travelers emerge from the pyramid they have been exploring, they discover that Pekuah, the princess's companion, has been abducted in romantic fashion by a band of Arab horsemen who have swooped down on them. Nekayah is disconsolate and discovers that "She who has no one to love or trust has little to hope. She wants the radical principle of happiness." She wishes to retire into a cloister, but Rasselas argues that time and activity will help to put her loss in perspective; and so they do, though "her real love of Pekuah was yet not diminished."

After some months news comes that Pekuah is being held captive by an Arab chieftain. She is ransomed and returns to tell her friends of life in the harem, where her captors (who use her very decently) have placed her. Pekuah discovers that life in this female "Happy Valley" is as boring as Rasselas had found his own: the inmates' "talk could take nothing from the tediousness of life"; and, as for their master, the Arab chief (who is an intelligent man and teaches Pekuah astronomy), "whatever pleasures he might find among them, they were not those of friendship or society." The main point of the section, of course, is the great importance to happiness of human friendship, which, Johnson insists, must be on a basis of intellectual and emotional, not merely physical, pleasure, for women as well as for men.

The fourth section, chapters 39 to 47, is the story of the mad astronomer—the most fully worked-out incident in the book. It is a remarkably modern case history of the development of a schizophrenic condition and its cure.[10] The immensely learned astronomer, who has withdrawn from human society to devote himself to his solitary research, astonishes Imlac by informing him that he now controls the movements of the heavenly bodies: "I reasoned long against my conviction, and laboured against truth with the utmost obstinacy. I sometimes suspected myself of madness," says the astronomer in a wonderful piece of irony. When Imlac asks for scientific proof of this remarkable fact, the astronomer replies, "It is sufficient that I feel this power." The friends pity him, and Imlac gives a dissertation on "the dangerous prevalence of imagination." This phrase has often been misinterpreted to mean that Johnson disapproves of imagination (although the whole point of

Rasselas's leaving the happy valley—with Johnson's hearty approval—is that there is nothing there to feed his human "hunger of imagination"!). But "prevalence" here does not have its modern meaning of "widespread occurrence"—as in "Colds are prevalent in winter"; it means the condition of "prevailing," "dominating"—the danger when fantasy comes to prevail over one's contact with reality, as much a definition of insanity today as in Johnson's. It is most likely to occur when the individual dissociates himself from other people and from concrete experience, as the astronomer has done.

And the cure is to introduce the patient again to experience. The friends have the ingenious thought of letting the two girls play the major role in the therapy (one thinks of Johnson's own debt, a few years later, to Mrs. Thrale). They dress in their prettiest clothes, visit the shy astronomer, and make a great fuss over him. He is flustered at first, but he gradually starts to respond: "The sage confessed to Imlac that, since he had mingled in the gay tumults of life . . . he found the conviction of his authority over the skies fade gradually from his mind." But there are setbacks. "If I am accidently left alone for a few hours," the astronomer says, "my inveterate persuasion rushes upon my soul. . . . I am sometimes afraid lest I indulge my quiet by criminal negligence and voluntarily forget the great charge with which I am entrusted." To which Imlac gravely replies with a fine insight, "No disease of the imagination is so difficult of cure as that which is complicated with the dread of guilt."

The whole account is startlingly modern psychiatry. It might be noted, however, that traditional Christian morality, with its emphasis on pride, or egocentricity, as the cause of human misery, is very close to some post-Freudian psychiatric teaching, notably that of Erich Fromm and Karen Horney. Horney sees pride, an attempt to maintain a favorable image of oneself that differs from the reality, at the bottom of all neuroses; and Fromm finds the origin of such egocentricity in insecurity, early damage to the ego which makes the sufferer unable to believe that he can ever be acceptable to anyone as he actually is. Johnson knew all about this condition: he once said to Mrs. Thrale that he "had never sought to please till past thirty years old, considering the matter as hopeless."[11] Imlac's final advice to the astronomer is "Keep this thought always prevalent, that you are only one atom of the mass of humanity, and have neither such virtue nor vice as that you should be singled out for super-natural favours or afflictions."

The story ends abruptly with a short metaphysical disquisition on the question of the immortality of the soul and with the difficult last chapter, in which Rasselas and his companions review their experiences and reflections. Each of the young people has chosen an ideal vocation. Pekuah is to enter a convent and "fill it with pious maidens and to be made prioress of the order; she . . . would gladly be fixed in some unvariable state." Princess Nekayah is going to be a teacher: "she desired to learn all [!] sciences," and in her college to "raise up for the next age models of prudence and patterns of piety." Rasselas wants to administer a little kingdom "in which he might . . . see all the parts of government with his own eyes"; but the little kingdom always keeps getting bigger as he thinks about it.

Johnson closes the story with a passage that has puzzled many readers: "Of these wishes that they had formed, they well knew that none could be obtained. They deliberated a while what was to be done, and resolved, when the inundation should cease, to return to Abyssinia." There has been much controversy about the exact meaning of this final paragraph and indeed the concluding chapter is so loosely worded as to admit a good deal of ambiguity—perhaps Johnson was in a hurry to get the book finished and the copy off to the printer. Those who are convinced of Johnson's "pessimism" think it means that the young people throw up their hands in despair and return to immure themselves again in the "Happy Valley" from which they started, having accomplished nothing. But surely this is a strained reading imposed on the text by the preconception. They return to Abyssinia, but nothing is said about the Happy Valley, which, in any case, they might find it difficult to re-enter even if they wanted to; and, if anything is made clear in the book, it is that one "choice of life" that Rasselas would *not* consider is the stultification of the "welfare state" he spent so much of his time and energy escaping from. Presumably they will return to live in their native land and strive *toward* the ideals they have in mind, in full (and healthy) realization that, like other ideals, they will not be completely attained. In this interpretation, the end of the book is similar to that of *Candide:* one should "cultivate one's garden"; do what is in one's power to make the world a better place; but one is not to be disheartened if in the end one does not accomplish miracles: "Leave to heav'n the measure and the choice." This doctrine is not a pessimistic, but a very sane and healthy one, which, as Johnson and Voltaire suggest, is likely to produce such imperfect happiness as the world is capable of.

The Rambler, The Adventurer, and The Idler

This chapter has so far dwelt at some length on certain shorter works more easily summarized than what is after all Johnson's greatest achievement as a practical moralist—his periodical essays. *The Rambler* made Johnson's name—he is oftener referred to during his lifetime as "the author of the *Rambler*" than by any other epithet. The 203 *Ramblers* Johnson wrote (five were contributed by friends) and published every Tuesday and Saturday for two years are a tremendous repository of acute thinking and excellent writing on subjects concerning the human condition; the seasoned reader of Johnson, faced with the challenge of selecting Johnson's greatest single work, may well find himself in the end going back to the *Rambler* as the most solid example of the essential Johnson.

The genre of the periodical essay is something almost peculiar to the eighteenth century. As everyone know, Steele and Addison in *The Tatler* and in *The Spectator* gave the genre an auspicious start. Literally hundreds followed—the *Cambridge Bibliography of English Literature* lists a total of 322 titles between 1697 and 1802. Almost everyone with literary aspirations tried his hand at a few numbers of a periodical essay; even Boswell put out a mediocre one which he characteristically called *The Hypochondriack*. As a genre, this type of essay should be carefully distinguished from other forms of prose writing. It is not journalism, since it does not profess to inform the reader about current events. (Steele, indeed, did begin *The Tatler* with a journalistic purpose, which did not last long.) It differs from what might be called "sporadic" essay-writing simply in being periodical: clearly, if the author has to sit down every Tuesday and Saturday, whether he feels like it or not, and produce two or three thousand words of wisdom for his readers, the end product is going to be very different from, say, the collected essays of Bacon or Lamb. The closest analogy is the work of the modern columnist. Except, however, for writers who specialize in a single subject—politics or economics or sports or "society"—and as a result take essentially a non-journalistic approach to their material, the modern newspaper and magazine column is feeble stuff compared with the work of Addison and Johnson.

What the eighteenth-century periodical essay has in common with the "column" is the creation of an "image" of its writer—a process recognized and facilitated by calling the essays by the name of the fictitious personality responsible for them: Mr. Spectator, Mr. Rambler, the Midwife, the Old Maid, the Hyp Doctor, the Man About Town, the North Briton, the Literary Fly. This device enables the writer to let his opinions and the way he expresses them range with more freedom and variety than if he signed them openly. Indeed, Johnson's "Mr. Rambler" and "Mr. Idler" turn out, on the whole, to be two quite different personalities. To get the real flavor, the proper way to read periodical essays is not to select a few at random, here and there, as one may legitimately do with an ordinary collection of essays, but continuously, from beginning to end (ideally, of course, one on Tuesday and the next on Saturday, as they originally appeared, though this is a counsel of perfection). This continuous reading is not always so difficult a task as it may seem to the modern reader; indeed, there is perhaps no more delightful or effective introduction to Johnson than to read the hundred or so *Idler* papers through from first to last in the order in which they occur.

Johnson's *Rambler* (1750–52) had a long run for a periodical essay, a genre whose mortality rate was naturally very high: of those listed in the *Cambridge Bibliography* few produced as many as two hundred numbers, and, of those that did, many were partisan political sheets written by a syndicate. *The Rambler*'s sales in London, when first issued, were not large; but it was widely read when reprinted in provincial papers and in book form.[12] It was inevitably compared with *The Spectator*—perhaps Johnson, who followed Addison's footsteps in so many other ways, intended it to be—and there were many readers, like Lady Mary Wortley Montagu, who preferred the comparative lightness of Addison's subject matter and the ease of his prose to Johnson's tougher thinking and highly condensed style. Lady Mary said that *The Rambler* "followed *The Spectator* with the same pace a pack-horse would do a hunter."[13] The Johnsonian devotee might retort that *The Rambler* is often more heavily laden with valuable material than *The Spectator*. The work does, in fact, require careful and sensitive reading; indeed, analytical study in depth of its contents has not yet been attempted.

In the year after *The Rambler* ceased publication, Johnson began to contribute regularly to another periodical essay, *The Adventurer*, a joint effort of Johnson, Hawkesworth, Joseph Warton, and Bonnell Thornton. Johnson wrote twenty-nine *Adventurers* in all, at intervals of about a fortnight, during 1753–54. In solidity, the essays are closer to those of *The Rambler* than to those of Johnson's later venture, the *Idler,* published once a week in the *Universal Chronicle* (*The Rambler* and *The Adventurer* had been issued as separate leaflets) between April 1758 and April 1760. Johnson wrote all but eleven of the 104 *Idler* numbers. They are really very readable and amusing and, as has been suggested, an excellent place to begin reading Johnson for the first time, but much lighter (deliberately so, no doubt) and less memorable than the *Ramblers*. It has also been discovered that Johnson began still another periodical essay, *The Weekly Correspondent,* which ran for three numbers in the *Public Ledger* in December 1760.[14] These essays are very short and light—their titles are "On Authors," "On the Coronation," and "Tom Stucco" (a builder)—but are amusing enough to repay digging them out and reading them, if only to see how well Johnson could perform as a humorist.

It is difficult to give any real idea of the wealth and variety of Johnson's periodical essays in such short space. One can perhaps attempt a rough classification. One important group deals with literary criticism. There is the account (*Idlers* 60, 61) of Dick Minim, or how to become a critic without actually doing any reading—a hilarious spoof of the then-popular critical clichés. There is a close examination of Milton's versification (*Ramblers* 86, 88, 90, 94); a critique of *Samson Agonistes* (*Ramblers* 139, 140); several on the pastoral (*Ramblers* 36, 37; *Adventurer* 92); two brilliant papers on biography (*Rambler* 60, *Idler* 84); a pioneering attempt at criticism of that very young genre, the novel (*Rambler* 4); of journalism (*Rambler* 145); of letter-writing (*Rambler* 152); of historiography (*Rambler* 122); on translation (*Idlers* 68, 69) and imitation (*Rambler* 121). There is an important essay on the connotation of words, illustrated from *Macbeth* (*Rambler* 168); a number about the nature of literary criticism itself (*Ramblers* 3, 92, 93, 125, 156, 158, 176)—two of these, 156 and 158, on the "rules" of writing, of which Johnson is suspicious; and a great many about the problems of writers and the literary life.

Another large group consists of essays that tell, often amusingly and often in the form of a letter to "The Rambler," cautionary tales of individuals who are the victims of various foibles of the human race: Melissa, who loses her money and consequently her admirers; Hilarius, the town wit whose cleverness is not appreciated in the backwoods; the apathetic Dick Linger; the cheese-paring Mrs. Savecharges; Misocapellus who can't live down in high society the fact that he was "brought up in trade"; Miss Gentle, "a good sort of woman" in the worst sense of the term; Tom Tempest and Jack Sneaker, the rabid political partisans, Tory and Whig, respectively. Finally, a very large group consists of essays that straightforwardly discuss specific matters of practical morality—politeness (*Rambler* 83), idleness (*Rambler* 134), memory (*Idler* 74), and so on.

Among these a remarkable number express "humanitarian" views that most students think of, wrongly, in connection with the nineteenth rather than the eighteenth century: a bitter attack against imprisonment of debtors (*Idler* 22); a plea for sympathy for the lot of prostitutes and a scheme for their rehabilitation (*Rambler* 171); a discussion of the barbarity of the criminal law (*Rambler* 114)—Johnson's plea that capital punishment be restricted to cases of murder was far ahead of his time; a protest against vivisection (*Idler* 17), with attacks elsewhere on Descartes's theory that animals are without feeling, a theory apparently used to justify their mutilation in the interests of scientific "research"; against the tyranny of brutal country squires over their tenants and neighbors (*Rambler* 142). One of the most "modern" is *Rambler* 148, where Johnson, far from demonstrating a "conservative" reverence for the institution of the family, anticipates modern psychiatrists in laying the blame for a great deal of misery at its door. *The Idler,* written in the early years of the Seven Years' War, is full of the pacifism and antimilitarism found in Johnson's contributions to the *Literary Magazine.*

An illustration of how vigorously Johnson can write in the cause of human morality is the original *Idler* 22, suppressed when the essays were published in book form, no doubt because Johnson or his printer felt it was too shocking for the general reader. It is an allegory in which a mother vulture instructs her young how to go about procuring human flesh for their diet. "The vultures would seldom feast upon [man's] flesh, had not nature, that devoted him to our uses, infused into him a strange ferocity." Wait, she says, until you see "two herds of men . . . meet and shake the earth with noise and fill the earth with fire." Then the young are to go down and take their fill. But why do the men themselves not eat their prey after they have killed it, the children ask? If they do not eat it, why do they kill other men at all? No one really knows, the mother replies; but one philosophical vulture (who has read Descartes, presumably) has a theory that men are not really living creatures at all, but merely automata created by a beneficent nature for the welfare of vultures. The piece is filled with the imagery of the butcher shop, and is as horribly effective as Swift's *A Modest Proposal.*

In many of these moral essays, especially in *The Rambler,* Johnson rises to generalizations of great thoughtfulness and beauty of language that reverberate deep in the reader's mind:

No vicious dispositions of the mind more obstinately resist both the counsels of philosophy and the injunctions of religion than those which are complicated with an opinion of [one's own] dignity. . . . All pride is abject and mean. Nothing which reason condemns can be suitable to the dignity of the human mind. (*Rambler* 185)

Reflections that may drive away despair cannot be wanting to him who considers how much life is now advanced beyond the state of naked undiscipline and unrestrained nature. (*Rambler* 129)

Whoever commits a fraud is guilty not only of the particular injury to him he deceives, but of the diminution of that confidence which constitutes not only the ease but the existence of society. (*Rambler* 79)

To be happy at home is the ultimate result of all ambition. (*Rambler* 68)

Curiosity is, in great and generous minds, the first passion and the last. . . . Such is the delight of mental superiority that none on whom nature or study have conferred it would purchase the gifts of fortune by its loss. (*Rambler* 150)

The common voice of the multitude, uninstructed by precept and unprejudiced by authority, in questions that relate to the heart of man, is, in my opinion, more decisive than the learning of Lipsius. (*Rambler* 52)

To immerse oneself in language and thought (and feeling) of this quality, responding fully to its overtones, can be an exciting experience for the reader. It is for this reason that Johnson's name would be a great one in the history of English literature on the strength of the *Rambler* essays alone.

Johnson's Moral Teaching

To try to formulate Johnson's "system of morality" in a short space would be presumptuous. Still, it can do no harm to present, as hypotheses for future investigation, some generalizations that seem to emerge. First, Johnson's is Augustinian Christian gospel morality. It is something that begins inside the individual and moves outward, not something that is imposed from the outside. Its supreme value is love, in the profoundest sense of the word—for God, and for one's neighbor (and, as will be discussed below, for one's self, in the way that some modern psychiatrists understand this process). The great and original sin, from which all the others stem, the source of hatred and cruelty and misery, both on a large scale (as in the worldwide warfare of Johnson's time—and later) and on a petty one (as in families and small communities), is pride—egocentricity, the overestimation of one's own importance in the scheme of things, involvement solely with the welfare of one's ego. Thus for the individual to be capable of love, he must cultivate true humility: his concern for his own ego must not be allowed to prevent the development of his capacity for emotional involvement with something outside himself.

Johnson's morality is anti-Stoic: it strives for involvement with life and other human beings, not for detachment from them;[15] for fulfillment of emotional potential, not for inhibition and repression of it. To be sure, it maintains that the self-centered passions that stem from pride—hatred, resentment, envy, self-pity—should be minimized because they themselves limit the complete fulfillment of the individual's capacity for feeling, for love. "Poverty of sentiment," Mrs. Thrale once remarked of Johnson, "in men who considered themselves to be company for the parlour, as he called it, was what he could not bear."[16]

Johnson's morality is rational, not obscurantist. Like Swift and Voltaire, he is convinced that knowledge and intelligence are, in themselves, good things; if people could be persuaded to use them fully, they would contribute much toward alleviating human misery. Johnson does not merely condemn follies: he analyzes them and accounts for their existence, and suggests programs for remedying them. Johnson's view is empiricist, in the great British philosophical tradition of the seventeenth and eighteenth centuries of Bacon and Locke. It holds that experience, direct contact with the fascinating variety of the world outside oneself, is supremely healthful and the source of genuine wisdom. It distrusts mere inward "intellectualizing," theorizing for its own sake, absorption in the ingenious constructions that man's mind, divorced from contact with outward reality, can spin for itself.

Finally, it is psychiatric, "soul-healing." In a remarkably modern way, Johnson is tremendously aware of how much self-inflicted human suffering stems from unhealthy mental and emotional habits, and he insistently tries to make his readers admit the possibility of such attitudes within themselves, try to eliminate them, and replace them with health-giving ones. (This attitude is also a very old moral tradition: constant spiritual self-inspection, the examination of one's own motives and bases for action has been recommended by Christian teachers since St. Augustine's own confessions.) Johnson's recipe for neurosis is the same as the modern psychotherapist's: work, occupation, involvement with things and persons outside oneself; steady contact with external reality.

Like the modern psychiatrist, Johnson knows that inner insecurity, a damaged ego, lies at the bottom of much misery inflicted on oneself and others. "Confidence" is one of his favorite words: "Self-confidence is the first requisite to great undertakings," he says in commendation of Pope's career; of scholars, "It were to be wished that they who devote their lives to study would at once believe nothing too great for their attainment and consider nothing too little for their regard." He knows the inner hindrances to achievement and happiness: "Fear is implanted in us as a preservative from evil; but its duty, like that of other passions, is not to overbear reason, but to assist it; nor should it be suffered to tyrannize in the imagination, to raise phantoms of horror, or beset life with supernumerary distresses." Or "No disease of the imagination is so difficult of cure as that which is complicated with the dread of guilt."

Erich Fromm, quoting the great commandment "Thou shalt love thy neighbour as thyself," points to the importance of the phrase "as thyself." The trouble with the neurotic, the egocentric, is that he does *not* love himself; he cannot love anything. Self-centeredness is not the same as self-love or self-respect, but its converse, self-contempt. From his own bitter experience Johnson knew this well, and was acute enough to see how innumerable others were hindered by it from realizing their full potential of accomplishment and happiness. As manuals of practical therapy for the ills of the mind and emotions, few bodies of writing rank higher than *The Rambler* and *Rasselas*.[17]

Chapter Six

The Political Writer

"Of political evil, if we suppose the origin of moral evil discovered," Johnson wrote in his review of Soame Jenyns, "the account is by no means difficult, polity being only the conduct of immoral men in public affairs." Johnson does his political thinking not in terms of entities and systems—"society," "classes," "economic groups"—but of concrete individuals. He will have nothing to do with lofty abstractions, "the will of the people," "the spirit of the nation," "the social contract," as the source of political power: government is simply certain human beings, who are fallible and greedy like the rest, invested with power over others; and Johnson has little faith in their superior ability to produce much happiness or virtue in those they govern. "How small, of all that human hearts endure, / The part which laws or kings can cause or cure," he wrote, in lines which he contributed to Goldsmith's *The Traveller.* His was not a point of view that appealed to "liberals" of the nineteenth and twentieth centuries, who were convinced that heaven can be created on earth by means of the judicious reform of a few social and economic institutions. To the modern psychiatrist, however, confronted with the "paradox" of increasing mental illness in "the affluent society," it may make considerable sense.

Government: The Use of Power

With the question of the origins, historical or theoretical, of political power, Johnson refuses to concern himself: theories of "divine right," original compacts, and "natural rights of man" he dismisses as useless and irrelevant speculation. One's concern must be to make political power work as well as it can for the greatest happiness of the greatest number of individual human beings. The only theoretical background needed is that government is preferable to anarchy, that power is necessary to make government work, and that in the various governmental systems some one institution ("the sovereign," in the technical sense of the word; "the legislative," to use Locke's term; in Great Britain, Parliament, consisting of its three components, the King, the Lords, the Commons) is the final repository of that power, and is legally omnicompetent. Johnson's statement "All government is ultimately and essentially absolute"[1] has sometimes been taken to mean that his "Toryism" is so preposterously reactionary that he is still advocating James I's theory that kings are answerable to God alone. This is a mistake: Johnson laughs at "divine right" theory—and indeed has rude things to say about the incompetence of monarchs generally—as much as he does at "natural rights." He is merely saying, what is the undoubted fact, that in Britain there is no appeal from an Act of Parliament (in the United States, from a constitutional decision of the Supreme Court). In the words of an American president, the "buck" stops somewhere in every form of government.

Talk of abstract political "rights" is therefore meaningless to Johnson except in the context of political power. Commenting on a declaration of the Continental Congress about inalienable rights to "life, liberty, and property"—an anticipation of the Declaration of Independence—Johnson points out that British subjects have "ceded to the King and Parliament, whether the right or not, at least the power of disposing without their consent, of their lives, liberties, and properties."[2] There is no legal way to prevent Parliament, the source of law, from depriving any individual of life, liberty, and property at its discretion: it does so all the time, by means of criminal and tax legislation, and will continue to do so (in the United States, Congress and the state legislatures, when supported by the Supreme Court, do so). How, then, can such abstract "rights" be called "inalienable," so far as the individual is concerned? And what meaning can this word have except as applied to the individual?

For Johnson to insist that the ultimate fact in political situations *is* power is not, as some students seem to think, a declaration on his part that he likes or advocates the use of power. The whole record of his life—his own rebelliousness as a youth, his toast to the next insurrection of the Negroes in the West Indies, and much more—indicates precisely the contrary: Johnson, like most decent people, is repelled by the actual use of power in itself. His insistence, then, that people recognize that, until the whole of the human race achieves sainthood, power *is* necessary to maintain some kind of peaceful society, is intended to minimize its actual use.

This attitude toward power is made very clear in the two most thoughtful statements Johnson composed on the subject of political theory: the sermons numbered XXIII and XXIV in the collection published after his death. In *Sermon* XXIII, on the duties of the governed, he begins by accepting individual self-interest as the motivating force of men in a political situation. It is fallacious to expect the individual's actions to be motivated by a love for society in the abstract: "Such a diffusion of interest, such sublimation of self-love is to all difficult . . . it is to many impossible." The pursuit of self-interest is therefore inevitable, and "in the prosecution of private interest . . . there must necessarily be some kind of strife . . . there must be constant struggle of emulation."

This being admitted, the need for government invested with power, and the need for the individual to conduct himself so as to minimize the use of that power, become apparent. *Sermon* XXIV, on the duties of governors, likewise directs attention to individual responsibilities: "It is the duty of those in authority to promote the happiness of the people. Their superiority is not to be considered a sanction for laziness, nor a privilege for vice." And Johnson is very far from recommending that subjects take a passive and uncritical attitude to the actions of their political superiors: "To be happy we must know our own rights; and we must know them to be safe," he says, in a good round declaration of "Whig" doctrine.

Politics thus resolves itself, for Johnson, into questions of morality dealing with the relations between individual human beings—questions to be decided by invoking general moral principles already established. Every situation must be regarded as a separate problem in morality, not to be decided (as the Americans wanted to decide the question of their independence from Britain) by the application of windy dogma, which probably conceals underlying motives of self-interest, but by the use of genuine moral responsibility by the individuals involved.

To say that Johnson uses a pragmatic or "positivistic" approach to political matters does not, of course, mean that he reaches the same conclusions in specific political questions that other political "positivists" such as Hobbes or Marx reach. It does mean, however, that when modern students try to assign Johnson's "place" in a spectrum of political ideology that has grown up in the nineteenth and twentieth century—to determine how far he is to the "right" or the "left"—they are bound to be baffled because the pattern simply does not apply to him. When he believes (along with the vast majority of his generation) that the English Civil War and the execution of Charles I were "a bad thing," he is called a reactionary conservative. When he toasts the next insurrection of the Negro slaves in the West Indies, he is acclaimed as an advanced, even a reckless, radical. But the difficulty here is of our creation, not Johnson's. He believed, after all, not in ideologies, in "package deals" in political theory, but in judging each political situation, as with each situation involving private individuals, on the basis of the principles of individual morality; and all the student can do is to follow him and see how he reacts to separate political situations as they occur.

Johnson's Political Involvements

Some older misconceptions about Johnson's political involvements need to be corrected. One is the judgment, formulated by Macaulay and repeated in more recent studies, that Johnson was not really much interested in political matters at all. This would be a very surprising thing if it were so, given his profound concern with morality and his belief that politics is individual morality on a larger scale. In fact, his writings and the records of his life and conversation disclose that there were few times in his adult life when he was not in close contact with the important political events of the day—and concerned about them.[3] Another notion is the one that, because Johnson allowed himself to be described as a Tory and because he often condemned Whiggism in pungent terms, he was violently and blindly partisan.

A little study reveals, however, that a great deal of his conversational "violence" against Whiggism is ironic and jocular. It is sometimes designed to take in duller and more solemn listeners—for instance, his remark to Mr. Langton's young niece: "My dear, I hope you are a Jacobite" (at which Mr. Langton was profoundly disturbed, as no doubt Johnson intended him to be). And there are others of this sort: "The first Whig was the devil" (perhaps a retort to Milton, whose Satan in *Paradise Lost* is a conservative, greatly upset at the changes God proposes to make in the politics of Heaven); "I do not like much to see a Whig in any dress; but I hate to see a Whig in a parson's gown."[4] Actually, one of Johnson's oldest and dearest friends was the Reverend John Taylor, staunchest of Whigs and a dependent of the great Whig magnate, the Duke of Devonshire. Indeed, Johnson's friends included many Whigs (and Scots and Americans). Garrick was a strong Whig; Burke was *the* great Whig theorist (though, to be sure, Johnson, while expressing his profound admiration of Burke as a man and a thinker, could be very caustic about his politics).

As for the Tories, Johnson's first political pamphlet of the famous group of four in the 1770s, *The False Alarm,* ends with a *condemnation* of the "frigid neutrality" of the Tories toward the issue the pamphlet deals with. In *Idler* 10, on political extremism, he satirizes Tom Tempest the Jacobite as vigorously as Jack Sneaker the Whig. His real views are expressed in the short "dissertation" he wrote on parties in 1781, at Boswell's request, which begins "A wise Tory and a wise Whig, I believe, will agree."[5] Much of the impression that readers have gained of Johnson's partisanship comes from Boswell, who himself cultivated a shallow and sentimental "Toryism" and transfers some of it to Johnson.

The third, and most troublesome, difficulty for the modern student has come from later misconceptions of what the term "Tory" actually meant in eighteenth-century England. Nothing shifts more confusingly than the meaning of political labels—for instance, "liberal," which in mid-Victorian England meant a believer in "free enterprise" and in noninterference by governments in the workings of a laissez-faire capitalist economy, has come in twentieth-century America to mean precisely the opposite: one who believes that governments should, where desirable for the welfare of the public, interfere in the conduct of private enterprise. Through various historical accidents in the nineteenth century, the term "Tory" in Great Britain came to designate the modern Conservative party. The history of the origin of that party, in the 1840s, is extremely complex, and still needs much careful research. (To complicate matters further, "Tory" in American history means a Loyalist, an opponent of the separation of the thirteen colonies from Britain.)

Likewise, during the mid-nineteenth century the concept of a universal dichotomy in political ideology, with everyone's political thinking being easily classifiable as either "left" (progressive, liberal) or "right" (reactionary, conservative), came to be accepted. For purposes of party propaganda, writers like Macaulay enthusiastically pushed these concepts backward in time, imposing the nineteenth-century "Whig interpretation" on the political history of the seventeenth and eighteenth centuries. It has taken a generation of careful research by historians like Sir Lewis Namier to expose the fallacy of this procedure, which is now completely discredited in reputable historiography but still lingers on in some old-fashioned school and literary histories.[6]

Actually, the Tories in most of eighteenth-century England seem to have been the rural, "agrarian" element in the politics of the time—the country gentlemen, the squires, the smaller landowners, who in any country tend to be suspicious of the central government, as too easily dominated by the "big interests" of industry and commerce and are anxious therefore to keep it from becoming too powerful. They tend to be "isolationist" and antiexpansionist in foreign policy since industry rather than agriculture profits from wars, foreign investments, and imperialist adventures. A fourth or a fifth of the members of the House of Commons in the eighteenth century were Tories in this sense (the House of Lords was much more Whiggish, since peerages were the reward of the central government for successful enterprise), and formed a permanent opposition to every government. No Tory ministry governed Britain in Johnson's lifetime after 1714. It is a mistake to think of Lord Bute and Lord North as Tories: they were orthodox Whigs; they were labeled "Tories" by disgruntled Whig opposition factions, just as extreme right-wing factions in the United States have charged moderate Republicans with having Communist tendencies.

Johnson's own background was not of the squirearchy, but he did grow up in a small town in the somewhat "isolationist" heart of the Midlands, where the scars of bitter Civil War fighting remained to add a confused legacy of history to the political divisions of the early eighteenth century. It must be added, however, that Johnson, though certainly hostile to the Puritan side in the Civil War, by no means romanticized the Stuarts as some "high Tories" of his time did—Boswell, for instance. Johnson has caustic things to say about James I, Charles II, James II, and Queen Anne; he makes very little fuss over Charles I; and he actually expresses admiration for Cromwell. There is not the slightest justification for calling Johnson a Jacobite, in the sense that a Jacobite was someone who wished to see the exiled Stuarts restored to the throne.

The origins of Johnson's Toryism, such as it was, are obscure. The evidence for the stories that he acquired it from his father, or his schoolmaster Hunter, is so slight as to be worthless. Considering what one knows of Johnson's rebelliousness as a youth, it is hard to conceive of his adopting any belief merely because someone in authority over him held it. Perhaps the best hypothesis is that Johnson, being "temperamentally always in revolt," intellectually a skeptic, naturally took to Toryism to show his intellectual independence of Whiggism, which was the majority, fashionable political attitude of his time. And, as has been noted, in *The False Alarm* he could announce his independence of the current Tory line as well.

The Walpole Era and Later

At any rate, Johnson first took a clearly defined political position in his writings of 1738 and 1739, shortly after his arrival in London. These were hectic days on the political scene, the days when Walpole, after twenty years of power, was tottering to his fall, bayed by a noisy opposition of "patriot" Whigs, such as William Pitt, with only halfhearted cooperation from the real Tories. The "patriots," more closely allied than Walpole to the commercial interests of London and Bristol, were intent on war with Spain to open overseas markets for British trade and to make Britain a worldwide naval and imperial (and therefore commercial) power. The opposition to Walpole had the support of the leading writers of the day, including such powerful ones as Pope and Swift. Johnson, resentful at his own neglect and perhaps encouraged by the neurotic Savage, joined in the attack. In *London* he furnished a vigorous and amusing versification of the stock opposition line that Walpole was corrupting all that was virtuous in English life. His two pamphlets of 1739 are equally vigorous and amusing and deserve to be read oftener than they are.

They are modeled on Swiftian satire, but the young Johnson's exuberance is so great that they are much untidier than Swift's. Johnson's full-blooded irony goes on and on until it sometimes becomes rather wearisome; he does not have Swift's talent for deadpan.

This criticism is particularly true of the first, *Marmor Norfolciense,* which was so uninhibited that the government, used as it was to lampooning by this time, is said to have issued a warrant for Johnson's arrest. In it, Johnson assumes the mask of a bumbling antiquarian scholar, a good party-line supporter of Walpole, who has unearthed an ancient stone in Norfolk (the home of the Walpoles) bearing a mysterious prophetic inscription in medieval Latin. The inscription consists of devastating innuendos against the ineptness and corruptness of Walpole's handling of British affairs, and George II's alleged subordination of British interests to those of his native Hanover. The antiquarian, however, has much difficulty interpreting the inscription; and his stupidity, his inability to see the clear meaning of the words, makes it the more obvious to the reader. In the end, he proposes the establishment of an academy of thirty loyal supporters of the government, half lawyers and half army officers (both professions were accused of having been suborned by Walpole to assist in his suppression of English liberty), to spend five years interpreting the inscription, at a cost of £650,000, which would be raised by various financial methods for which Walpole had been criticized—for instance, an excise tax on bread.

A Compleat Vindication of the Licensers of the Stage from the Malicious and Scandalous Aspersions of Mr. Brooke is more smoothly and effectively done—and even more violent in its innuendoes. Henry Brooke had written a play called *Gustavus Vasa,* a thinly veiled allegory from Swedish history, suggesting that Walpole and George II had treasonably subverted the state and that the only remedy was a civil war. Walpole, perhaps with justification, defended himself by means of the recently passed Stage Licensing Act (the provisions of which were in force until 1968), whereby no play could be publicly performed in London without first being read, approved, and licensed by the Lord Chamberlain's office; and the Lord Chamberlain's examiners vetoed *Gustavus Vasa.* Brooke then printed it by subscription with an inflammatory preface, and there was a great hullabaloo about liberty of the stage and of speech. Johnson's pamphlet uses the Swiftian technique of purporting to be a defense of the censorship of the stage, in which the most contemptibly despotic motives are urged by the "defender" for such censorship. What makes the work interesting is that it becomes, by indirection, a blistering attack on the obscurantism fostered by repressive governments to keep the people of a country submissive by starving their minds—by "thought control." The "vindication" ends by suggesting that not only the stage and the press should be subject to censorship, but schools as well:

There are scattered over this kingdom several little seminaries, in which the lower ranks of people, and the youngest sons of our nobility and gentry are taught, from their earliest infancy, the pernicious arts of spelling and reading, which they afterwards continue to practice, very much to the disturbance of their own quiet, and the interruption of ministerial measures. These seminaries may, by an act of parliament, be at once suppressed, and that our posterity be deprived of all means of reviving this corrupt method of education, it may be made a felony to teach to read without a license from the Lord Chamberlain . . . and the nation will rest at length in ignorance and peace.

For at least three years most of Johnson's literary energy was devoted to the compilation of the *Debates in the Senate of Magna Lilliputia,* a work totaling some half-million words (at least), and containing much excellent prose, wit, and thought.[7] It has been unjustifiably neglected by students of Johnson. There have been two—contradictory—misconceptions about the *Debate.* One, found in some older histories, is that they represent the actual words of the speakers in Parliament. This came about because, since there was no official reporting of parliamentary debates at the time—indeed, it was illegal to report them openly—Johnson's "debates" are reprinted in the volumes of the *Parliamentary History,* the forerunner of *Hansard,* as furnishing at least some evidence of what was said in Parliament at the time. Some historians and biographers have mistakenly thought them to be verbatim reports; indeed, even during Johnson's own lifetime, William Pitt and (ironically) Lord Chesterfield were praised for their command of rhetoric in speeches whose wording was Johnson's. The amusing story is told of how Pitt, at the height of his fame, was being praised for an early oration—perhaps the one which begins "Sir, the atrocious crime of being a young man I shall neither attempt to palliate nor deny"—when Johnson broke in, "That speech I wrote in a garret in Exeter Street."[8]

The opposite mistake, fostered perhaps by some loose remarks of Johnson himself, such as the notorious "I took care that the Whig dogs should not have the best of it,"[9] is to think that the *Debates* are completely the product of Johnson's imagination. Recent careful checking of Johnson's *Debates* against other independent evidence, such as private memoranda by members of Parliament, has shown that in fact they are quite an accurate record of who spoke, what the gist of his speech was, and even, occasionally, of some of the phraseology actually used by the speaker. But there can be no doubt that, on the whole, the idiom in which they are couched and perhaps even some of the argumentation are Johnson's. As specimens of Johnson's ability to compose excellent English prose, they should not be disregarded.

And certainly as evidence that Johnson was *not* unconcerned or unconversant with political issues, both great and small, they are conclusive. He knew these issues intimately. A great deal of his reporting, perhaps two-thirds of the accepted canon, is of debates on two subjects: the attempt to remove Walpole from office, and the state of the armed forces. The first group contains some magnificent oratorical invective put into the mouths of Pitt and other opposition speakers,[10] and equally magnificent defense on the part of Hardwicke, Walpole's Lord Chancellor, and Walpole himself. It might be noted that the quip about taking care "that the Whig dogs should not have the best of it" really makes very little sense: virtually *all* the speakers whom Johnson reports were Whigs, either for or against Walpole—the Tories, the back-bencher country gentlemen, took, as usual, very little part in the proceedings; and, on the vote for the removal of Walpole, many of them either abstained or voted for Walpole.

One minor debate, however, on a motion to set the daily allowance of "small beer or cyder" for a soldier at three quarts, gives Johnson an opportunity to display amusingly the political habits of back-benchers, who have a wonderful time squabbling over the merits of the beer and cider brewed in their respective constituencies. Debates on bills for paving the streets of Westminster and for controlling the sale of liquor show Johnson's ability to compose vivid, almost Hogarthian, pictures of contemporary life. At the other end of the scale, the motion for an inquiry into the alleged political corruption practiced by Walpole's treasury officials provides a discussion of the highly complex matter of self-incrimination (the subject of the Fifth Amendment to the U.S. Constitution), involving profound questions of basic jurisprudence and constitutional law.

Tradition has it that the idea of reporting the debates in Parliament during the exciting years prior to Walpole's downfall was one of Johnson's contributions to the welfare of the *Gentleman's Magazine,* whose sales did indeed profit greatly from their inclusion. Earlier attempts by periodicals to report the debates "in clear" had resulted in punitive action by Parliament, and Johnson is said to have conceived the scheme by which the magazine evaded such action.

The *Gentleman's Magazine*'s series of debates was introduced in 1738 by a long "continuation" of *Gulliver's Travels,* almost certainly from Johnson's own pen and one of his most readable and incendiary pieces of political writing. Lemuel Gulliver's grandson, who has recently made a journey back to

Lilliput, has discovered that the country has undergone a revolution and that its constitution has been resettled on exactly the same basis as that of Great Britain. Young Gulliver stays there for three years, and returns with a cargo of "histories, memoirs, tracts, speeches, treaties, debates, letters, and instructions" concerning the political life of the country. The magazine proposes to furnish its readers with regular installments of this treasure. The prime minister of Lilliput turns out to be a gentleman named Walelop, one of his chief opponents Ptit, and so on.

In this introduction, *The State of Affairs in Lilliput,*[11] Johnson has much to say about colonialism and imperial expansion, matters that greatly concerned him throughout his life and of which he had the deepest distrust. This was the period of the creation of British Empire, chiefly under the inspiration of Pitt. Young Gulliver writes:

The people of Degulia, or the Lilliputian Europe . . . have made conquests, and settled colonies in very distant regions, the inhabitants of which they look upon as barbarous, tho' in simplicity of manners, probity, and temperance superior to themselves; and seem to think that they have a right to treat them as passion, interest, or caprice shall direct, without much regard to the rules of justice or humanity; they have carried this imaginary sovereignty so far, that they have sometimes proceeded to rapine, bloodshed, and desolation. . . . It is observable that their conquests and acquisitions in Columbia (which is the Lilliputian name for the country that answers our America) have very little contributed to the power of those nations which have, to obtain them, broke through all the ties of human nature.

One can see the force of Johnson's argument that the principles of political morality are only those of individual morality writ large. It took Europe another century and a half after Johnson's death to learn this lesson regarding imperialism.

The State of Affairs in Lilliput also contains much jingoism against Spain—part of the standard opposition line at the time—and bitter attacks on Walpole and George II. Johnson was later to retract his anti-Walpolianism: "Of Sir Robert Walpole, notwithstanding that he had written against him in the early part of his life, he had a high opinion: he said of him that he was a fine fellow . . . he honoured his memory for having kept this country in peace many years, as also for his goodness and placability of his temper."[12] Perhaps the experience of reporting the parliamentary debates for three or four years, of being in close contact with the practical business of politics, and of learning, to use one of Johnson's favorite quotations, "with how little wisdom the world is governed," cured Johnson of some of the starry-eyed view of politics he had had when he and Savage tramped the streets of London at night, "establishing new forms of government, and giving laws to the several states of Europe." And, when Walpole fell from power in 1742, his place was taken by a coalition of Walpolians and former anti-Walpolians, who, once they got into office, proceeded, as politicians will, to continue along exactly the same lines they had recently been breathing fire against Walpole for pursuing.

Johnson may later have retracted his hostility to Walpole personally, but he never became a "Walpolian." The tradition of the Walpolian group of Whigs was carried on after Walpole's retirement by Henry Pelham, prime minister until his death in 1754, and by his brother the Duke of Newcastle, later by Lord Rockingham (with his official publicist Edmund Burke), and by Charles James Fox. They represented the old established "big interests" of the British scene, the large landed aristocracy with dukedoms and marquessates conferred by William III and the early Georges. They, the "haves" of Great Britain, tended to be cautiously conservative, so as not to endanger their privileged position. The younger business interests, with their fortunes still to make and therefore more enterprising, were represented by William Pitt and his small but effective group of allies. Of this group, who called themselves "the Patriots," Johnson made his memorable remark: "Patriotism is the last refuge of a scoundrel."[13] If Johnson had little love for the philosophy of Walpolian and of Burkean Whiggism, which was in essence "What is good for the Walpoles and Pelhams and Rockinghams is good for Britain," he detested even more the noisy imperialism and unabashed expansionism of Pittite Whiggism, with its program of profit-seeking exploitation and worldwide aggression.

When, after a decade or more of squabbling among themselves, Pitt and Newcastle joined forces in 1756 to conduct the Seven Years' War against France, which was to add Canada and India to the empire, Johnson's violent opposition was recorded in the series of articles in the *Literary Magazine* already described in chapter 3. As a result, Johnson's editorship of the *Literary Magazine* did not last long, nor did the weekly column of equally anti-"patriotic" "Observations" on the war, which he started in the *Universal Chronicle* in 1757. It came to an abrupt close after he was taken to task by an outraged patriot for refusing to rejoice over the capture of Louisbourg. The point Johnson repeats again and again is that no decent person can be expected to work up much patriotic ardor for either the English or the French in a war over lands that both sides have stolen from their original owners, the Indians. No one listened to him at the time, but at least he managed to have his say, and this brilliant series of essays, puncturing the high-flown *Gott mit uns* attitudinizing of the "Patriots," makes remarkable sense at a time when both Pitt's and Choiseul's empires have crumbled into dust and the folly of a colonialism that ignores the feelings of the indigenous peoples has long been proven; when the principle Johnson insisted upon at the end of his *Introduction to the Political State of Great Britain,* 1756, has been amply demonstrated by history:

It is ridiculous to imagine that the friendship of nations, whether civil or barbarous, can be gained and kept but by kind treatment; and surely they who intrude, uncalled, upon the country of a distant people, ought to consider the natives as worthy of common kindness, and content themselves to rob without insulting them. . . . We continue every day to show by new proofs that no people can be great who have ceased to be virtuous.

The Reign of George III

In 1760 the death of George II (aged seventy-seven) and the accession of his grandson George III (aged twenty-two) caused an important rearrangement of the terms of political life in Britain. This change was not the legendary one described by the Whig historians of the nineteenth century—that George III, brought up on the teachings of the Tory Lord Bolingbroke, began a campaign to restore to the Crown powers that had lapsed under the "democratic" regime of Walpole and the first two Georges, and to make himself into an absolute monarch. This fable, useful as political propaganda, has now been completely discredited: George III was a scrupulously constitutional monarch. The constitutional position, however, was still what it was to be until the mid-nineteenth century (and had been under George I and II): the king was still supposed to be the effective head of the executive branch of government, and it was his responsibility to initiate executive action to the best advantage of his subjects. George tried to do so, conscientiously though ineptly. His utter sincerity, and his piety and domestic virtue, were recognized by the great majority of his subjects; and, during his long reign, he was probably the most widely beloved monarch in many centuries of English history.

But a change did take place. George III's father, Frederick, Prince of Wales (who had died in 1751), had been, like most heirs to the British throne, at loggerheads with his father, George II, and of course with George II's minister, Walpole, and the Walpolian Whigs. Frederick to some extent espoused the "Patriot" cause, and he collaborated with Pitt and other opposition Whigs to overthrow Walpole. George III, only thirteen when his father died, inherited from Frederick and Frederick's adviser, the Scottish Lord

Bute, the distrust of the Walpolian Whigs. Believing (like Johnson and many others) in the cynically self-seeking and corrupt character of the long-entrenched Walpole-Pelham Whig faction, George sought, when he came to the throne, to appoint ministers outside this old ruling class, ones who would have some regard for the interests of the country as a whole, not merely for their own special interests.

George's idealism was that of a very young, inexperienced, and far-from-clever person; and he had to rule with the aid of one combination or another of Whig groups. But the freshness of his position appealed to men like Johnson and Goldsmith, themselves very much "have-nots," who saw in it the possibility of a "New Deal" for the average man. Goldsmith put it thus:

> Wealth, in all commercial states, is found to accumulate, and all such have hitherto in time become aristocratical. . . . In such a state . . . all that the middle order has left is to preserve the prerogative of the one principal governor with the most sacred circumspection. For he divides the power of the rich, and calls off the great from falling with tenfold weight on the middle order placed beneath them. . . . I am then for, and would die for monarchy. . . . Every diminution of [the monarch's] power . . . is an infringement upon the real liberties of the subject.[14]

In other words, Johnson's and Goldsmith's support of George III was closely analogous to the American "liberal's" support of the authority of the federal government under Franklin D. Roosevelt, as a bulwark against the power of the vested interests of the National Association of Manufacturers.

Johnson's acceptance of his pension from Lord Bute in 1762 was a public declaration of his support of George III's "New Deal," and it marked him out for constant abuse, to which he was subjected all the rest of his life (and long after) from Whigs of the type of Macaulay. Many of the preposterous distortions of the plain facts about Johnson that still circulate today are relics from that vilification. Johnson, having done what he thought was right, sturdily ignored his abusers. In his obscure middle years he seems to have had a number of political involvements, about the details of which little is known: for instance, being solicited by Charles Jenkinson, one of Bute's assistants, to help him compose a pamphlet defending the Peace of Paris, which closed the Seven Years' War (perhaps Bute and Jenkinson remembered his antiwar writings of 1756 and 1757?); planning some work to defend the East India Company against a raid by Chatham's (Pitt's) administration. Some of his writing projects at this time deserve more than passing mention, though they have been little studied. One, a manuscript in Johnson's hand, entitled "Considerations on Corn," found after his death among the papers of the Anglo-

Irish politician William Gerard Hamilton (for whom Burke too had written), reminds one that Johnson, like everyone seriously interested in politics, was also concerned with economics. A number of careful commentaries on the important wool trade, in early volumes of the *Gentleman's Magazine,* may well be Johnson's too. An essay, "Further Thoughts on Agriculture," in the *Universal Visiter* in 1756, is a powerful statement of the central position in Johnson's economic thinking. As might be expected, it is an argument (as are the "Considerations on Corn") for the advisability of careful control by the central government of the national economy in order to keep it well balanced and to make Britain as far as possible economically self-sufficient.[15]

Britain in the 1750s was still able to feed her own population, and Johnson looked with distrust on the grandiose schemes of Pitt and others that would set her on a course of uncontrolled commercial expansion. Pittite policies did indeed imply the free-trade and laissez-faire attitudes that Adam Smith was later to illustrate in *The Wealth of Nations,* that the younger Pitt was to incorporate into the national system, and that in the mid-nineteenth century became British government dogma. The system resulted in great prosperity for Britain during the nineteenth century, when she was far in advance of the rest of the world in technology and was able to import raw material, manufacture it cheaply, and sell it back to the rest of the world at a profit sufficient to buy food for her greatly increased population.

Johnson, however, predicted with remarkable foresight what in fact came to pass in the twentieth century: "It is apparent that every trading nation flourishes, while it can be said to flourish, by the courtesy of others. We cannot compel any people to buy from us, or to sell to us. A thousand accidents may prejudice them in favour of our rivals; the workmen of another nation may labour for less price. . . . The natives of Lombardy might easily resolve to retain their silk at home, and employ workmen of their own to weave it. And this will certainly be done when they grow wise and industrious, when they have sagacity to discern their true interest and vigour to pursue it."[16] Or, as Johnson was to versify in the four lines he contributed to the end of Goldsmith's *The Deserted Village:*

> Trade's proud empire hastes to swift decay,
> As oceans sweep the labour'd mole away;
> While self-dependent power can time defy,
> As rocks resist the billows and the sky.

Only a few years ago it was discovered that Johnson had made large and important contributions to the massive series of lectures delivered before the

Oxford law school by his friend Sir Robert Chambers, the Vinerian Professor of English Law.[17] These lectures were the sequel to those of Chambers's predecessor, the great Blackstone, which were published as his famous *Commentaries*. They show Johnson's lifelong interest in law and an excellent grasp of the theoretical bases of it. The Vinerian Lectures are an important part of Johnson's work, and they need careful study and analysis to determine their relation to his thinking on politics and general morality. It is curious to reflect that so seemingly improbable a person as Johnson influenced the legal thinking of a generation or more of English lawyers.

The Pamphlets of the 1770s

When Johnson's "political writings" are mentioned, however, one usually thinks of the four pamphlets he wrote in the 1770s in support of certain policies of the administrations of the Duke of Grafton and Lord North (*not,* it must be repeated, of the Tories," who were not in office, and whose "frigid neutrality" in the Wilkes case Johnson specifically condemns in *The False Alarm*). These pamphlets represent only a fraction of his total political writing; and, though vividly written, they tell little about his basic political attitudes not expressed more thoughtfully elsewhere. They are lively reading, however; and, couched in the idiom of violent invective he had learned in the robust days of Walpole, they were a little shocking to the more delicate ears of the 1770s.

The False Alarm (1770) deals with the famous affair of John Wilkes. Wilkes, a clever, amusing, and unscrupulous adventurer in politics, had earlier been convicted of seditious libel because of his virulent periodical, the *North Briton,* and his obscene *Essay on Woman;* he had been expelled from the House of Commons and outlawed. A few years later he returned to England, got his outlawry reversed, and was elected to the Commons from Middlesex; but the House pronounced him ineligible to sit. He was reelected twice with larger majorities; the second time the House declared his opponent Colonel Luttrell elected, as the *eligible* candidate with the largest number of votes. A great outcry arose (effectively fostered by a clever "public relations" campaign organized by Wilkes and his allies); there was much demonstration by mobs; but the government stood its ground.

Johnson's pamphlet, as its title indicates, argues that the "alarm" about liberty is factitious and that no one's "liberties" are being endangered by Wilkes's expulsion. He draws on a learned series of precedents to show that the House of Commons has an uncontrolled right to determine its own membership,[18] and has a good deal to say about *vox populi*—at least, the voice of illiterate mobs cleverly manipulated by unscrupulous demagogues—not being *vox Dei*. Johnson's point of view seems more valid to the twentieth century, experienced in how the voice of the people may be in fact the voice of a Goebbels, than it did to the more innocent nineteenth. He describes the ease with which petitions, like those drawn up in favor of Wilkes, are assembled; and he also recounts the scenes of an election year, no doubt drawing on his early memories of Staffordshire elections:

The year of the election is a year of jollity; and what is still more desirable, a year of equality. The glutton now eats the delicacies for which he longed when he could not purchase them, and the drunkard has the pleasure of wine without the cost. The drone lives a while without work, and the shopkeeper, in the flow of money, raises his price. The mechanic that trembled at the presence of Sir Joseph now bids him come again for an answer; and the poacher whose gun has been seized now finds an opportunity to reclaim it.

Thoughts on the Late Transactions Respecting Falkland's Islands (1771) is a lucid account of the history of a current dispute with Spain over the title to these South Atlantic islands.[19] North's administration had at last arrived at a peaceful settlement with Spain, to the disgust of the opposition, some of whom were clamoring for war—in order to profiteer from it. Johnson charges that "These are the men who, without virtue, labour, or hazard, are growing rich as their country is impoverished; they rejoice when obstinacy or ambition adds another year to slaughter and devastation; and laugh from their desks at bravery and science, while they are adding figure to figure, and cipher to cipher, hoping for a new contract from a new armament, and computing the profits of a siege or tempest." As in *The False Alarm,* there is much abuse of "the rabble," which has led students to talk about Johnson's revulsion from "the rising tide of democracy." But the violence of the London mob, to culminate a few years later in the disgraceful Gordon Riots, can hardly be equated with responsible "democracy."

The Patriot (1774)—a short election pamphlet written perhaps at the request of his friend Henry Thrale, government member of Parliament for Southwark (Johnson wrote many brief election addresses for him)—plays skillfully on the distinction between true patriotism and the noisy self-proclaimed "patriotism" of men like Wilkes: "A man sometimes starts up a patriot only by disseminating discontent, and propagating reports of secret influence, or dangerous counsels, of violated rights, and encroaching usurpation. This practice is no certain note of patriotism." *The Patriot* includes a defense of the Quebec Act, recently passed by the North government, which guaranteed the religious and civil rights of the French-speaking population of this newly acquired region. This act is now regarded by historians as a piece of farsighted legislation, one much in advance of its time; but, because of the inflamed state of America at the time, it was denounced as an attempt by the government in London to subvert the welfare of the thirteen colonies. "In an age," Johnson comments, "when every month is open for 'liberty of conscience,' it is equitable to show some regard to the conscience of a papist."

The "liberty" for which the publicists of the American Revolution were clamoring did not much impress Johnson, when it seemed to him, as has been noted, that this was not a liberty to be extended to Negroes, Indians, French Canadians, or Loyalists. The Quebec Act was one of the grievances mentioned in the resolutions of the American Continental Congress at Philadelphia in 1775, to which Johnson's last and most notorious political pamphlet, *Taxation No Tyranny,* was a reply. To try to defend this work to Americans reared on the traditional teachings of their school histories about the War of Independence is an unprofitable task. But it does contain political theory that at least deserves to be taken seriously—and, if the reader disagrees, seriously rebutted. Given the on-the-whole meek acceptance of modern methods of taxation by Americans, it is hard for them to argue, contrary to Johnson's title, that taxation is, in itself, tyranny.

What makes taxation tyranny, some Americans at the time argued, is for the taxed to be unrepresented in the taxing institution—in this case, the Parliament at Westminster. It is not hard, of course, to show that taxation without representation is still continually practiced: no government has the slightest qualms about taxing, say, workers under the age of eighteen, who have no vote. If it is argued that they are "virtually represented" through their elders, this is Johnson's reply to the Americans in 1775: countless Britons who have no right to vote are compelled to pay taxes on the grounds that they are "virtually represented"—why not the Americans? But Johnson is not really much interested in the metaphysical problem of political representation. What annoys him about the American publicists of 1775, as he was annoyed by the publicists of the Seven Years' War in 1756, is the use of patriotic "cant"—the outcry about love of country, liberty, and the rights of man to conceal what are ultimately motives of self-interest. The war between the French and the English in 1756 was, he said, "only the quarrel of two robbers for the spoils of a passenger"—the Indians, to whom the land originally belonged.

Conceivably, Johnson would have been willing to discuss the problems of taxation and representation in America as simple questions of practicality and expediency, to be solved by a compromise fair to all parties. But, when men's minds become swollen with windy slogans, Johnson's first thought is to deflate them. A passage in *The Patriot* provides a key to much of his later political writing:

A man may hate his king, yet not love his country. He that has been refused a reason-able or unreasonable request, who thinks his merit underrated, and sees his influence declining, begins soon to talk of natural equality, the absurdity of *many made for one,* the original compact, the foundation of authority, and the majesty of the people. As his political melancholy increases, he tells, and perhaps dreams, of the advances of the prerogative, and the dangers of arbitrary power; yet his design in all his declama-tion is not to benefit his country, but to gratify his malice.

Johnson is primarily a moralist and psychiatrist; political evil is the activity of immoral and irrational individuals in public affairs. His first concern, there-fore, is to try to cure "political melancholy"—fantasy, madness—on the part of the individual. Perhaps his concern is the greater because his early political writings against Walpole, which he later recanted, contained a good deal of the same sort of "political melancholy" that he reprobates in the later "patri-ots"; as the saying goes, it takes one to know one. Nevertheless, the "shock treatment" Johnson administers in *The False Alarm* and *Taxation No Tyr-anny* does not seem to have been very effective in its immediate results.

Johnson as Social Anthropologist

The modern term "social anthropologist" is a fairly accurate description of Johnson's attitude toward distant cultures, in which he took a great interest all his life. His earliest published book (1735) deals with Ethiopia; one of his last (1775) with the Highlands of Scotland, almost as little known to eighteenth-century Englishmen as Ethiopia. He is tremendously interested in how the Ethiopians and the Highlanders actually *live;* his attitude toward them is neither the romantic Rousseauism of "the noble savage" nor the insu-larity of his fellow Englishmen (even though he once amused himself by quoting "old Meynell," a fox-hunting country squire, "For anything I see, foreigners are fools").[20] Johnson, like the modern anthropologist, makes his observations objectively yet sympathetically. He is not attempting to prove a thesis, either that "savages" are superior to "us" or that "we" are superior to "savages": he is concerned to add to man's store of knowledge about the infi-nite variety of human behavior simply because he is "interested in people." "A generous and elevated mind," Johnson says in the dedication to his version of Lobo, "is distinguished by nothing more certainly than an eminent degree of curiosity; nor is that curiosity ever more agreeably or usefully employed than in examining the laws and customs of foreign nations."

The circumstances of Johnson's translation (and abridgment, and, often, rewriting) of the Le Grand-Lobo book about Abyssinia have been described in chapter 1, and something has been said about the context of religious controversy in which it appeared. But Johnson is equally fascinated by the description it gives of primitive African life, and in his preface he praises Father Lobo for the sober realism of his reporting (the tradition of Sir John Mandeville was not yet dead in contemporary "travel" literature, as the burlesque of it in *Gulliver's Travels* shows): "The Portuguese traveller, contrary to the general vein of his countrymen, has amused his readers with no romantick absurdities or incredible fictions. . . . He appears by his modest and unaffected narrative to have described things as he saw them, to have copied nature from life, and to have consulted his senses not his imagination."

The refusal to believe that, whatever the superficial differences may be, basic human nature varies greatly from one part of the world to another, is very important in Johnson's thinking; and he applauds Lobo's shrewd observation of the Ethiopians that supports that conclusion:

The reader will here find no regions cursed with irremediable barrenness, or blessed with spontaneous fecundity, no perpetual gloom, or unceasing sunshine; nor are the nations here described either devoid of all sense of humanity, or consummate in all private and social virtues; here are no Hottentots without religion, polity, or articulate language, no Chinese perfectly polite, and compleatly skill'd in all sciences: he will discover what will always be discover'd by a diligent and impartial observer, that wherever human nature is to be found, there is a mixture of vice and virtue, a contest of passion and reason.

Simply as a description of a remote and unfamiliar culture, Lobo's *Voyage to Abyssinia,* as reworked by Johnson, is still highly readable and interesting; and it is a pity so few, even among professional Johnsonians, have thoroughly read it.

As already seen, Johnson, in his *Life of Drake,* condemned the treatment of the natives of South America by the Spanish invaders of the sixteenth century; and, in his articles on the Seven Years' War, the treatment of the Indians of North America by the British and (less severely, for their own treatment of the Indians was more humane) the French. His strongest statement of condemnation of the exploitation of native populations by Europeans is found in his long introduction to the *The World Displayed* (1759), a collection of works on travel and exploration:

We are openly told that they [the Portuguese] had the less scruple concerning their treatment of the savage people, because they scarcely considered them as distinct from beasts; and indeed the practice of all the European nations, and among others of the English barbarians [!] that cultivate the southern islands of America [the West Indies], proves that this opinion, however absurd and foolish, however wicked and injurious, still continues to prevail. Interest and pride harden the heart, and it is vain to dispute against avarice and power.

Johnson condemns the aggressive Catholic missionaries in Africa and South America: they are unlike the first propagators of Christianity, "who recommended their doctrine by their sufferings and virtues; they entered no defenceless territories with swords in their hands; they built no forts upon ground to which they had no right, nor polluted the purity of religion with avarice of trade, or insolence of power." And he summarizes this whole depressing chapter of European history thus: "The Europeans have scarcely visited any coast but to gratify avarice, and extend corruption; to arrogate dominion without right, and practise cruelty without incentive. Happy had it then been for the oppressed, if the designs of Henry [the Navigator] had slept in his bosom, and surely more happy for the oppressors."

It was not, however, until 1773 that Johnson was to have the opportunity of displaying his own talent for observing a strange culture. At that time Boswell tempted him, old as he was and rugged and indeed dangerous as the expedition was, to tour the Highlands of Scotland, only recently "pacified" after the 1745 rebellion and, as Johnson says, "To the southern inhabitants of Scotland . . . equally unknown with . . . Borneo or Sumatra." Not that Boswell had to do much coaxing, for Johnson himself confesses: "I had desired to visit the Hebrides, or Western Islands of Scotland, so long that I scarcely remember how the wish was originally excited." One wonders whether, paradoxically, the famous and evocative reference to the Hebrides in *Lycidas* may have had something to do with it.

If one thinks that he can get all he needs to know about Johnson in Boswell, there is no better way for him to judge what he is missing than by reading, first, Boswell's *Journal of a Tour to the Hebrides,* and then Johnson's *Journey to the Western Islands of Scotland.* Boswell's is the work of one who has made a consummate art out of gossip, delightfully imparting the curiosity of seeing "the great Doctor Johnson" in a strange setting; though, in the end, Johnson does not seem as out of place in that setting as Boswell perhaps hoped he would. It was Boswell, not Johnson, who got seasick and suffered agonies in the small boats in which they crossed the angry seas; indeed, Johnson turns the tables and pokes fun at Boswell from time to time, as when he describes the primitive conditions of the inn at Glenelg: "Sleep, however, was necessary. Our Highlanders had at last found some hay, with which the inn could not supply them. I directed them to bring a bundle into the room, and slept upon it in my riding coat. Mr. Boswell being more delicate, laid himself sheets, with hay over and under him, and lay in linen like a gentleman." Johnson's book, however, is not about Johnson but about Scotland: the record of a first-rate mind, tremendously concerned about the human situation, seriously and acutely reporting a way of life new to him and his readers. He reports it, moreover, in a superbly "journalistic" style—direct, clear, economical, vivid, and personal. The work is an "Inside Scotland" by an observer and far greater artist with words than the modern writers who have tried to write such books.

In a famous passage Johnson tells how he decided to write the book—and it is typical of the highly personal quality of so much of his writing that he should do so: "I sat down on a bank such as a writer of romance might have delighted to feign. I had, indeed, no trees to whisper over my head, but a clear rivulet streamed at my feet. The day was calm, the air was soft, and all was rudeness, silence, and solitude. Before me, and on either side, were high hills, which, by hindering the eye from ranging, forced the mind to find entertainment for itself. Whether I spent the hour well I know not; for here I first conceived the thought of this narration."

If this passage seems "romantic," one should read on, where Johnson explains how very "realistic" his reflections are:

We were in this place at ease and by choice . . . yet the imaginations excited by the view of an unknown and untravelled wilderness are not such as arise in the artificial solitude of parks and gardens [such as his "romantic" contemporaries like Shenstone were busily creating]. . . . The phantoms which haunt a desert are want, and misery, and dangers: the evils of dereliction rush upon the thoughts; man is made unwillingly acquainted with his own weakness, and meditation shows him only how little he can sustain, and how little he can perform. . . . Whoever had been in the place where I then sat, unprovided with provisions, and ignorant of the country, might, at least before the roads were made [very recently], have wandered among the rocks, till he had perished with hardship, before he could have found either food or shelter. Yet what are these . . . spots of wilderness to the deserts of America?

What makes the book great is this power of "creative imagination," and of empathy, that enables him to see the Highlanders not, as Boswell does, as "quaint natives" for a tourist to enjoy on an outing and then forget, but against the background of the somber total situation of the human race.

These few puny but amazing creatures continually battle against the overwhelming forces of nature; and, by dint of their intelligence and effort, they
wrest from it the conditions for a life of some kind of decency.

The whole of Johnson's *Journey* is informed with his awareness of this continual struggle. He scathingly reprobates the Scottish religious "reformers" of
the sixteenth century, who in their fanatic zeal destroyed the old cathedrals
and abbeys—not because Johnson is an admirer of the Middle Ages, "ages so
long accustomed to darkness," as he calls them, but because these monuments are precious to him as rare outposts of learning and religion in that wilderness of ignorance and barbarity. He notes carefully the books and other
evidences of learning he finds in the houses he visits in the Hebrides; he expresses his admiration of the enlightened chiefs and clergymen he encounters;
and he vigorously condemns those other landowners whose want of a feeling
of responsibility for their tenants has led to mass emigration to America. It
makes Johnson unhappy to see the Highlands, already suffering from under-
population, becoming still less populated. "Emigration," he says to Boswell,
"spreads mankind, which weakens the defence of a nation, and lessens the
comfort of living."

And yet, when Johnson puts himself in the position of the individual
Highlander (the sort of thing he almost always does when he considers a political question), he can understand that position very vividly:

The traveller wanders through a naked desert . . . and now and then finds a heap of
loose stones and turfs in a cavity between rocks, where a being, born with all those
powers which education expands, and all those sensations which culture refines, is
condemned to shelter itself from the wind and rain. Philosophers there are who try to
make themselves believe that this life is happy, but they believe it only while they are
saying it. . . . The Highlanders have learned that there are countries less bleak and
barren than their own, where instead of working for the Laird, every man may till his
own ground, and eat all the produce of his own labour. Great numbers have been in-
duced by this discovery to go every year, for some time past, to America.[21]

In a long discussion of the old clan system, now broken down, one sees that
the idea in itself appeals to him—the ties of loyalty, the feeling of "belong-
ing," the chief's sense of responsibility for the welfare of the members of the
clan. And yet, in the end, his summing up is that "The system of insular subordination . . . having little variety, cannot afford much delight in the
view. . . . The inhabitants were for a long time perhaps not unhappy; but
their content was a muddy mixture of pride and ignorance, an indifference
for pleasures which they did not know, and a strong conviction of their own

importance." Once when Boswell, a genuinely "romantic" conservative of the kind that Sir Walter Scott and Edmund Burke were to foster, was babbling in a starry-eyed way about the delights of the clan—"I said I believed mankind were happier in the ancient feudal state of subordination than they are in the modern state of independency"—Johnson broke in: "To be sure, the *Chief* was: but we must think of the number of individuals. That *they* were less happy seems plain; for that state from which all escape as soon as they can, and to which none return after they have left it, must be less happy; and this is the case with the state of dependence on a chief or great man."[22]

Johnson was no believer in unrestricted laissez-faire and the devil take the hindmost, as he saw it developing under Pitt and as it was to develop further in Britain during the next century: his view was the Christian one that each man is his brother's keeper. On the other hand, his own individualism and love of independence are always strong enough to keep him from wanting to turn his or any society into a complete welfare state, organized and administered from the top down. His basic political position, that is to say, is remarkably like that of many modern moderate "liberals" and liberal "conservatives."

Chapter Seven

The Student of Language and Literature: Lexicographer and Critic

There was a time, in the heyday of "romantic" taste, when readers would have asked, "What can Johnson's lexicography have to do with his criticism?" This was the time when one applied Matthew Arnold's "touchstones" to a poem and decided whether the "ideas" embodied in it possessed "high seriousness" or not. In more recent times, readers and critics have come around to Mallarmé's and Eliot's way of thinking: in criticism the spirit killeth, but the letter giveth life. Johnson would have agreed. His aim in compiling his great *Dictionary of the English Language* is stated in his preface to his abridgment (published the following year, 1756) of the full work: "I lately published a Dictionary like those compiled by the academies of Italy and France, *for the use of such as aspire to exactness of criticism, or elegance of style.*"

The abridged dictionary is for "the greater number of readers, who, seldom intending to write or presuming to judge, turn over books only to amuse their leisure"—"escape reading"—"and to gain degrees of knowledge suitable to lower characters, or necessary to the common business of life: these know not any other use of a dictionary than of adjusting orthography, and explaining terms of science, or words of infrequent occurrence, or remote derivation." A small dictionary is, therefore, all that is needed for "common readers," but Johnson says (what is quite true) that the many smaller dictionaries already published for just this market are unsatisfactory: "and, as I may without arrogance claim to myself a longer acquaintance with the lexicography of our language than any other writer has had," he is well qualified "to accommodate the nation with a vocabulary of daily use."

Method and Intent

Indeed Johnson's small octavo dictionary was *the* household dictionary for many decades. It was undoubtedly a copy of the octavo edition of the

"Dixonary" that Miss Pinkerton presented to her pupils when they left her school and that Becky Sharp hurled back at her benefactor. But, as Johnson makes clear, the great original dictionary, in two massive folio volumes, had a higher purpose than merely to help clerks to spell and schoolboys to look up meanings of unfamiliar words. Like the Tuscan dictionary of the Accademia della Crusca in 1612 and the great dictionary of the Académie Française in 1694, Johnson's was intended to facilitate "exactness of criticism and elegance of style." How was it to accomplish this? By being, like the other famous ones, a dictionary on historical, empirical, scientific principles; that is to say, by examining minutely how words had been used by the most highly regarded English writers in the past. It is firmly based, like the French and Italian dictionaries, and like important modern English dictionaries, on "usage." But, unlike some modern English dictionaries, it is not so much concerned with colloquial usage as with the literary usage of those writers who are regarded as having most fully realized the potential of the English language. Johnson nevertheless does include a surprisingly large number of colloquial words and expressions in the *Dictionary*.

This concern can be made clearer by noting how Johnson went about compiling the *Dictionary*. He first read through the works of the great English writers of the sixteenth and seventeenth centuries, men like Shakespeare, Spenser, Hooker, Bacon, Milton, Boyle the "Father of Chemistry." He selects the last four for special mention in his preface, and the diversity of the "fields" in which they wrote should be noted—theology, philosophy, poetry, natural science. As he read, whenever he encountered a word whose signification was clearly illustrated by its context, he marked it; and eventually he handed the book to his amanuenses, who copied the passage down under the initial letter of the word. Finally, all the passages illustrating a single word were brought together, studied, and compared; then the various shades of meaning of the word were sorted out; and finally a definition of each shade of meaning was formulated, with the passages exemplifying it annexed in support of the definition. It was, in fact, the way great modern dictionaries are compiled, except that they have the assistance of typewriters, photocopying machines, computers, and filing cards instead of quills and ledgers, and of a clerical staff of hundreds instead of Johnson's faithful six.

Johnson's attitude toward language generally is remarkably "modern." Much has been said (sometimes by linguistic specialists who should know better) of Johnson's "foolish" determination to "fix" the English language. This aim he did accept at first in his *Plan of an English Dictionary*, published in 1747 when he was just beginning work on his project. "All change is of itself an evil, which ought not to be hazarded but for evident advantage," he says; and he reprehends those "who despise the inconveniences of confusion, who seem to take pleasure in departing from custom, and to think alteration desirable for its own sake"—an attitude sometimes found among modern writers on linguistics.

Johnson, however, thinks stability in language is desirable, and he is perfectly right. He shows some awareness in his political and lexicographical writing of the linguistic trends of his time. With the tremendous geographical expansion of the sphere of European culture since the Renaissance, through exploration, colonization, and trade, English was rapidly becoming a world language; and in such a situation lack of stability and standardization must cause much greater inconvenience to communication than it would when English was merely the language of a handful of people in a small isolated island off the western coast of Europe. Indeed, since the time of the publication of Johnson's *Dictionary,* the rate of linguistic change in written English, at least, has been notably retarded; and with modern methods of communication—radio, television, motion pictures—the tendency of the language has been to standardization. For instance, Anglo-American differences of idiom—"lift/elevator," "radio/wireless," "movies/cinema"—have tended to disappear, much to the advantage of ease of communication among the far-flung community of writers and speakers of "standard English."

Yet Johnson, whatever the aim he announced in his *Plan,* was not so naïve as to think that "fixing" a living language is possible. Eight years later, when he had finished the *Dictionary,* he declared in the preface that such an aim is impossible to achieve. Although still affirming (rightly) that stability is, in itself, a good thing, "Those who have been persuaded to think well of my design will require that it should fix our language, and put a stop to those alterations which time and chance have hitherto been suffered to make in it without opposition. With this consequence I will confess that I flattered myself for a while; but now begin to fear that I have indulged expectation which neither reason nor experience can justify." And he makes fun of the struggles of national academies ("which," he bursts out, "I, who can never wish to see dependance multiplied, hope the spirit of English liberty will hinder or destroy") against reason and experience. "Their vigilance and activity have hitherto been vain; sounds are too volatile and subtile for legal restraints; to enchain syllables and to lash the wind are equally the undertakings of pride."

Johnson's rejection of the purpose of "fixing" a language is based, as he himself says, on his theory of the nature of language, which is firmly "nominalist" in the tradition of the British empiricist philosophy of Bacon, Locke, Berkeley, and Hume. He refuses to be taken in by exalted Platonic notions that words are representations of permanent and transcendental "ideas" in the mind of God: "This recommendation of steadiness and uniformity does not proceed from an opinion that particular combinations of letters have much influence on human happiness, or that truth may not be successfully taught by modes of spelling fanciful and erroneous; I am not yet so lost in lexicography as to forget that *words are the daughters of earth and that things are the sons of heaven.* Language is only the instrument of science, and words are but the signs of ideas"—"ideas" here in the Berkeleyan sense, not the Platonic: that is to say, sense impressions. And, as the empiricist knows, apart from divine revelation, sense impressions are the ultimate source of all true knowledge ("science").

This passage is of great importance in understanding Johnson's literary theory. Words in themselves are meaningless sounds and marks. "Meaning" becomes attached to them when they are used, in context, by human beings and when other human beings respond to them. Criticism, then, is primarily a branch of human psychology: an examination of how men respond to certain combinations of linguistic elements, and how those elements can be most effectively combined to achieve a desired psychological response. The business of the lexicographer is ancillary to that of the critic: it is to observe and tabulate, as well as he can, on the basis of recorded linguistic behavior, the various kinds of usage and response to individual linguistic forms.

Johnson emphatically states that this inquiry is always an a posteriori and approximate, never an a priori and exact, inquiry. The vagueness of meaning of some words, he says, "is not to be imputed to me, who do not form, but register the language": "The shades of meaning sometimes pass imperceptibly into each other, so that though on one side they apparently differ, yet it is impossible to mark the point of contact. Ideas of the same race, though not exactly alike, are sometimes so little different that no words can express the dissimilitude. . . . Sometimes there is such a confusion of acceptations that discernment is wearied, and distinction puzzled, and perseverance herself hurries to an end by crowding together what she cannot separate." This problem can be illustrated by the number of significations Johnson manages to distinguish for certain common words, almost as many in some cases as the *Oxford English Dictionary* discovers. For *give* (transitive) he has thirty-seven meanings; for *go*, seventy; for *good,* thirty-six; and for the transitive verb *set,* he lists seventy-one meanings, and at definition 72 he throws up his hands in despair and declares, "This is one of the words that can hardly be examined otherwise than by various and multiplied exemplification."

It is clear that the habit of talking about Johnson's lexicography as "normative" or "dictatorial" or "authoritarian" is completely wrong. He does not "assign" rigid definitions to words: he collects examples of their usage and then tries to classify those examples, as a botanist collects and then classifies different varieties of plants. It follows, also, that the practice of quoting Johnson's "definitions" in isolation, as examples of his idiosyncratic ways of thinking, is to misrepresent him and his work. As with any dictionary compiled in an empirical, scientific manner, what is important is not the definition but the illustration; and to quote the definition without reference to the illustration is perverse. For instance, the entry under "Whig" is often cited as an example of Johnson's prejudice—merely "The name of a faction." When one looks at the entry, however, it is obvious that the function of this definition is merely to direct the reader to the illustration that follows it—a long and detailed exposition by the historian Gilbert Burnet (himself a staunch "Whig") of how the word came into use.

The habit of citing "funny" definitions from the *Dictionary* as evidence of Johnson's eccentricity—always suppressing the fact that the definitions are followed by quotations showing the word used in context—was one of the various types of distortion popularized by Boswell. It is true that Johnson occasionally relieved the tedium of dictionary-making by indulging in personal reflections: under *lich*, a dead body, mentioning "Lichfield . . . *salve magna parens*"; under *irony*, "A mode of speech in which the meaning is contrary to the words: as, *Bolingbroke was a holy man.*" But many of Boswell's "amusing" examples have been shown to be not nearly so idiosyncratic as he thought. In his definitions of *Tory*, *Whig*, and *oats*, Johnson is merely following accepted lexicographical tradition; the polysyllables in his definition of "network" come from Sir Thomas Browne's *The Garden of Cyrus*, a treatise on "networks"; in the hostile definition of *excise*, he is only repeating a large body of sentiment of his time, expressed with equal vigor in, for example, Sir William Blackstone's *Commentaries;* and so on.

To sum up, Johnson's *Dictionary* is a very great and serious achievement in the history of the study of the English language. It is not merely a curious whim of a quaint eccentric, but a most important landmark in the development of English, from a set of unimportant local dialects spoken by a small group of islanders on the fringe of civilization, to a great world language. It represents the necessary application to English of the systematic and scientific technique of linguistic recording and investigation used earlier in the famous academic dictionaries of Italian and French, and is itself the direct ancestor of such modern scientifically compiled dictionaries as the *Oxford English Dictionary* and *Webster's New International*. All this is now recognized in modern accounts by professional students of linguistics—for instance, in the important book by J. H. Sledd and Gwin J. Kolb commemorating the two-hundredth anniversary of the publication of the *Dictionary*.[1]

Criticism and Language

"What . . . was it that made Dr. Johnson such a unique judge of poetic merit?" one recent student of Johnson's literary criticism asks; and his answer begins, "He well knew that the study of literature must be founded on an exact knowledge of the language."[2]

Johnson's close attention to the hard facts of a literary text, his insistence on asking, again and again, "What does this word, this phrase, this sentence, *mean?* What are the emotional associations it evokes? What is the precise picture that this image brings into our mind?," his refusal to be led away from the facts of that text into nebulous pseudo-philosophical speculation, were treated very superciliously by the romantic critics of the nineteenth and early twentieth centuries. But in the mid-twentieth, through the influence of Eliot, Leavis, and others, Johnson's approach came again to be the prevailing mode in literary criticism; and the student unwise enough meekly to follow nineteenth-century literary historians in their low estimate of Johnson's criticism; will find himself very much out of date. The reputation of Johnson as a critic has never been higher than in the last half-century, and some recent opinions of him are worth quoting. To Yvor Winters, "A great critic is the rarest of all literary geniuses; perhaps the only critic in English who deserves that epithet is Samuel Johnson."[3] F. R. Leavis finds that

Johnson's criticism . . . is alive and life-giving. . . . We read it for the vigour and weight that comes from a powerful mind and a profoundly serious nature, and the weight that seems to be a matter of bringing to bear at every point the ordered experience of a lifetime. . . . When we read him we know, beyond question, that we have here a powerful and distinguished mind operating at first hand upon literature. This, we can say with emphatic conviction (the emphasis registering the rarity), really *is* criticism. . . . So powerful an intelligence, associated with so intense an interest both in letters and in human nature, could no more be narrow than shallow.[4]

Edmund Wilson writes, "The *Lives of the Poets* and the preface and commentary on Shakespeare are among the most brilliant and the most acute documents in the whole range of English criticism, and the products of a mind which, so far from being parochially local and hopelessly cramped by the taste of its age, saw literature in a long perspective and could respond to the humanity of Shakespeare as well as to the wit of Pope."[5]

It must be said, to begin with, that Johnson is not, and does not wish to be, a critical *theorist*. He is not interested in constructing an ingenious and rigid "system" of critical or aesthetic doctrine. Instead, he is always the "practical critic" who is intensely interested in how he and other readers respond to certain works and kinds of literature. If one wishes to examine his reactions and deduce from them systematic principles and patterns that unconsciously underlie them, one is presumably welcome to do so; but this activity is not one that appeals to Johnson. In this preference, of course, he is like other great critics, Dryden, Arnold, Sainte-Beuve, Eliot, whose point of departure is always the work of art itself; it is the lesser men who start with some ingenious a priori set of theories and fit the work of art into them. Many such were devised in Johnson's own time, and had their short day; only the rare specialist now cares to turn to Lord Kames's *Elements of Criticism*, Archibald Allison's *Essays on the Nature and Principles of Taste*, and the like; but Johnson's critical writing is still, as Leavis says, alive and life-giving.

Like his writings on politics and morality, Johnson's critical writings are diverse and scattered; and they are difficult, therefore, to arrange in a neat pattern for purposes of discussion. For convenience we may consider them in three groups:

(1) His work on Shakespeare—the great edition of the plays in 1765, with important revisions in the fourth edition, 1773; together with such earlier work as the *Miscellaneous Observations on Macbeth* (1745), intended as a specimen of a full edition of the plays, although the project was postponed until after the *Dictionary* was finished; *Proposals* (1756) for the 1765 edition; the important dedication to his friend Charlotte Lennox's *Shakespear Illustrated*, 1753.

(2) The critical portions of *The Lives of the Poets*, written chiefly between 1777 and 1781, although some, like the *Life of Savage*, were composed earlier.

(3) A large group of smaller miscellaneous critical writings, some of them too much neglected: for instance, important papers in the *Rambler* and *Idler*, on such subjects as fiction, biography, Milton's versification, *Samson Agonistes*, problems of "diction," pastoral poetry, and other subjects; a fine "Essay on Epitaphs" (1740) and another on Pope's verse epitaphs (1756); the preface to Maurice's translation of *Oedipus Tyrannus* (1780), which contains some challenging remarks on tragedy; several important reviews, in particular that of Joseph Warton's *Essay on Pope* (1756); chapter 10 of *Rasselas*, in which Imlac (not Johnson) gives his famous "character" of the ideal poet.

No student has yet undertaken a really systematic account, in chronological order, of Johnson's critical writings.[6] This is a pity, for it causes much confusion if one assumes that all the critical ideas put forward in his writings were held simultaneously and permanently. In fact, Johnson changed his mind, as he grew older, on a number of subjects, including (as will be noted) the vexed one of "poetical justice" in drama.

Criticism of Shakespeare

Johnson's motto "Always fly at the eagle" was exemplified by his issuing proposals, at the age of thirty-five, for a new edition of Shakespeare. The *Miscellaneous Observations on Macbeth* which he published at the same time provided a specimen of the kind of annotation he proposed to furnish. The annotation is, in fact, quite similar to that which actually appeared twenty years later—notes historical, linguistic, explanatory of difficult readings in the text, critical of the explanations of other critics. One thing that is apparent, however, by comparing the 1745 and the 1765 notes on *Macbeth* is that in the later version Johnson becomes much more reluctant to introduce conjectural emendations of the folio text in order to remove seeming infelicities in the readings of that text. In the 1753 dedication of Mrs. Lennox's *Shakespear Illustrated* (a pioneering collection of the sources from which Shakespeare took his plots) and the 1756 *Proposals*, he says in briefer form (but most effectively) some of the things he was later to say in the 1765 *Preface*. For instance, he writes about Shakespeare's use of idiomatic language, "If Shakespeare has difficulties above other writers, it is to be imputed to the nature of his work, which required the use of the common colloquial language, and consequently admitted many phrases allusive, elliptical, and proverbial, such as we speak and hear every hour without observing them: and of which, being now familiar, we do not suspect that they can ever grow uncouth, or that, being now obvious, they can ever seem remote," and of Shakespeare's characterization, he comments, "Among his other excellences it ought to be remarked, because it has hitherto been unnoticed, that his *heroes are men*, that the love and hatred, the hopes and fears, of his chief personages are such as are common to other human beings, and not like those which later times have exhibited, peculiar to phantoms that strut upon the stage. . . . Shakespeare's excellence is not the fiction of a tale, but the representation of life: and his reputation is therefore safe, till human nature shall be changed."

The *Preface* to the 1765 edition of Shakespeare is, of course, one of Johnson's greatest and most famous performances. It is a beautiful and memorable piece of writing; historically, it is important as publicizing the rejection of the "rules" of the "three unities" as a requisite to effective drama; one of the most amusing ironies of literary history is that Stendhal's *Racine et Shakespeare*, published in the 1820s and regarded as one of the revolutionary manifestos of high "romanticism," cribs largely from it. Moreover, Johnson's statement about how to edit a Shakespearean text is almost modern in its approach. Although recent investigation has been inclined to discount somewhat the originality of the views set forth in the *Preface*, many of which can be found in the work of earlier and contemporary critics,[7] it can be safely said that Johnson gave them their first really effective and memorable expression.

The *Preface*, more carefully organized than many of Johnson's writings, begins with a section in praise of Shakespeare: the greatness of his reputation has stood the test of time; his highest praise is that he "holds up to his readers a faithful mirror of manners and of life"; his characters, unlike "the phantoms which other writers raise up," are real men and women. That he mingled tragedy and comedy together is not a count against him, for he "exhibits the real state of sublunary nature, which partakes of good and evil, joy and sorrow. . . . That this is a practice contrary to the rules of criticism will be readily allowed: but there is always an appeal open from criticism to nature." Finally, his dialogue is convincing—he "deserves to be studied as one of the original masters of our language."

The second section lists Shakespeare's faults—"faults sufficient to obscure and overwhelm any other merit." No system of morality can be detected in his plays; the plots are careless; he is full of anachronisms; his jests are gross; he has much tedious and tumid language; he falls into bathos ("What he does best, he soon ceases to do. He is not soft and pathetic without some idle conceit, or contemptible equivocation. He no sooner begins to move than he counteracts himself"); he can never resist a pun.

There follows, as a third section, Johnson's thoughtful, ingenious, and compelling defense of Shakespeare against the charge of violating the unities of time and place. The justification for the unities is that they are supposed to maintain verisimilitude; to ask the audience to imagine that they are in Rome in one scene and a few minutes later in Alexandria is to put too great a strain on the willing suspension of disbelief. But how can this matter, Johnson asks, when the spectators know perfectly well that they are not in Rome to begin with, but in a playhouse in London? If their imagination is powerful enough to convey them to Rome in the first place, it can be relied on to convey them as easily from Rome to Alexandria.

The fourth section is a long consideration of Shakespeare in the context of his age, and it amounts, therefore, to a defense of him against some of the strictures listed in the second section. The crudeness and crowded incident of his plots is understandable, given the reading tastes of his public—for "adventures, giants, dragons, and enchantments." Voltaire's preference for the "regularity" of *Cato* is answered by "Addison speaks the language of poets, and Shakespeare of men." The problem of "Shakespeare's learning" is canvassed, and Johnson concludes that he learned not from books but from experience: "Shakespeare, whether life or nature be his object, shows plainly that he has seen with his own eyes; he gives the image which he receives, not weakened or distorted by the intervention of any other mind."

The fifth and final section is a careful review of the history of the editing and criticism of Shakespeare up to the date of Johnson's edition, and a statement of his own principles of editing. Most notable is his condemnation of the indiscriminate use of conjectural emendation of the early Shakespearean texts. It is true that the printing of the quartos and the first folio is abominable. Johnson rightly points out that the first is the only folio with any authority, since variations in the later ones can only be errors introduced by the printers; one of Johnson's qualifications for editing Shakespeare is that, as a bookseller's son and a Grub Street hack, he knows much more than, say, Warburton, about the concrete details of the bookmaking process.

But to think, as earlier editors had done, that every passage they did not at once understand must be a misprint and to change the difficult word to an easy one is, as Johnson insists, a most dangerous practice: one must first search through Elizabethan English to make sure that there is not some now-obsolete but then accepted meaning of the word that makes sense of the passage. And, of course, Johnson was qualified to edit Shakespeare as none of his predecessors had been: he not only had, for the first time, a competent dictionary of Elizabethan English at his disposal, but had compiled it himself during eight years of minutely reading and examining Elizabethan texts. He concludes the *Preface* with an exhortation to read Shakespeare, in the first instance, *without* the copious notes ("necessary evils") he has provided— "When [the reader's] fancy is once on the wing, let it not stoop at correction or explanation"—and with the quotation of Dryden's tribute to Shakespeare in the *Essay of Dramatic Poesy.*

Much has been written in an attempt to "place" Johnson's *Preface to Shakespeare* in the history of criticism. Is it fundamentally an expression of "neoclassic" or of "romantic" literary theory, or a mixture, or transition, or what? The emphatic rejection of "rules" about the unities and tragicomedy has been thought to be "pre-romantic." On the other hand, the second section of the *Preface*, in which Johnson complains of Shakespeare's messy plotting, irrelevant clowning, and occasional turgidity of language, has shocked those who came to believe, with Coleridge, that Shakespeare "never did wrong but with just cause"; that he was something more than merely a human, if very great, writer. This section caused critics to insist that Johnson is, after all, basically "neoclassic."

As time goes on, such controversy seems more and more pointless and sterile. There is little evidence that Johnson subscribed to any formulated "neoclassic" critical theory, or was even aware that one existed (if one actually *did* exist at all in England in the eighteenth century). As always, he is simply saying what he thinks as he goes along; one senses that he does not worry a great deal about whether or not this happens to agree with what others before him have thought or what those after him are going to think. True, after he has disposed of the "unities," he exclaims, "I am almost frighted at my own temerity; and when I estimate the fame and the strength of those that maintain the contrary opinion, am ready to sink down in reverential silence." If he really is, it is the only recorded occasion when this could be said of Johnson. The most "famed" of those who maintained the contrary opinion at the time was, of course, Voltaire, of whose opinions Johnson remarks at another point in the *Preface* in a startlingly different tone: "These are the petty cavils of petty minds." In fact, this passage, which then continues with a pompous and hackneyed allusion to classical mythology, a device of which Johnson often expressed his contempt—"as Æneas withdrew from the defence of Troy, when he saw Neptune shaking the wall and Juno heading the besiegers"—is one of the best examples of Johnson's occasional talent for boisterous humor.

The *Preface* and the delightful but desultory "General Observations" at the ends of the plays have often been reprinted. The running annotations, however, have not;[8] and it has recently been argued, with considerable plausibility, that they—not the *Preface*, fine as it is—are the supreme example of Johnson's competence as a critic. Here, as Professor Sherbo says, one sees "Johnson's criticism in operation," actively applied to words, images, action, and characterization, attempting to elucidate for the reader the *meaning*—in the widest sense of the term, of emotional as well as intellectual effect—of this great monument, thirty-seven plays in all, of some of the world's most subtle, most difficult, and most rewarding literature. David Nichol Smith once remarked that when reading Shakespeare in a variorum edition, with commentary by a host of editors at the bottom of the page, one asks, "when baffled by a difficult passage, 'What does Johnson say?'"[9] Johnson's own edition is, of course, a pioneering "variorum" edition: as well as his own comments, he reprints notes by Pope, Theobald, Hanmer, Warburton, and others. Sometimes he makes no comment (when he agrees with their explanations); very frequently, he argues with them; and, occasionally, in spite of his remarks in the *Preface* deprecating the tendency of critics to squabble with one another, he loses his temper, as when he appends to some farfetched reading of Warburton's, "Of the finding of such beauties there is no end."

In the notes Johnson brings to the service of readers of Shakespeare his knowledge of older English—

Yield his engrossments] His accumulations—[10]

of other languages—

Fig me like / The bragging Spaniard] *To fig,* in Spanish *Higas dar,* is to insult by putting the thumb between the fore and middle finger. From this Spanish custom we yet say in contempt, *a fig for you*—

of other early literature—

I was then Sir Dagonet in Arthur's show] The story of Sir Dagonet is to be found in *La Mort d'Arthur* [Johnson goes on to tell who Sir Dagonet was, and quotes Ascham to show the popularity of the work in Elizabethan times.]

Many of his notes elucidate Shakespeare's compressed language, and he is properly severe on those editors who would "regularize" the rich and subtle texture of its imagery by conjectural emendation—

We come within our awful banks again] *Awful banks* are the proper limits of reverence [Warburton had wanted to emend "awful" to "lawful."]

Who falling in the flaws of her own youth, / Hath blister'd her report.] Who doth not see that the integrity of the metaphor requires we should read FLAMES of youth?— *Warburton.* Who does not see that upon such principles there is no end of correction?

He often assists the reader to visualize Shakespeare's imagery: on Hamlet's calling Osric "this water-fly," he comments that "A waterfly skips up and down upon the surface of the water, without any apparent purpose or reason, and is thence the proper emblem of a busy trifler." And on " 'Tis seldom, when the bee doth leave her comb / In the dead carrion," he writes: "As the bee, having once placed her comb in a carcase, stays by her honey, so he that has once taken pleasure in bad company, will continue to associate with those that have the art of pleasing him."

In longer notes Johnson calls attention to beauties of expression—

Thou hast nor youth, nor age; / But as it were an after dinner's sleep, / Dreaming on both.] This is exquisitely imagined. When we are young we busy ourselves in forming schemes for succeeding time, and miss the gratifications that are before us; when we are old we amuse the languor of age with the recollection of youthful pleasures or performances; so our life, of which no part is filled with the business of the present time, resembles our dreams after dinner, when the events of the morning are mingled with the designs of the evening—

and subtleties of characterization and psychology—

If it were damnable, he being so wise, / Why would he for the momentary trick / Be perdurably fin'd] Shakespeare shows his knowledge of human nature in the conduct of Claudio. When Isabella first tells him of Angelo's proposal he answers with honest indignation, agreeably to his settled principles, *thou shalt not do't.* But the love of life being permitted to operate, soon furnishes him with sophistical arguments, he believes it cannot be very dangerous to the soul, since Angelo, who is so wise, will venture it.

He frequently expostulates on what seems to him Shakespeare's negligence of morality: on Lancaster's execution of Hastings and Mowbray (in *II Henry IV*), "It cannot but raise some indignation to find this horrible violation of faith passed over thus slightly by the poet, without any note of censure or detestation"; and on the end of *Measure for Measure,* "Angelo's crimes were such as must sufficiently justify punishment, whether its end be to secure the innocent from wrong, or to deter guilt by examples; and I believe every reader feels some indignation when he finds him spared."

And so he comments throughout the thirty-seven plays of the folio. But no short sampling can do justice to the rich *texture* of Johnson's commentary; as with the *Dictionary,* the student should do some *continuous* reading, making his way through at least one complete play in Johnson's edition. What Johnson wrote of the qualifications of the ideal textual editor may be applied to Johnson's work as a commentator on Shakespeare generally: "In perusing a corrupted piece, he must have before him all possibilities of meaning, with all possibilities of expression. Such must be his comprehension of thought, and such his copiousness of language. Out of many readings possible, he must be able to select that which best suits with the state of opinions and modes of language prevailing in every age, and with his author's particular cast of thought and turn of expression. Such must be his knowledge and such his taste. . . . Let us now be told no more of 'the dull duty of an editor.'"

Whether or not we agree with all Johnson's comments, we cannot follow them intelligently without becoming intimately *involved* with the play itself and with Shakespeare the poet—and that, of course, is what Johnson wants the reader to do. His sensitive reading is the stuff of which great criticism is made.

Critical Attitudes

The critical portions of the fifty-two *Prefaces, Biographical and Critical, to the Works of the English Poets* (later known as *The Lives of the Poets*) vary a great deal in length and concentration—as one might expect. Some of the poets are very great ones; others (the majority), quite unimportant. Indeed, if one reads through them consecutively, one is a little depressed (as Johnson himself no doubt was) by the amount of mediocrity one encounters—Duke, King, Smith, Stepney, Hughes, Fenton, Yalden, Broome, Pitt, Hammond: the roll call of forgotten poetasters seems to go on forever. Of course, if one had to select fifty poets from any other century, the last thirty or so in the list would be as dreary.

The work to which Johnson's *Lives* formed the prefatory remarks was an anthology of English poetry from about 1650 to 1750. The poets to be included were selected by the publishers, although Johnson made a few suggestions for additions, the most striking being, as has been observed, the very fine hymn-writer Isaac Watts. For the bulk of these poets Johnson conscientiously deals out a few scant critical paragraphs of perfunctory praise and blame. But when he comes to a great poet like Milton or Pope, he carefully examines, one by one, his major productions; and then he gives a long and thoughtful assessment of his total achievement. In one essay, the first (on Cowley), one finds something unusual—the dissertation on "metaphysical poetry," the term Johnson popularized for the work of Donne, Cowley, Crashaw, and the rest. Of this, a modern Donne scholar comments, "By his copious quotations from Donne, and his declaration that to write in the metaphysical manner 'it was at least necessary to read and think,' Johnson brought back into literary discussion a body of poetry that had largely sunk into oblivion. . . . The Donne revival begins with Johnson."[11]

The third group of Johnson's critical writings, the short miscellaneous and occasional essays, are too various in subject to lend themselves to a summary description. Perhaps it will be worthwhile at this point to attempt some kind of comprehensive statement of what appear to be the more important critical attitudes that emerge from a reading of Johnson's criticism as a whole, and to try to fit into it significant statements found in the miscellaneous criticism. A genuinely exhaustive synthesis of Johnson's total critical position would be a task far too great to embark on here, but some attitudes that appear from even a rapid survey of his critical writings are these:

Empiricism.   Johnson is an empirical, not a dogmatic, critic. His activity as a critic begins, not with the assertion of certain rigid predetermined criteria of what is good or bad in literature, but with his own reaction to a work. "Of this tragedy many particular passages deserve regard," he begins his concluding "General Observation" on *Julius Caesar;* "and the contention and reconcilement of Brutus and Cassius is universally celebrated: but *I have never been strongly agitated in perusing it.*" So much for *Julius Caesar.* The work must make an emotional impact of some kind on him to begin with for it to be worth expending paper on at all. He never hesitates to be extremely personal and impressionistic in his criticism. "I was many years ago so shocked by Cordelia's death," he confesses, at the end of *King Lear,* "that I know not whether I ever endured to read again the last scenes of the play till I undertook to revise them as an editor." As he finishes annotating *Othello,* he exclaims, "I am glad that I have ended my revisal of this dreadful scene. It is not to be endured."

His "empiricism"—in the sense that the individual aesthetic experience comes first—is summarized in the scornful remark he makes apropos of someone's criticism that Pope's versification is "too uniformly musical": "I suspect this objection to be the cant of those who judge by principles rather than perception." He quotes the charge against Addison that he "decided by taste rather than principles"; and, although he does not answer it (perhaps as not deserving an answer), he makes it clear that he regards Addison highly as a critic. Johnson is enough of a rationalist to concede that principles, regularities, "rules" are at least possible, and may emerge (tentatively, as working hypotheses) from an examination of literature. But clearly he has not much faith in their usefulness. *Idlers* 60 and 61 are an amusing lampoon on Dick Minim, the "petty critic," who has learned by heart and parrots the fashionable critical cant of his day (he is still with us).

Perhaps Johnson's fullest statement of the kind of critic he tried to be is the remark recorded by Fanny Burney: "There are three distinct kinds of judges upon all new authors or productions: The first are those who know no rules, but pronounce entirely from their natural taste and feelings; the second are those who know and judge by rules; and the third are those who know, but are above the rules. These last are those you should wish to satisfy. Next to them rate the natural judges; but ever despise those opinions that are formed by the rules."[12]

Psychology.   Johnson is a psychological critic. Literature for him is an activity having to do with the human nervous system. Literature is constructed out of language, and "Language is only the instrument of science, and words are but the signs of ideas"—of sense impressions registered in the human mind. In considering language he is an associationist of the school of Locke. His *Rambler* 168 on "low words" is interesting: "No word is naturally or intrinsically meaner than another; our opinion therefore of words, as of other things arbitrarily and capriciously established, depends wholly upon accident and custom. . . . Words become low by the occasions to which they are applied . . . the disgust which they produce arises from the revival of those images with which they are commonly found."

The "low" words Johnson uses to illustrate his thesis—"dun," "knife," "blanket" from Macbeth's speech before he kills Duncan—have not much impressed modern readers, for whom they have largely lost the connotations of the stable, the kitchen, and the squalid bedroom that they had for Johnson. These associations have, in fact, changed in general usage; and Johnson's ear for the overtones of words is probably more sensitive than that of the average modern reader. But it is difficult to refute the thesis itself.

One of the most striking statements of the psychological basis of Johnson's view of literature is that found at the beginning of *Rambler* 60 (already noted in connection with Johnson's work as biographer): "All joy or sorrow for the happiness or calamities of others is produced by an act of the imagination that realizes the event, however fictitious, or approximates it, however remote, by placing us, for a time, in the condition of him whose fortune we contemplate; so that we feel, while the deception lasts, whatever motions would be excited by the same good or evil happening to ourselves." This concept of empathy, as one might call it, as the source of the emotional effect of much literature is clearly fundamental to Johnson's critical thinking. (It is also very important in his morality: "To feel sincere and honest joy at the success of another . . . is necessary to true friendship. . . . As cruelty looks upon misery without partaking pain, so envy beholds increase of happiness without partaking joy.")[13] The concept, involving "deception," is perhaps not very different from Coleridge's "willing suspension of disbelief."

Johnson's rejection of the unities of time and place is based on a somewhat similar notion: since setting a play in a different country and time to begin with involves an effort of the reader's imagination, there is no reason why one should not expect a similar effort from it when the scene is changed in the middle of the play. In his virtual rejection of the common view of onomatopoeia, making "the sound an echo to the sense," he likewise argues in psychological terms. He doubts the theory that certain combinations of sounds in themselves inevitably produce specified emotional states in the hearer; he thinks that the effectiveness of "representative metre" has been much exaggerated and is complicated by wishful thinking and fashionable cant: "It is scarcely to be doubted that on many occasions we make the music which we imagine ourselves to hear; that we modulate the poem by our own disposition, and ascribe to the numbers the effects of the sense." He has little difficulty showing that Pope's famous "representative" line, "Flies o'er th' unbending corn and skims along the main," far from being rapid, is in "a tardy and stately measure, and the word 'unbending' one of the most sluggish and slow which our language affords."[14] (It is also clear that, contrary to the usual legend, Johnson had an extremely acute and sensitive poetic ear.)

Mimesis. Johnson firmly believes that literature is valuable only insofar as it communicates the truth about things as they are, as it rests ultimately on "nature," or reality. Shakespeare's greatness is that he (like Hamlet's players) "holds up to his readers a faithful mirror of manners and of life." The value of critical "rules" is limited, since "There is always an appeal open from criticism to nature"—and the infinite variety of "nature" (reality) is difficult to reduce to rules. "The end of writing is to instruct," Johnson continues; "the end of poetry is to instruct by pleasing." And "instruction," in the end, means bringing the reader into contact with reality. This is the highest morality: "Let us endeavour to see things as they are. . . . Whether to see life as it is will give us much consolation, I know not; but the consolation which is drawn from truth, if any there be, is solid and durable; that which may be derived from error must be, like its original, fallacious and fugitive."

But the "imitation of life" in literature Johnson well knows to be, at best, a pale replica which does not really take anyone completely in; it produces its effect not through sheer verisimilitude, but by association and empathy—the reader or audience must still exercise his own imagination: "It will be asked, how the drama moves, if it is not credited. It is credited with all the credit due to a drama. It is credited, whenever it moves, as a just picture of a real original; as representing to the auditor what he would himself feel, if he were to do or suffer what is there feigned to be suffered or to be done. . . . Imitations produce pain or pleasure, not because they are mistaken for realities, but because they bring realities to mind."[15]

Morality. Since literature and life are inseparable—"The only end of writing is to enable the readers better to enjoy life, or better to endure it"[16]— literary criticism is in the end (like political criticism) a branch of general human morality. (It may be pointed out that most other important critics, from Aristotle to Eliot and Leavis, would not disagree: the greatest critics have also been great moralists.) In chapter 4 it was suggested that Johnson was not so naïve as to imagine that the moral end of literature is effected in any way so simple as by writing cautionary tales with precepts tacked on to the end; rather, his dictum that "The end of poetry is to instruct by pleasing"[17] is to be interpreted as "Literature, by involving the reader emotionally, effects desirable changes in the patterns in his nervous system."

The emotional involvement, the surrender, is indispensable; and Johnson insists again and again: "What a man reads as a task will do him little good"; "Tediousness is the most fatal of all faults"; "Works of imagination excel by their allurement and delight; by their power of attracting and detaining the attention. That book is good in vain which the reader throws away."[18] It will not hurt to repeat Lionel Trilling's description of the function of the modern novel as a useful paraphrase of Johnson's idea of the function of literature generally—"involving the reader himself in the moral life, inviting him to put his own motives under examination, suggesting that reality is not as his conventional education has led him to see it."

Johnson indeed goes farther and suggests that even "escape" literature serves a moral purpose: "The author is not wholly useless who provides innocent amusement for minds like these [who 'seek in books refuge from' themselves]. There are in the present state of things so many more instigations to evil than incitements to good that he who keeps men in a neutral state may be justly considered as a benefactor to life."[19] This observation is not a completely trivial one; for to divert men from self-centeredness—to get them to involve themselves in *anything* outside themselves—is desirable from the point of view of Augustinian and empiricist morality. "Let a man seek pleasure everywhere except in himself," as Walt Whitman wrote: "Let a woman seek happiness everywhere except in herself."

There is one problem in the relations between literature and morality that has caused difficulty for some readers of Johnson: the question of "poetical justice." It seems a little simpleminded of Johnson to condemn Shakespeare for "sacrificing virtue to convenience," for not being "always careful to show in the virtuous a disapprobation of the wicked," and for complaining that in *King Lear* it was unnecessary to have killed the virtuous Cordelia: "A play in which the wicked prosper and the virtuous miscarry may doubtless be good, because it is a just representation of the common events of human life: but since all reasonable beings naturally love justice, I cannot easily be persuaded that the observation of justice makes a play worse; or that, if other excellencies are equal, the audience will not always rise better pleased from the final triumph of persecuted virtue." "Better pleased, but worse instructed," the modern reader may growl, throwing Johnson's own principle back at him. Perhaps one can partly forgive Johnson this passage on account of his intense love for Cordelia and his horror at her death. Johnson's critical "lapses"—in

Lycidas as well—seem often to stem from a sensitivity of response to the work greater than that of most modern readers.

At any rate, if Johnson's attitude to "poetical justice" in the edition of Shakespeare was a fault, he made ample amends for it in his preface to Addison (in *The Lives of the Poets*) sixteen years later, where he completely reverses his position. He quotes John Dennis's complaint that Addison's *Cato* violates "poetical justice"—the virtuous Cato is defeated—in precisely the same spirit as Johnson complained about *Lear*. "It is certainly the duty of every tragic poet," Dennis asserted, "by the exact distribution of poetical justice, to imitate the divine dispensation and to inculcate a particular providence."

Johnson lustily pooh-poohs the whole idea: "Whatever pleasure there may be in seeing crimes punished and virtue rewarded, yet, since wickedness often prospers in real life, the poet is certainly at liberty to give it prosperity on the stage. For if poetry has an imitation of reality, how are its laws broken by exhibiting the world in its true form? The stage may sometimes gratify our wishes; but, if it be truly the 'mirror of life,' it ought to show us sometimes what we are to expect." The recantation could not be more complete; and one wonders whether Johnson, by making use of the phrase "mirror of life" that he employed in the preface to Shakespeare, does not want it to be taken as a conscious retraction of his earlier words.

Contemporaneity of language; originality.   As was pointed out in chapter 2, Johnson sets his face relentlessly against what seems to him "gimmickry" in poetic language—the use of archaisms, inversions of normal sentence order, outmoded and affected verse forms (as he sees them), "ode and elegy and sonnet." These, he thinks (perhaps with justice in the case of academic poetasters like the Wartons), are easy devices whereby men with no poetic talent can acquire some sort of reputation as poets without engaging in the great labor the real poet must endure in order to communicate effectively to his readers something worth communicating. In answer to the old charge that his failure to appreciate Gray's and some of Milton's verse was the result of his personal prejudice against their Whiggish politics, it may be pointed out that Johnson's most scathing denunciation of "contrived" language is in regard to Collins, for whom he had deep personal affection (and who is certainly the weakest talent of the three poets): "His diction was often harsh, unskillfully labored, and injudiciously selected. He affected the obsolete when it was not worthy of revival; and he puts his words out of the common order, seeming to think, with some later candidates for fame, that not to write prose is certainly to write poetry."

By contrast, the language of Shakespeare is given his highest praise:

If there be, what I believe there is, in every nation, a style which never becomes obsolete, a certain mode of phraseology so consonant and congenial to the analogy and principles of its respective language as to remain settled and unaltered, this style is probably to be sought in the common intercourse of life, among those who speak only to be understood, without ambition of elegance. . . . There is a conversation above grossness and below refinement where propriety resides, and where this poet seems to have gathered his comic dialogue. He is therefore more agreeable to the ears of the present age than any other author equally remote, and among his other excellencies deserves to be studied as one of the original masters of our language.[20]

Johnson's dislike of the pastoral convention and the use of allusion to classical mythology undoubtedly stems from a similar motive. His notorious comment on *Lycidas* that its "form is that of a pastoral, easy [everyone can do it], vulgar [everyone *does* do it], and therefore disgusting [boring]" is only one of many insults he directs at that form. But if his thorough and thoughtful critique of the pastoral in *Ramblers* 36 and 37 is read, it will be seen that he has a very high regard for the pastorals of Virgil, if not of later imitators. As for the "puerilities of mythology," "the machinery of the pagans is uninteresting to us"; "criticism disdains to chase a school-boy to his commonplaces" (it must be remembered that in Johnson's day and later, every schoolboy in England was expected to introduce Jupiter, Venus, and the rest into his exercises in Latin verse). To Johnson's distaste for clichés generally was joined, when the subject was the death of a Christian, as in *Lycidas* and Pope's epitaphs, a feeling, for which there is at least an arguable case, that the introduction of pagan mythology is blasphemous.

But the primary attitude is no doubt that which he expressed when he wrote "No man ever yet became great by imitation." Like Pope, and like every genuine lover of literature in every age, Johnson is troubled by the number of ambitious but artistically untalented people who, having nothing of importance to say in verse, still grind it out by dint of sheer ingenuity and assiduity. For such, the pastoral, the sonnet, and the classical allusion are easy substitutes for genuine communication and artistry. So too, Johnson discovered, were blank verse and the ballad—too easy. As he rightly says of blank verse, it takes the exuberant imagination of a Milton to make it successful: "It can hardly support itself without bold figures and striking images."

What Johnson wants in any writer is, first, "originality," or "invention." Invention, "by which new trains of events are formed and new scenes of imagery displayed . . . and by which extrinsic and adventitious embellishments and illustrations are connected with a known subject," is one of three qualities, along with imagination and judgment, that constitute genius in Pope. Origi-

nality and invention are almost impossible to define, but everyone recognizes
them when they are present and recognizes their absence when they are not;
and clearly "hereditary similes, traditional imagery," stock phraseology, pedantic archaisms, and mechanical inversion of normal sentence order do not
require or give the impression of much originality. In all this, Johnson is saying nothing very different from what Wordsworth said when he talked about
"a selection of the language really spoken by men" or Ezra Pound when he
said "Make it new."

The Concrete and the General.   In chapter 2 attention was called
to the richness of imagery in Johnson's best poetry (something will presently
be said about the imagery in his prose), and to the amount of concern he gives
to imagery in his criticism of other poets. As one thumbs through the *Lives of
the Poets* one is struck by the frequency with which the words "images," "imagery," and "imagination" recur. The reader is told, of the pastoral genre to
which *Lycidas* belongs, "Whatever images it can supply are long ago exhausted"; of *L'Allegro* and *Il Penseroso*, "the images are properly selected and
nicely distinguished"; and of Milton generally, "He never fails to fill the
imagination; but his images and descriptions of the scenes of operations of
Nature do not seem to be always copied from original forms, nor to have the
freshness, raciness, and energy of immediate observation." Of Congreve's
comedies, Johnson writes that "They are the works of a mind replete with images and quick in combination"; of Prior, "The act of composition fills and
delights the mind with change of language and succession of images"; of
Akenside's lyric poetry, "He has no longer his luxuriance of expression, nor
variety of images"; that Hammond "has few images drawn from modern
life"; that Thomson "imparts to us much of his own enthusiasm that our
thoughts expand with his imagery and kindle with his sentiments."

In view of Johnson's insistence—both in his own writing and in his criticism of that of others—on the importance of "concretizing" ideas by the use
of imagery, it would seem very strange to find him at other times playing the
role of the great "abstractionist," as he has sometimes been termed. In fact,
Johnson never seems to have used the word *abstract* as a critical term. What
he does use frequently is the word *general*, which has (mistakenly) been taken
to mean "universal" (in the platonic sense of "transcendent, something tran-
scending human sensory experience").[21] In context "general" seems to mean
nothing of the kind. Johnson's uses of the word as a critical term can be divided into two groups. The first consists of those occasions when he uses it as
a derogatory term. Among these are his praise of Pope's line "Hills peep o'er
hills, and Alps on Alps arise" because "it makes particular what was before
general"; his recommendation that in epitaphs "the praise ought not to be

general, because the mind is lost in the extent of any indefinite idea, and cannot be affected with what it cannot comprehend"; his disparagement of Rowe's plays, because there cannot be found in them "any deep search into nature, any accurate discriminations of kindred qualities, or nice display of passion in its progress: all is general and undefined." "The general and rapid narratives of history," he says in *Rambler* 60, "afford few lessons applicable to private life." Fenton's critique of Roscommon is "too general to be critically just." In *Comus* "the invitations to pleasure are so general that they excite no distinct images of corrupt enjoyment and take no dangerous hold on the fancy." Johnson censures one of Pope's epitaphs, which "contains of the brother only a general indiscriminate character. . . . The difficulty in writing epitaphs is to give a particular and appropriate praise."[22] In all these passages "general" seems to mean "vague, indefinite, unable to be grasped by the senses"—"abstract," in the sense that vivid and concrete sensory impressions are absent. It seems clear from such remarks that Johnson (like Blake and many others) feels that "particulars" rather than "generalities" are the proper material of literary art.

The trouble comes from some other passages where Johnson uses "general" as a term of praise, three of which are always cited. One is his praise of Shakespeare's characterization: "His characters are not modified by the customs of particular places, unpracticed by the rest of the world; by the peculiarities of studies or professions. . . . His persons act and speak by the influence of those general passions and principles by which all minds are agitated. . . . His adherence to general nature has exposed him to the censure of critics. . . . His story requires Romans or kings, but he thinks only on men." Another is Imlac's remark in chapter 10 of *Rasselas:* "The business of a poet is to examine not the individual but the species; to remark general properties and large appearances; he does not number the streaks of the tulip, or describe the different shades in the verdure of the forest. He is to exhibit in his portraits of nature such prominent and striking features as recall the original to every mind; and must neglect the minuter discriminations which one may have remarked and another have neglected." A third is from the *Life of Cowley:* "Great thoughts are always general, and consist in positions not limited by exceptions, and in descriptions not descending to minuteness."

All these passages must, of course, be read in full context. If one thinks about just *what* Johnson is praising in Shakespeare's characterization, one sees that it is certainly not the *abstractness* of Claudius and other characters. Rather, it is what one might call (following E. M. Forster) the "roundness" of Claudius, by contrast with the "flatness," the quality of caricature, in, say, Ben Jonson's characters. One laughs at a freak like the noise-hating Morose, but one does not expect to meet anyone like him. A Claudius is much more disturbing (and, therefore, more "instructive") precisely because he *is* so much like men one meets every day—like oneself. To make Claudius more "general," Shakespeare provides him with a very "concrete" trait—he gets drunk. Johnson approves. It is the critics whom Johnson attacks—Voltaire, in particular—who *dis*approve, who complain that, by having such a trait, Claudius fails to comply with the abstract, platonic "idea" of a king, to manifest "essential" kingliness. It is Johnson who dismisses these complaints as "the petty cavils of petty minds."

It is surely clear that Johnson is not recommending a reduction in the degree of *concreteness* in the writing. "General" in this latter group of passages obviously means "of widespread occurrence, recognizable as corresponding to something in the reader's experience." If something is so recherché that there is nothing like it in the reader's experience, he cannot respond to it; and, if he cannot respond to it, it is useless as literature: all this, like so much in Johnson's criticism, is pure Lockean psychology. The opposite of "general" in this sense is not "concrete" nor "particular," in the sense of "something definite"; rather, it is "particular" in the sense of "singularity" (Keats's term), of what is idiosyncratic, esoteric, of limited availability.

For all the superciliousness that critics have displayed toward the "streaks of the tulip" passage, it is surely true (and surely what Johnson meant) that the *numbering* of the tulip's streaks (such-and-such a species has X stripes, such-and-such has Y) is not an activity likely to arouse much emotion in any heart but that of the dedicated botanist. When Blake writes "O Rose, thou art sick!" and talks of "The invisible worm / That flies in the night," he does not number the streaks of the rose, or specify the family of *Annelida*. His rose and worm are very "general" indeed—Blake merely says enough about them to "recall the original to every mind" and "neglects the minuter discriminations" which would be of interest only to the scientist. So does Wordsworth with his daffodils. Nor does Keats advocate the "numbering of the streaks" in the rainbow:

> Do not all charms fly
> At the mere touch of cold philosophy?
> There was an awful rainbow once in heaven:
> We know her woof, her texture. . . .

Johnson indeed makes the identical complaint, using the same metaphor from spectroanalysis, against the metaphysical poets: "They broke every image into fragments, and could no more represent, by their slender conceits and laboured particularities, the prospects of nature, or the scenes of life, than he who dissects a sunbeam with a prism can exhibit the wide effulgence of a summer noon."[23]

All Johnson is saying in these passages is what has been said many times by many critics in many ages—mere jejune, plodding enumeration of detail is not enough for the poet, though it may be for the scientist. Virginia Woolf said it in connection with the "laboured particularities" of Arnold Bennett's novels: "They [the Edwardian novelists] said, 'Begin by saying that her father kept a shop in Harrogate. Ascertain the rent. Ascertain the wages of shop assistants in the year 1878. Discover what her mother died of. Describe cancer. Describe calico. Describe—' But I cried, 'Stop, stop! . . . I knew that if I began by describing the cancer and the calico, my Mrs. Brown, that vision to which I cling though I know no way of imparting it to you, would have been dulled and tarnished for ever."[24]

And what Johnson said about Shakespeare, Ezra Pound said about Joyce's *Ulysses* and Eliot's *Prufrock*: "James Joyce has written the best novel of the decade, and perhaps the best criticism of it has come from a Belgian who said, 'All this is as true of my country as of Ireland.' Eliot has a like ubiquity of application. Art does not avoid universals, it strikes at them all the harder in that it strikes through particularities. . . . His men in shirt-sleeves and his society ladies are not a local manifestation: they are the stuff of our modern world, and true of more countries than one."[25]

This position is precisely Johnson's. "Generality" in the last group of quotations from his criticism is exactly equivalent to Pound's "ubiquity of application." It certainly does *not* mean "abstractness," something Johnson never in his life recommended in imaginative writing, but something that he with perfect consistency condemned. And the way to achieve it is not by laborious and unimaginative "numbering of the streaks of the tulip" but by artistically inspired *selection* of detail—detail that corresponds to something in the experience of the general reader, to which he can respond—such as makes Shakespeare's character drawing so triumphantly great.

If this reading of these much-cited passages from Johnson's criticism deprives him of his chief claim to be considered a "neoclassic" critic, then he will have to be so deprived. Indeed, Johnson can no more be pigeonholed into some such compartment than any other great and dedicated critic, from Aristotle to Eliot. He is intensely, passionately interested in the whole range of literature, in the way literature affects men's thoughts and emotions and lives; and he despises formulas, gimmicks, rigid "rules," which would narrow its potential range. Literature, for Johnson, is not an ingenious and, in itself, meaningless exercise within the framework of some predetermined intellectual system, but part, and an important part, of human life itself. Like other great critics, he sometimes maintained positions with which one finds it difficult to agree—his less than complete enthusiasm for the metaphysical poets (though he was almost the only critic for some two centuries who took them seriously enough to write at length about them) and his dislike of *Lycidas*[26] and of the ending of *King Lear* (in these latter two instances, it is possible that his response was the result of what seems to us—and we may be at fault here—a hypersensitivity to the fact of human death).

But these small puzzles are unimportant in comparison with the vast range of literature into which his insight penetrated with what strikes one, when one encounters it, as complete *rightness*. What Johnson said of Bacon's *Essays* applies to Johnson's own critical writings (it is paraphrased, perhaps unconsciously, in Leavis's comment on Johnson's criticism quoted above): "Their excellence and their value consists in being the observations of a strong mind operating upon life; and in consequence you find there what you seldom find in other books."[27]

A Note on Johnson's Prose

To talk of Johnson's "prose style," as though he had only one, is unjust to his immense versatility with language. The bare, direct, moving prose he uses in his fragmentary autobiography has already been noted: "She [my mother] bought me a silver cup and spoon, marked SAM. I. lest if they had been marked S.I., they should, upon her death, have been taken from me. She bought me a speckled linen frock, which I knew afterwards by the name of my London frock. The cup was one of the last pieces of plate which dear Tetty sold in our distress."[28] And he uses the same clear, lively, simple style in writing to children and to very intimate adult friends, as in this letter to John Taylor:

My eye is almost recovered, but is yet a little dim, and does not much like a small print by candle light. You will however believe that I think myself pretty well, when I tell you my design. I have long promised to visit Scotland, and shall set out tomorrow on the journey. I have Mr. Chambers' company as far as Newcastle, and Mr. Boswell, an active lively fellow, is to conduct me round the country. What I shall see, I know not, but hope to have entertainment for my curiosity, and I shall be sure at least of air and motion. When I come back, perhaps a little invitation may call me into Derbyshire, to compare the mountains of the two countries.

One notices the little whimsy, the dry but friendly humor. Taylor is proud of the mildly rugged scenery of his home; Johnson knows that he will not mind being rallied a little about it and that the "invitation" he asks for will be forthcoming ("perhaps" he will come—that is, virtually certainly).

He can write perfectly straightforward, lucid, unornamented "reportorial" prose for publication when the occasion calls for it:

> The principal beast of burden is the camel, of which the species are four, the Turkman camel, the Arab, the dromedary, and the camel with two bunches. The Turkman camel is the largest; his common load is 800 pounds, but he cannot bear heat, and therefore lies still in the summer months. The Arab being smaller carries about 500 pounds. He can endure heat, and scarcely needs any sustenance but the thistles which he crops as he goes along loaded. They have been known to travel fifteen days without water, but then drank so eagerly that many died.

Much of *The Journey to the Western Islands* is written in this simple idiom, but somewhat greater elaboration marks what may be called Johnson's "controversial" style, which he frequently uses when he is examining and demolishing the arguments of others. It maintains a surface of massive politeness, while underneath lies a deadly irony. Its most impressive use is in the review of Soame Jenyns, but it is also the staple of the political pamphlets and many other reviews, such as the amusing one of Jonas Hanway's diatribe against tea. Hanway has expressed the hope that the Foundling Hospital will protect its wards from the evils of tea-drinking:

> I know not upon what observation Mr. Hanway founds his confidence in the Governors of the Foundling Hospital, men of whom I have not any knowledge, but whom I intreat to consider a little the minds as well as the bodies of the children. I am inclined to believe irreligion equally pernicious with gin and tea, and therefore think it not unseasonable to mention that when a few months ago I wandered through the Hospital, I found not a child that seemed to have heard of his creed or the commandments. To breed up children in this manner is to rescue them from an early grave that they may find employment for the gibbet; from dying in innocence that they may perish by their crimes.

One notices the introduction of balance; of meiosis ("I am inclined to believe"); of alliteration, of which Johnson uses much, often subtly, in his prose ("grave—gibbet" is imperfect, of course, but no doubt intended as alliteration if only to the eye); and of a satisfying rhythmic cadence to end the passage—"from dying in innocence that they may perish by their crimes." Johnson's sensitivity to rhythm in his more elaborate prose is one of its delights.

Other degrees of elaboration might be detected, if one wanted to try to classify them. There is, for example, his "sermon" style, which has a quite distinctive quality, no doubt the result of following the accepted sermon idiom of the time. Finally, one reaches the high alembication of many of the *Ramblers* or of this sentence, astonishing in its baroque magnificence, from the Vinerian lectures at Oxford:

When we consider in abstracted speculation the unequal distribution of the pleasures of life, when we observe that pride, the most general of all human passions, is gratified in one order of men only because it is ungratified in another and that the great pleasure of many possessions arises from the reflection that the possessor enjoys what multitudes desire, when it is apparent that many want the necessaries of nature, and many more the comforts and conveniences of life, that the idle live at ease by the fatigues of the diligent and the luxurious are pampered with delicacies untasted by those who supply them, when to him that glitters with jewels and slumbers in a palace multitudes may say what was said to Pompey, *Nostrâ miseriâ tu es magnus*, when the greater number must always want what the smaller are enjoying and squandering, enjoying often without merit and squandering without use, it seems impossible to conceive that the peace of society can long subsist; it were natural to expect that no man would be left long in possession of superfluous enjoyments while such numbers are destitute of real necessaries, but that the wardrobe of Lucullus should be rifled by the naked and the dainties of Apicius dispersed among the hungry, that almost every man should attempt to regulate that distribution which he thinks injurious to himself and supply his wants from the common stock.

It is sometimes said that Johnson's prose style became simpler as he grew older. The reason for this statement is probably that those who make it are familiar chiefly with the early *Rambler* (1750–52) and the late *Lives of the Poets* (1777-81) among his prose writings. It is true that the style of the *Rambler* is more elaborate than that of the *Lives;* but no one who knows the rest of Johnson's prose writings could maintain that his simplification is the result merely of the mellowing effect of time. The last piece of prose he wrote for publication, a few months before his death, contains some of his most formidable sentence structure: "Thus in those lands of unprovided wretchedness, which Your Majesty's encouragement of naval investigation has brought lately to the knowledge of the polished world, though all things else were wanted, every nation had its music; an art of which the rudiments accompany the commencements, and the refinements adorn the completion of civility, in which the inhabitants of the earth seek their first refuge from evil, and, perhaps, may find at last the most elegant of their pleasures." And the sentence that follows is even longer and more complex.

On the other hand, in early journalistic writings such as the *Life of Blake*, there occurs straightforward reportage as plain, clear, and loose as that of Defoe:

It was not long before he had an opportunity of revenging his loss and restraining the insolence of the Dutch. On the 18th of February, 1652/3, Blake being at the head of eighty sail, and assisted, at his own request, by Colonels Monk and Dean, espied Van Tromp with a fleet of above 100 men of war, as Clarendon relates, of 70 by their own public accounts, and 300 merchant ships under his convoy. The English, with their usual intrepidity, advanced towards them; and Blake in the Triumph, in which he always led his fleet, with twelve ships more, came to an engagement with the main body of the Dutch fleet, and by the disparity of their force was reduced to the last extremity, having received in his hull no fewer than 700 shots, when Lawson in the Fairfax came to his assistance. The rest of the English fleet now came in, and the fight was continued with the utmost degree of vigour and resolution, till the night gave the Dutch an opportunity of retiring, with the loss of one flagship and six other men of war. The English had many vessels damaged but none lost. On board Lawson's ship were killed 100 men, and as many on board Blake's, who lost his captain and secretary, and himself received a wound in the thigh.

The difference in style, of course, has little or nothing to do with chronology; but it does have a great deal to do with the occasion, the intention, and the audience. In the *Ramblers* (or at least many of them) Johnson wants to create an atmosphere of serious, dignified reflection; in the *Lives of the Poets*—again, it helps to give them their proper title, *Prefaces to the Works of the English Poets*—Johnson *is* writing prefaces, not labored dissertations, and the casualness of the style is perfectly appropriate to the situation. A dedication to the king obviously calls for a more heightened style than a piece of popular journalism like the *Life of Blake*, and so on. Indeed, the versatility of Johnson's handling of English prose is one of the delights of the reader familiar with the full canon of his writings.

Accounts given in the past of "Johnson's prose style" usually refer to the fairly ornate *Rambler* style (found in other writings too, of course). Certain elements in this are readily apparent: his use of elaborately balanced phrases and clauses, usually in pairs or triads:

> The notice which you have been pleased to take of my labours,
> had it been early, had been kind; but it has been delayed
>   till I am indifferent, and cannot enjoy it;
>   till I am solitary, and cannot impart it;
>   till I am known, and do not want [need] it.

One should notice the effective use of climax in this triad. He is fond of beginning a piece with a long noun clause—"That every man should regulate his actions by his own conscience, without any regard to the opinions of the rest of the world, is one of the first precepts of moral prudence" (*Rambler* 23) —or a phrase in "of" or "among"—"Among the innumerable follies by which we lay up in our youth repentance and remorse for the succeeding part of our life, there is scarce any against which warnings are of less efficacy than the neglect of health" (*Rambler* 48).

He also delights in long, elaborately organized sentences, often alternating, for emphatic contrast, with short ones, and in alliteration, often so subtly handled as to be unnoticed until it is pointed out. These and other features of this style have been analyzed in considerable detail by W.K. Wimsatt, Jr., whose most striking contribution, however, to the study of Johnson has perhaps been his noting what a large number of "philosophic words" (technical terms from the sciences of Johnson's day) were used metaphorically by him, and in that metaphorical sense have passed into everyday language.[29]

This is not the place for a synopsis or expansion of Wimsatt's work, but there are three things about Johnson's "*Rambler* style" that may be worth emphasizing. The first is that it is essentially *poetic*. One reads it, as one does Sir Thomas Browne's prose, for the rich involvement of skillfully controlled sound (both rhythm and the handling of vowel and consonant sounds), imagery, and syntax. It seems clearly to be a deliberate attempt on Johnson's part to recapture something of the baroque prose beauty of the time of Donne, Andrewes, and Browne, which had been lost in the excellent but very different prose of Dryden, Swift, and Addison (though, as has been seen, Johnson can also use the "unadorned" prose idiom effectively on occasion).

The second point has to do with one of the most egregiously mistaken, and at the same time most influential, pieces of criticism ever written: Macaulay's remark concerning what he calls "Johnsonese." Macaulay used as his text two quips by Johnson about Buckingham's play *The Rehearsal:* "It has not wit enough to keep it sweet. It has not vitality enough to preserve it from putrefaction." Boswell reported these sentences as delivered in succession—there may be a question whether they actually were, since each remark is recorded separately by another witness on another occasion—and he inserts after the first the editorial comment, "This was easy—he therefore caught himself, and pronounced a more rounded sentence." Macaulay, who stigmatized this language as "Johnsonese," calls it Johnson's "translating aloud" and an example of "his constant practice of padding out a sentence with useless epithets."

This is obtuse reading. Johnson is *not* merely repeating in longer words what he said before. He is using two distinct, though related, images to convey his meaning vividly. The first metaphor is drawn from the household and is couched in domestic phraseology; in another extant report, the remark is given as "There was too little salt in it to keep it sweet." In those days before refrigeration Johnson and his audience were very familiar with the practice of soaking meat in brine to preserve it. *The Rehearsal*, unlike, say, *The Way of the World*, has failed to retain its charm because it does not contain a strong enough infusion of salt, or wit.

The meaning of the second statement is likewise clearer in Mrs. Thrale's report of it: "The greatness of Dryden's reputation is now the only principle of vitality which keeps the Duke of Buckingham's *Rehearsal* from putrefaction."[30] Johnson's mind has turned to the scientific problem of the decay of animal bodies after death, and it naturally turns also to scientific ("philosophical") terminology: the life-giving "principle of vitality" having gone, the corpse undergoes "putrefaction." Even if Johnson were making the identical criticism of the play in both remarks (and in Mrs. Thrale's version of the second one, it is not its wit but its topicality that is being discussed), the one is a scene from the kitchen, the other a scene from the biologist's laboratory. If the use of a series of varying metaphoric "vehicles" to convey the same "tenor" is padding, then Shakespeare and the metaphysical poets are likewise flagrantly guilty of it. The fact is that no English prose writer is less given than Johnson to "padding out" sentences with "useless epithets." Every word counts, and only the reader too lazy to think about the precise meaning of each of Johnson's words can accuse him of tautology.

The third point is that Johnson, in his ornate prose, revels in imagery. The most obvious instance is the *Preface to Shakespeare*, where he seems consciously to introduce an elaborate and striking image for emphasis at an average of every ten sentences or so. One views past writers, he says, "through the shades of age, as the eye surveys the sun through artificial opacity." As "no man can call a river deep or a mountain high without the knowledge of many mountains and many rivers," so extraordinary works of literature have to wait for an assessment until we have read other similar ones. Shakespeare "holds the mirror up to life" (this is consciously borrowed from Shakespeare himself, of course, in Hamlet's speech to the players). To illustrate Shakespeare by a few select quotations is like the fool "who, when he offered his house for sale, carried a brick in his pocket as a specimen." And much more.

The most memorable use of imagery is probably in that paragraph where Johnson condemns Shakespeare's fondness for puns, and it almost seems that he is trying to demonstrate that he, too, can make use of extravagant wordplay when he wants to: "A quibble is to Shakespeare what luminous vapours are to the traveller. . . . A quibble is the golden apple for which he will always turn aside from his career [like a racer] or stoop from his elevation [like a falcon]. . . . A quibble was to him the fatal Cleopatra for which he lost the world and was content to lose it." At times Johnson seems to revel in extended, "conceited" metaphor, sometimes letting alliteration run away with him:

The work of a correct and regular writer is a garden accurately formed and diligently planted, varied with shades, and scented with flowers; the composition of Shakespeare is a forest, in which oaks extend their branches, and pines tower in the air, interspersed sometimes with weeds and brambles, and sometimes giving shelter to myrtle and roses; filling the eye with awful pomp, and gratifying the mind with endless diversity. Other poets display cabinets of precious rarities, minutely finished, wrought into shape, and polished into brightness. Shakespeare opens a mine which contains gold and diamonds in unexhaustible plenty, though clouded by incrustations' debased by impurities, and mingled with a mass of meaner minerals.

The image with which he concludes the first section of the *Preface*, setting forth Shakespeare's praise, is a noble one: "The sand heaped by one flood is scattered by another, but the rock always continues in its place. The stream of time, which is continually washing the dissoluble fabrics of other poets passes without injury by the adamant of Shakespeare." And the imagery in Johnson's "famous sayings" made them memorable. "Hell is paved with good intentions," "A woman's preaching is like a dog's walking on its hinderlegs," "I have sailed a long and painful voyage round the world of the English language; and does he [Chesterfield] now send out two cock-boats to tow me into harbour?" Imagery is almost equally conspicuous in his more ornate prose, if the reader looks at it with eyes not dimmed by preconceptions about Johnson's "abstractness."

Chapter Eight

The Modernity of Samuel Johnson: A Recapitulation

"What does he have to say to *us?* In what way is he relevant today?" These are questions that the student of literature has a right—indeed, a duty—to ask of any earlier writer whom he is recommended to study. Too often, however, the student, like Pontius Pilate, stays not for an answer. Human laziness being what it is, even those who pride themselves on being particularly well qualified to explore older literature and to interpret it to the modern world are not always as eager as one might expect to enlarge the horizons of their reading in hope of finding such relevance. It consumes time and energy to cope with the difficult language of some earlier author, to become familiar with the intellectual context in which he is writing, to follow the subtle intricacies of his thought and feeling, even though the effort may be rewarded in the end with a rich increase of insight into the problems not only of his time but of one's own. Moreover, these new insights are at first sometimes upsetting to one's complacent preconceptions—the expansion of the mind is for many a far from painless process. The result is that the student often welcomes any seemingly authoritative pronouncement that such and such a writer, whose work would take some time and intellectual effort to get to know, is valueless, or (much the same thing) "only of historical interest." And there have usually been critics, themselves not always too fond of the effort of acquainting themselves with something new and strange, to provide such comforting assurances.

The roster of great writers who have been disposed of in this way for a very considerable period of time is a long one. Few readers (with the conspicuous exception of Samuel Johnson) took the poetry of John Donne at all seriously between Donne's own time and the 1920s—his crabbed versification and diction and his tortuous "conceits" were regarded as quaint foibles of a bygone day, and that he had anything relevant to say to "modern" man would have been thought preposterous until a few decades ago. Throughout much of the nineteenth century William Blake was regarded as an amusingly naive crackpot, Swift was dismissed from serious consideration by Macaulay and

Thackeray as a madman, and so on. The point is that what Donne, Blake, and Swift have to say, if taken seriously, would have proved only *too* relevant, too disturbing, to nineteenth-century man; it was better to put them away in a safe pigeonhole marked "of historical interest," where they would be given no more than a cursory and patronizing glance and so could do no harm.

No major writer of English literature has been subjected to a more strenuous course of such neutralization than Johnson. There is probably no use spending much time speculating on the psychological and other motives behind this, though they might be interesting. Boswell, who converted Johnson from a great writer and fine thinker into an amusing conversationalist and tavern companion, may have been following the well-known course of the disciple: if you find yourself emotionally dependent on some individual of greater talents than your own, there is an almost irresistible urge (unconscious, no doubt) to cut him down to something nearer your own size, to point out (with all reverence, of course) his little weaknesses and mistakes, to dwell on small (but surely significant) incidents where you proved to be right and the Master wrong. Macaulay, whose perverse review of Croker's edition of Boswell's *Life* was prescribed as a school textbook for several generations of students in the English-speaking world, used it as an opportunity for a coruscating display of the talent for paradox that was his journalistic stock in trade. To make the startling and brilliant discovery that Boswell was (a) an imbecile and at the same time (b) author of the greatest biography ever written was certainly the way to increase the circulation of the *Edinburgh Review* and with it Macaulay's reputation. It was equally brilliant to announce to the world the discovery, hitherto unsuspected except by Macaulay, that Johnson, who had been regarded as one of the greatest of English writers, was in fact worthless except as his eccentric personality provided material for the central character in Boswell's book. This judgment no doubt comforted teachers of the new school subject of English literature and the pioneer writers of textbooks in that subject, which were just beginning to be produced—there was one less body of difficult writing for them to have to struggle through.

The nadir of Johnson's reputation was probably reached around the time of the centenary of his death, when such wonderfully supercilious judgments were published as this in the *Times*: "The infatuated admiration which he inspired . . . is not wholly comprehensible to this generation. . . . He had but little disposition towards abstract thinking and no lively imagination, so that he cannot be ranked high as a philosopher or poet"; and this in the "advanced" *Westminster Review*: "We cannot refrain from expressing our gratitude that our lot is cast in a time when in society such a man as Samuel Johnson is an impossibility."[1] One might think that such anathematization by the Establishment would commend Johnson to the modern reader—and, to be sure, Johnson often succeeded in annoying the Establishment during his lifetime, as well as after his death. But sometimes other, not too reputable motives may influence even the modern reader. As I have written elsewhere,

It is not merely that "Johnson the Great Clubman," to use Leavis's phrase, is a manifesto of anti-intellectualism, a defense against "Johnson the great highbrow." . . . For many people the legendary [that is, the Boswellian and Macaulayan] "Doctor Johnson" seems to assuage some deep-seated emotional need; essentially, I suppose, a need for some older, publicly-honored figure whom one can bolster one's shaky ego by patronizing; a surrogate father. And no doubt there is a pleasure, if a mildly paranoid one, to be derived from erecting an image of Johnson as a conceited "Great Cham," a "literary dictator," contemplating it with resentment and righteous indignation—or, worse, understanding forgiveness—and then allowing one's superior taste and literary insight to deflate it.[2]

But all *this* is "only of historical interest," the record of the embarrassment and, sometimes, resentment of the smaller-minded in the presence of greatness. It is well to repeat the words of the distinguished modern critic printed at the beginning of this volume: "That Johnson himself was really one of the best English writers of his time, that he deserved his great reputation, is a fact that we are likely to lose sight of"; and it may be useful here to rehearse some of the things that this book has tried to show go to make up Johnson's perennial excellence.

He was a great artist with words and was immensely knowledgeable about them. He had a clear understanding of what poetry is, and throughout his life poetry was very close to him. One of his contemporaries, not noted for her generally high opinion of Johnson, went so far as to say, "*Everything* Johnson wrote was poetry."[3] In this statement she no doubt referred to the intense sensitivity to language, the profound respect for its ability, when skillfully handled, to communicate truth and pleasure, that shines out perhaps even more from Johnson's prose than from his verse. The quantity of competent verse that he did compose, especially in his earliest and latest years, is impressive. True, much of it was written in unmemorable forms—juvenile translations and mild "love poems" (often done at the request of a friend), half-jocular impromptus, prayers and personal meditations in Latin. But he did leave one great longer poem (*The Vanity of Human Wishes*, a searching and unforgettable comment on the human condition), an amusingly exuberant diatribe on life in "the big city," with stridently political overtones (*London*), and half a dozen shorter pieces (the Levet and Sir John Lade poems, the *Prologues*, the moving epitaphs on Hogarth and Claudy Phillips) that will remain permanently in the canon of the works in English verse that are read and respected by those who take poetry seriously and care about it. One wishes there were more; but, as T. S. Eliot said (apropos of these very poems), "How little, how very little good poetry there is anyway!" As for Johnson's prose, those who think it consists in using inflated polysyllables and sneer at "Johnsonese" merely convict themselves of inability to respond to the rhythmical and semantic subtleties of which the English language is capable, and of a philistine attitude to the artistic handling of prose which, carried out logically, would also result in the rejection of Sir Thomas Browne on one hand and James Joyce on the other.

Johnson's tremendous sensitivity to language places him in the small handful of literary critics of the very highest rank in the English language—some, like Yvor Winters, have not hesitated to place him, alone, at the top. His preparation as a critic was unequalled—some nine years spent in minutely examining the texts of masterpieces of English from the sixteenth to early eighteenth centuries, noting the subtle semantic differences of English words and phrases, finally assembling the results of his labors into the first modern dictionary of the language: a dictionary, as he put it, "for the use of such as aspire to exactness of criticism or elegance of style," a dictionary whose method formed the basis of all later scientific and historical study of the language. And the first application he made of that knowledge, to the explication of the difficult and often corrupt text of the greatest of English writers, Shakespeare, laid a monumental foundation for all future explication of it.

Nowhere is Johnson more modern than in his criticism of poetry. Students now identify the close scrutiny of poetic text with "the new critics" of the twentieth century, and applaud as "modern" Mallarmé's dictum that poetry is made up of words, not ideas, and Eliot's footnote to it, that in criticism "The spirit killeth, but the letter giveth life." They have only rediscovered what Johnson, long before, preached and practiced, in his rejection of archaism of vocabulary and distortion of syntax—of writers like Gray who "thought his language more poetical as it was more remote from common use" and Collins who "affected the obsolete when it was not worthy of revival, and . . . puts his words out of the common order, seeming to think, with some later candidates for fame, that not to write prose is certainly to write poetry." With Wordsworth and Pound and Eliot, Johnson believed that the language of serious poetry, addressed to the contemporary reader, must be essentially contemporary. We think of a concern with imagery in poetry as a characteristic of modern criticism, but no critic has been more intent than

Johnson on fully realizing the imagery of the poetry he studied. The words "image," "imagery," and "imagination" (the image-creating faculty) occur many dozens of times in *The Lives of the Poets*, and Johnson has no greater praise for a poem than to say that its imagery is novel and effective, and no greater censure than that its imagery is inept or trite.

Johnson is much *more* modern than some twentieth-century critics in his sturdy rejection of classical mythology, whose impact on the incredulous modern reader can be at best literary and factitious, unworthy of the serious modern poet. So too is his dismissal of the conventions of such classical *genres* as the pastoral, which has caused one recent student to affirm, apropos of his critique of *Lycidas*, "Johnson, then, is a pivot in the transition from a Renaissance to a 'romantic'—a modern—point of view; modern criticism begins with Johnson."[4] This, to be sure, is not true of some modern academic criticism, which, like that of the Wartons in Johnson's own day, has a vested interest in antiquarianism. Whether, a hundred years from now, that poetry of the twentieth century produced by the self-conscious revival of mythopoeia will prove to have been as enduring as that which, as Johnson preferred, deals with contemporary emotions in contemporary terms, only time will tell. In eighteenth-century poetry, at any rate, it has not been the myth-laden odes of Gray and Collins, but the poetry of contemporary reference, that of Dryden, Pope, Swift, and Johnson himself, that has made the greatest impact on posterity. In modern drama the circumscription of the audience's and the playwright's imagination by the Renaissance "rules" of the theater and the ban on "mingling the kinds" in tragicomedy has long been abandoned and forgotten: it is well to recall that it was Johnson who gave them their deathblow. (The phrase may remind us of Carlyle's remark that Johnson's tremendous letter to Chesterfield sounded the death-knell of literary patronage; although this is hardly fair to Pope, who had at least as much to do with it as Johnson, the modern concept of the independence of the literary artist does begin with the eighteenth century, and no writer more fiercely insisted on that independence than Johnson.)

Language and literature are, however, aspects of human behavior, not isolated entities; means, though tremendously important means, not ends. The end of linguistic communication Johnson never lost sight of: to increase the sum total of human happiness. "The only end of writing is to enable the readers better to enjoy life, or better to endure it," he told Soame Jenyns. That human happiness can be increased, Johnson had little doubt—so long as one does not cherish the delusion that on this imperfect earth one can attain, or is entitled to, the uninterrupted felicity that is reserved for an afterlife; for to entertain that delusion is to destroy whatever possibility of happiness does exist here. Accepting one's imperfect state without useless repining, one can, by the willingness to learn from observation and experience, find ways of making it somewhat less imperfect, and one of these ways is through responsible and effective writing. Thus biography, of which Johnson was perhaps the first "modern" practitioner, is important—and enjoyable—if one approaches it with the right values—biography which passes quickly over "those performances and incidents which produce vulgar greatness," but dwells on "those relations . . . which tell not how any man became great, but how he was made happy; not how he lost the favour of his prince, but how he became discontented with himself." Such values are as sound in the twentieth century as in the eighteenth, as the psychotherapist well knows, and Johnson, as his account of the cause and cure of schizophrenia in the astronomer of *Rasselas* testifies, was no mean psychotherapist. His high regard for biography led him to a distrust of conventional history, with its emphasis on "vulgar greatness" and its willingness to make facile generalizations. This attitude has won for Johnson the hostility of a number of professional historians; yet there is the interesting fact that at least one powerful school of modern historians of Britain, that of the late Sir Lewis Namier, has maintained that political history is indeed little or nothing more than the collective biography of politically active individuals. As so often, Johnson has got into trouble for being too far ahead of his time.

In no respect was Johnson more harshly condemned by the nineteenth century than as a writer on politics. He shortsightedly opposed William Pitt's Seven Years' War, "the Great War for the Empire," that brought into existence not only the Victorian British Empire, on which the sun never set, but also (by eliminating the French barrier to westward expansion) the modern United States of America. Worse, he dismissed as cant the lofty professions of exalted libertarian ideals of the American revolutionaries. With the fading of some of the complacency of the nineteenth century—in particular, with the rapid disappearance in the twentieth century of Pitt's British Empire—one begins to wonder whether Johnson was not much more farsighted, more modern, than his critics. And to some American readers of the 1960s, Johnson's contempt for a declaration of the equality of all men and their inalienable rights to life, liberty, and property that calmly excluded Negroes, Indians, and other lesser breeds may seem very modern indeed. "How is it that we hear the loudest yelps for liberty from the drivers of Negroes?" is a question that can still be pertinently asked. In many other matters—his ferocious assault on the Stage Licensing Act, whose provisions were repealed only in 1968; his plea for humane treatment of prisoners of war, something officially implemented only a century or more after he wrote; his arguments for mitigation of the laws against prostitutes and debtors and for the suspension of the death penalty for forgery—he was equally "modern."

Of perhaps the most popular and widely influential English political writer of the twentieth century it has been said that to him, "Political issues were moral issues. He understood that peace and social justice would descend on the world, if at all, from a moral impulse."[5] Two centuries earlier Johnson has written, "Of political evil, if we suppose the origin of moral evil discovered, the account is by no means difficult, polity being only the conduct of immoral men in public affairs." Indeed, from Johnson's (and Orwell's) point of view, most human activity (including literary activity) reduces in the end to material for the moralist—to questions of value concerning the behavior of one individual to another. Questions of value for human beings in turn depend for their answer on the individual's view of the nature of man and his place and destiny in the universe. Johnson's view of these matters was the strictly orthodox one of Augustinian Christianity, found in the theology of his church (and many other Christian churches), the view held by the great majority of earlier English writers on the human condition—Spenser, Milton, Donne, Herbert, Swift, to mention some—the view insisted on again in the twentieth century by such theologians as Karl Barth, Paul Tillich, and Reinhold Niebuhr and found in the writings of, say, T. S. Eliot and C. S. Lewis (though implicit in those of many other twentieth-century writers, including some like Orwell seemingly very far removed from the orthodox Christianity professed by Eliot and Lewis). Johnson most clearly expresses that view in *Rasselas* and *The Vanity of Human Wishes*. Man is by no means the "naturally good" being of Rousseau and the Victorian liberals, who, if left alone, will inevitably tend toward perfection—and it is hard to see how anyone who has witnessed the events of the twentieth century with its gas chambers and nuclear bombs can easily continue to hold that view. Rather, he is an incurably imperfect being, endowed nevertheless with a longing for perfection which cannot be attained here on earth, a "hunger of imagination" which cannot be filled by bread alone—witness the gloomy boredom of the welfare state of the "Happy Valley." To live as a man, not an animal, he must pursue ideals—and he will be very foolish if the ideals he chooses are the worldly, material, self-seeking ones of wealth, power, and fame, which in the end always prove illusory and unable to provide happiness. Rather, they should be those that can create a measure of inner peace: "a healthy mind," patience, faith, "love, which scarce collective man can fill."

That love must manifest itself in involvement with others—thus the Stoic recipe of detachment, "dull Suspense," is fallacious and must be rejected. At the same time, as an imperfect creature in an imperfect world, man must rec-

oncile himself to "a conclusion in which nothing is concluded," in which perfection is never achieved. The perfect government, the perfect educational
system, the perfect society are ideals not attainable on an earth peopled by
fallen man. Yet Johnson's most urgent plea is that we do not jeopardize our
chances for such imperfect happiness as *is* attainable by ego-centered repining at our lack of perfectibility: there *are* things that can be done to make life
somewhat more of a state to be enjoyed and less to be endured. The techno-
logical advances of the Europeans—their improvements in the healing of disease, in communication between friends, in mitigating the physical rigors of
life—have not made them happy, says Imlac (and of course never will); yet
"they are less unhappy" than the primitive Africans.

On this very sensible basis Johnson's vigorous campaigns for social
amelioration—for the abolition of Negro slavery, for a recognition of the
rights of Indians and other indigenous peoples oppressed by European col-
onizers, for a mitigation of the harsh treatment of prostitutes, debtors, and
forgers—his interest in scientific advances and in economic and political
questions, his ability to see the defects of the Scottish clan system (while understanding its appeal) are easily explicable. He is very far from being the
stereotyped "Tory reactionary" that some have wanted to make him, lamenting everything that has happened since the Renaissance and longing
for a return to medieval authoritarianism in political and intellectual matters. Nor is he a "pessimist" (even one "with an enormous zest for living," as
he has been described), if a pessimist, as various dictionaries define the
word, is one "who believes that all things tend to evil." Johnson clearly believed that a great many things were susceptible of improvement, from textual editing to the writing of poetry, from the censorship of the London
stage to Britain's international relations, and was highly active in trying to
improve them. If he spoke out against perfectibilism, it was because of a
well-founded suspicion that perfectibilism is the enemy of meliorism, and
there were few areas of human existence where Johnson did not display
himself actively as a meliorist.

Yet even if Johnson believed that the external circumstances of life ought
to be and generally can be improved, and that very often there are external
circumstances—slavery, grinding poverty, oppression—that make happiness
impossible for its victims, he was well aware that the creation of an "affluent
society," a Happy Valley for all, would not in itself guarantee the happiness of
the individual, a mistake made by some modern "liberals": "How small, of
all that human hearts endure, / That part which laws or kings can cause or
cure!" he wrote. When the minimum of physical comfort necessary for happiness *is* attained, it then becomes the task of the individual to order his

thinking, his values, his emotional responses so as to maximize his happiness—that happiness which, as Johnson says in the last line of *The Vanity of Human Wishes*, the mind *can* "make," though not "find." It is perhaps as a psychotherapist, as we should call it, that Johnson—like some other English writers in the same Augustinian tradition, Donne, Herbert, Swift, Eliot—is of most direct relevance to the modern reader. What is needed first is to reduce one's egoism, to estimate one's individual importance in clear perspective against the whole immense range of existence. Eliot's diagnosis is worth repeating:

> Half the harm that is done in this world
> Is due to people who want to feel important.
> They don't mean to do harm—but the harm does not interest them,
> Or they do not see it, or they justify it
> Because they are absorbed in the endless struggle
> To think well of themselves.[6]

In the *Rambler* especially, but in many of his other writings as well, Johnson provides an encyclopedia of the various ways in which people's desire to feel important falsifies their values, blinds their vision, and harms themselves and others. It is a perennial lesson that human beings of every generation have to be taught again and again, and one that is as relevant to the twentieth century as to the eighteenth. Indeed, as one surveys the ghastly toll of needless misery inflicted by human beings on themselves and others that the history of the twentieth century records, one is inclined to say even more relevant.

Chapter Nine
Johnsonian Studies since 1970

It cannot be said that in the years since 1970, when the first edition of this work was published, there have been revolutionary or even very striking discoveries concerning Samuel Johnson. The preceding account of his life and work remains much the same as it was. Nevertheless, there have been some new attributions to him of journalistic pieces, some reconsideration of attributions of others, new editions of his works, and a great deal of biographical and critical commentary. What follows is a summation of at least the highlights of this activity.

Conferences and Exhibitions

The year 1984, the bicentenary of Johnson's death, saw a host of commemorative events. The most spectacular of these was a week-long conference in July at Oxford University, with Johnson's old college, Pembroke, as host. Some 170 people from around the world attended, and some applications had to be turned away because of shortage of accommodations. A total of fifty papers were given, many of which have since been published (see the selected Bibliography under Wahba and Korshin). At the same time the Arts Council of Great Britain mounted a splendid exhibition in London of Johnsonian portraits and other memorabilia.

Most of the various local Johnson societies throughout the world likewise arranged special exhibitions and programs. A list of these societies (with the dates of their founding) follows, with the thought that students may wish to take part in the proceedings of societies in their vicinities.

- The Johnson Society (Lichfield, England), 1909
- The Johnson Society of London, 1928
- The Johnsonians (eastern United States), 1948
- The Johnson Society of the Central Region (incorporating the Johnson Society of the Great Lakes Region and the Johnson Society of the Midwest), 1966

- The Johnson Society of the North West (western Canadian provinces and northwest United States), 1969
- The Johnson Society of Evansville (Indiana; birthplace of the great Johnsonian scholar James L. Clifford), 1982
- The Johnson Society of Southern California, 1984
- The Johnson Society of India, 1986

Addresses of these can be found in the Clifford/Greene/Vance bibliographies. Many publish newsletters, *Transactions*, and other pamphlets.

The 1984 commemorations by non-Johnsonians were not equally enlightened. The best the London *Times* and *Punch* could do was to print feeble parodies of what they thought to be Johnson's prose style, crammed with polysyllabic words—an old gimmick that goes back to Johnson's own lifetime and demonstrates gross ignorance of the subtleties of his prose. When the British Post Office was approached with the suggestion that it might issue stamps bearing Johnson's portrait, it turned it down, and instead issued a series bearing, ironically, pictures of Scottish cattle.

Bibliography

James L. Clifford and Donald Greene, *Samuel Johnson: A Survey and Bibliography of Critical Studies* (1970) has been supplemented by Donald Greene and John A. Vance, *A Bibliography of Johnson Studies, 1970–1985* (1987). In spite of these dates, the supplement includes some titles from 1968 and 1969 overlooked in Clifford and Greene, as well as many from 1986 and even some "expected 1987." The arrangement of entries is the same as in Clifford/Greene, and the numbering of entries follows consecutively from that in the earlier work.

A full checklist of writings attributed to Johnson, by Donald Greene and John L. Abbott, is in preparation.

A new annual journal, *The Age of Johnson*, edited by Paul J. Korshin, began publication in 1988. Several other volumes of collected essays on Johnson and his times, inspired by the events of 1984, have been published.

Editions

Four more volumes of *The Yale Edition of the Works of Samuel Johnson* have appeared: Vol. 9. *A Journey to the Western Islands of Scotland*, edited by Mary Lascelles (1971); Vol. 10. *Political Writings*, edited by Donald Greene (1977); Vol. 14. *Sermons*, edited by Jean H. Hagstrum and James Gray

(1978); Vol. 15. *A Voyage to Abyssinia*, edited by Joel J. Gold (1985). Volume numbers 11 to 13 are reserved for the Parliamentary Debates. The next volume to appear is *Rasselas*, edited by Gwin J. Kolb. Comment on these and other editions of individual works is given below.

Two substantial volumes of selections were published in this period: *Samuel Johnson: Selected Poetry and Prose*, edited by Frank Brady and W. K. Wimsatt (1977). Mainly critical and biographical writings. *Samuel Johnson* (The Oxford Authors), edited by Donald Greene (1984). A wider selection, including much early journalism.

Biography

Three important one-volume biographies were published in the 1970s: John Wain, *Samuel Johnson* (1974); W. Jackson Bate, *Samuel Johnson* (1977); James L. Clifford, *Dictionary Johnson: Samuel Johnson's Middle Years* (1979).

Wain, like Johnson, grew up in Staffordshire, attended Oxford University, and made his living as a journalist, so that his book is engagingly personal. Bate emphasizes Johnson's psychological troubles—perhaps overemphasizes them; his psychoanalytic approach has not won entire favor from professional psychoanalysts. Clifford's book, published posthumously, is a sequel to his *Young Sam Johnson* (1955) and takes Johnson from 1749 to 1762.

Two useful books are O M Brack, Jr., and Robert Kelley, *Johnson's Early Biographers* (1971) and *The Early Biographies of Samuel Johnson* (1974). The latter reprints fourteen early biographies and biographical sketches between 1762 and 1786, antedating the publications of Mrs. Piozzi, Sir John Hawkins, and James Boswell. It is interesting that many small incidents found in Boswell and the other later biographers were first recorded in these early ones.

Other recent studies have filled in gaps in our knowledge of Johnson's life. One is by Bertram Davis (in *Johnson After Two Hundred Years*, edited by Paul Korshin), which gives an almost day-by-day account of the two months' visit in 1764 by Johnson, Anna Williams, and Frank Barber to Thomas Percy at Easton Maudit, Northamptonshire. Johnson and Percy were hard at work on important books, Johnson's edition of Shakespeare and Percy's *Reliques of Ancient English Poetry*. (Clifford, in *Dictionary Johnson*, has a similarly detailed account of Johnson's six-week tour to Devonshire in the late summer of 1762. Johnson's willingness to absent himself for substantial periods from London has often been underestimated.) Thomas Curley, in his introduction to his edition of Sir Robert Chambers's Vinerian Lectures on the English Law, gives a preliminary sketch of Johnson's many involvements with his young friend Chambers in the late 1760s, helping him prepare his course of lectures at Oxford. These are parts of Johnson's life not to be found in Boswell, since Boswell knew little or nothing about them. In *Samuel Johnson: A Personality in Conflict* (1971) George Irwin gives a shrewd analysis of the harmful influence of Johnson's domineering mother on young Sam. William W. Fee's article, "Samuel Johnson's 'Wonderful' Remission of Dropsy" (1973), throws useful medical light on Johnson's "late conversion" in the year before his death.

A new edition of Johnson's letters in five volumes, sponsored by Mary Hyde (Viscountess Eccles) and edited by Bruce Redford, is in preparation and will supersede the three-volume Chapman edition.

Intellectual Life

It is perhaps indicative of modern approaches to Johnson's thought that in 1975 J. D. Fleeman published a facsimile edition of the sale catalog of Johnson's library and Donald Greene a companion volume containing an analysis of its contents, showing the amazingly wide range of Johnson's intellectual interests. Many of the books deal with contemporary science and medicine, and in 1971 Richard B. Schwartz published *Samuel Johnson and the New Science*, rescuing him from the myth that he had no interest in science. Similarly, John A. Vance in *Samuel Johnson and the Sense of History* (1984) demolishes the ignorant charge that he despised history. Work has been done on Johnson's relations with the arts, including a forthcoming book on the subject by Morris Brownell. At last the full text of Sir Robert Chambers's Vinerian Lectures on the English Law (2 vols., 1986), in which Johnson collaborated, has been published under the editorship of Thomas M. Curley, so that we now have the necessary material to try to determine just what was Johnson's share in this impressive introduction to English (and American) law, the successor to Sir William Blackstone's *Commentaries*, which was for so long the standard textbook on the subject for beginning law students in both countries.

Johnson's Acquaintances

Much good work has recently been done in recording the lives of those with whom Johnson's overlapped. In *The Thrales of Streatham Park* (1977) Mary Hyde (Viscountess Eccles) has printed Mrs. Thrale's "Family Book," beginning in 1764, with extensive commentary. Her earlier work, *The Impossible Friendship* (1971)—that between Mrs. Thrale and Boswell—adds some details to that picture. Bertram H. Davis's *A Proof of Eminence: The Life of Sir John Hawkins* (1971) gives a minutely researched account of Johnson's early friend and biographer, a pioneering historian of music and a London magistrate. Davis has also published (1981) in Twayne's English Authors series a brief account of Thomas Percy, later Bishop of Dromore, and a fuller biography is in progress. John L. Abbott's *John Hawkesworth: Eighteenth-Century Man of Letters* (1982) tells the story of another early colleague of Johnson's on the *Gentleman's Magazine*.

The last volume of Boswell's journals composed during Johnson's lifetime was published in 1981. We are still awaiting the publication of the manuscript of the *Life*, edited by Marshall Waingrow—the intermediate stage between the journals and the printed *Life*. According to James L. Clifford, the changes and additions to the manuscript were "a major creative effort, almost an entire rewriting of the manuscript. Boswell at the start had written on one side of the quarto leaves with the verso reserved for later corrections and additions. . . . By the time the final version was complete, many of these versos were completely filled and very few were blank." Johnson scholars are anxious to be able to scrutinize these "creative" additions, to see to what extent they correspond with Boswell's original journal entries, made sometimes decades earlier, and inquire to what extent they can be trusted as an authentic record of Johnson. The old myth of Boswell's constantly following Johnson around with pen and notebook at the alert has pretty well been exploded. After all, during the last twenty-two years of Johnson's life, Boswell, apart from the three months they were together on the Scottish tour in 1773, was in Johnson's company on only around three hundred days. It is often forgotten that Boswell's home was in Edinburgh, and that he came down to London for only two or three months of the year, and by no means every year, so that it is hard to regard him as the final authority on Johnson's life during those later years.

The Poet

It is indicative of shifts in readers' attitudes toward Johnson that in the Greene/Vance bibliography of Johnsonian studies, 1970 to 1985, much the largest number of entries in the various classifications of Johnson's works is devoted to studies of his poetry. Still, it is over fifty years ago that T. S. Eliot proclaimed Johnson's excellence as a poet and declared that *London* and *The Vanity of Human Wishes* are among the finest verse satires in any language.

As well as supervising a second edition (1974) of the pioneering collection, *The Poems of Samuel Johnson*, edited by D. Nichol Smith and E. L. McAdam, Jr. (1941), in which the contents are rearranged in chronological order, J. D. Fleeman published his own edition of *The Complete English Poems* (1971), which also usefully includes much of Johnson's Latin poetry, with English prose translations. John Wain has also rendered some of these in modern English verse forms. A concordance to Johnson's poetry by Helen Harrold Naugle was published in 1973.

The Journalist and Occasional Writer

Students continue to hunt, sometimes with success, among unsigned contributions to periodicals with which Johnson is known to have had a connection, and among obscure pamphlets for traces of Johnson's hand. One fascinating such new attribution is his assistance with a biography of Nadir Shah, also called Kouli Khan—a "robber chief" who in the 1730s and 1740s seized power in Persia, one of many such adventurers who have done so during the course of history. Johnson's involvement is further proof of his journalistic preoccupation with contemporary affairs. On the other hand, some earlier attributions have been questioned. The many entries concerning ancient physicians in James's *Medicinal Dictionary* have been argued, on stylistic grounds, to be by James himself rather than by Johnson, leaving Johnson's only substantial contribution to the work the life of Boerhaave, reprinted and revised from its original appearance in the *Gentleman's Magazine*.

Joel J. Gold's fine edition (volume 15 of the Yale *Works*) of *A Voyage to Abyssinia* (1985), the first edition of it since 1789, shows clearly how well acquainted Johnson was with the international situation in Africa and the Middle East in the seventeenth century, and with the theological controversies involved in the Jesuit mission to Ethiopia. Gold establishes that this, Johnson's first book, composed when he was in his early twenties, is much more than a bare translation: there is much adaptation of the statements of its authors, Jeronimo Lobo and Joachim le Grand, often modifying their Roman Catholic idiom in a Protestant direction.

An interesting article by Ruth K. McClure (1976) discloses that, not for the first time, Johnson was in trouble with the authorities for a piece of journalism—in this case, the review of Jonas Hanway's *Journey*. The governors of the Foundling Hospital, outraged at Johnson's suggestion that its inmates were not receiving proper Christian instruction, applied to the attorney general for a formal prosecution of the author of the review. The attorney general, however, declined, and Johnson went on to hit harder than ever at Hanway and the governors.

The Biographer

At last the definitive edition of the *Life of Savage* has been published, superbly edited and annotated by Clarence Tracy (1971). It is unlikely to be soon superseded. The truth about Savage's story of his birth and childhood remains as much a mystery as ever. An interesting study by Mark Temmer relates the *Life* to the work of Denis Diderot, who reviewed a French translation of it. Temmer suggests that Diderot's famous *Le Neveu de Rameau (Rameau's Nephew)* may be based to some extent on Savage.

In 1971 J. D. Fleeman published in facsimile a collection of twenty early biographies by Johnson. It is convenient to have them assembled in one volume, but the typography of the *Gentleman's Magazine* and other early journals is hard on the eyes. Robert Folkenflik's *Samuel Johnson, Biographer* (1978) is a thorough study of Johnson's biographical techniques.

The Moralist

A fine edition of Johnson's *Sermons* by Jean H. Hagstrum and James Gray (Yale *Works*, vol. 14, 1978) and a monograph on the sermons by James Gray (1972) have been published. J. D. Fleeman has prepared a splendid set of facsimiles of the manuscripts of the *Prayers and Meditations* in the possession of Pembroke College.

A number of recent monographs and articles have probed the foundations of Johnson's religion more deeply than in the past. Richard B. Schwartz's *Samuel Johnson and the Problem of Evil* (1975) gives the fullest discussion yet of the review of Soame Jenyns's *Free Inquiry into the Nature and Origin of Evil*, together with a facsimile of the original printing in the *Literary Magazine*. Robert G. Walker's *Eighteenth-Century Arguments for Immortality and Johnson's Rasselas* (1977) concentrates on chapter 48 of the tale. Owen Chadwick's "The Religion of Samuel Johnson" (1986) is a splendid summing up by a famous theologian and ecclesiastical historian. Donald Greene's "Johnson, Stoicism, and the Good Life" (in Burke and Kay, 1983) lists Johnson's unceasing attacks on Stoicism and points out that the much disputed phrase, so prominent in chapter 22 of *Rasselas*, "To live according to nature," is no more than the translation of a famous Greek tag much used by the Stoics and supposed to have been invented by their founder Zeno, "to homologoumenos tei physei zen."

The Political Writer and Traveler

Volume 10 of the Yale *Works, Political Writings*, edited by Donald Greene, appeared in 1977 and contains twenty-four items, ranging over forty years, from early anti-Walpolian lampoons to the longer anti-Wilkes and anti-American pamphlets of the 1770s. The introduction makes it clear that the title of the volume is not "*the* political writings": to have given it that title would have necessitated the inclusion of *London*, entries in the "Foreign News" reports of the *Gentleman's Magazine*, and some reviews included, or planned to be included, in other volumes of the series. Annotation is heavy, with the expectation that modern readers will be unfamiliar with the details of current political history that form the context of these pieces.

One of the later pamphlets, *Thoughts on the Late Transactions Respecting Falkland's Islands* (1771), became well known in the 1980s, when the islands were invaded by Argentine troops—a duplication of the events of 1770 that gave rise to Johnson's pamphlet. A large number of British and American journalists made reference to it, for it gives a most lucid account of the origins of the quarrel between Britain and Spain (later Argentina) over possession and sovereignty of the islands, a quarrel that has not yet been resolved. Unfortunately, some journalists, not having taken the trouble to read the work carefully, and extrapolating from the Macaulayan image of Johnson as a narrow-minded High Tory John Bull, thought the point of the pamphlet was to support Britain's claim to the islands. Of course, it does not: Johnson deplores the suggestion that Britain establish that claim by military action, as happened in 1982.

There are hints of a recrudescence of the old Macaulayan slander (and that of polemicists of his own day) that Johnson was a Jacobite. How that position can be maintained in face of Johnson's uncompromising statement (in *An Introduction to the Political State of Great Britain*, 1756) that "the necessity of self-preservation had impelled the subjects of James [II] to drive him from the throne" is hard to see.

Two important new editions of *A Journey to the Western Islands of Scotland* have appeared—one by Mary Lascelles (Yale *Works*, vol. 9, 1971) and the other by J. D. Fleeman (1985), which contains much ancillary material concerning the people Johnson met on the tour. Thomas M. Curley's *Samuel Johnson and the Age of Travel* (1976) gives a general discussion of Johnson as traveler.

The Student of Language and Literature

Facsimiles of the first edition (1755) of the *Dictionary of the English Language* have been printed in West Germany (1968), Tokyo (1983), and New York (1979). The last is not entirely reliable, since it incorporates parts of the second edition. A valuable facsimile of the revised fourth edition (1773), with an introduction by James L. Clifford, was printed in Beirut, Lebanon, in 1979. Robert DeMaria, Jr.'s *Johnson's Dictionary and the Language of Learning* (1986) is a careful study of the content of the *Dictionary*.

Volumes of selections from the edition of Shakespeare have appeared, as have many critical essays about it, but it cannot be said that any very striking new approaches have yet emerged. The ignorant depreciation of the value of Johnson's work is, however, being eroded. Among the best of recent studies are Arthur Sherbo's *The Birth of Shakespeare Studies: Commentary from Rowe (1789) to Boswell-Malone (1821)* (1986), and a number of articles by Shirley White Johnston, who is at work on a book that will give a careful analysis of Johnson's editorial work on Shakespeare.

The Yale Edition's *Lives of the Poets* has been long awaited: a great deal of textual work is still needed. Meanwhile, we have to make do with the unsatisfactory G. Birkbeck Hill edition. Since *The Lives of the Poets* is a misnomer —it is not a collection of biographies—there is a movement to revert to the original title of the work, *Prefaces, Biographical and Critical, to the Works of the English Poets*, which better describes its nature. When a new edition was proposed, Johnson suggested as its title either "An Account of the Lives and Works of the Most Eminent English Poets" or "The English Poets Biographically and Critically Considered." He left the decision, however, up to the printer, who chose *The Lives of the Most Eminent English Poets; with Critical Observations on Their Works*, demoting the critical part of the prefaces to secondary status. Even this addition was soon abandoned, and Hill's title page reads merely *The Lives of the English Poets*.

Oddly, Johnson's first substantial piece of literary criticism has been almost completely neglected until recently. This is his translation and annotation of Jean-Pierre Crousaz's *Commentary on Mr. Pope's Principles of Morality, or Essay on Man*. Its notes contain pungent comments on what Johnson thinks to have been Crousaz's misunderstanding of Pope's poem, and, in particular, on the mistranslations in the French version of the poem by Du Resnel that Crousaz worked from. The work is very rare; only one copy of the first edition, 1739, is known to survive. Fortunately, a facsimile was published in 1974, and the work will surely receive more attention than in the past.

The Greene/Vance (selective) bibliography of Johnsonian studies, 1970–

85, contains twelve hundred items, an average of eighty a year. Details of publication of works mentioned in this chapter not listed in the Selected Bibliography can be found there. It seems likely that the study of Johnson will continue at at least the same rate in the foreseeable future.

Notes and References

Preface

1. See P. A. W. Collins, "Boswell's Contact with Johnson," *Notes and Queries,* April 1956, p 163.

2. There is little point in the student's constantly referring to "Doctor Johnson." Like other sensible holders of honorary doctorates, Johnson, when using the third person, always wrote "Mr. Johnson." In *A Journey to the Western Islands of Scotland* Johnson reprobates "The indiscriminate collation of degrees" and suggests that the best criterion for awarding doctorates is longevity, hoping that "He who is by age qualified to be a doctor has in so much time gained learning sufficient not to disgrace it, or wit sufficient not to desire it." It is perhaps significant that he made this remark apropos of the University of Aberdeen, which had conferred an LL.D. on Johnson's attacker, the scurrilous William Kenrick, for a translation of Rousseau. Boswell once saw a letter addressed to "Samuel Johnson, Esquire" and protested that it should be "Doctor"; Johnson, he says, "checked" him (*Dictionary: "check*: a reproof, a slight"). Although Johnson always figures as "Mr." in the original journal of Boswell's *Tour to the Hebrides*, in the version published after Johnson's death Boswell changed all the "Mr.s" to "Dr.s"—why, it is hard to say, except to make Johnson appear more pompous. Clearly it shows more respect for Johnson to address him in the way he wished to be addressed.

3. Samuel Parr (1747–1825), the classical scholar (sometimes called "the Whig Johnson"), apparently projected something of this kind: "I conversed with him upon numberless subjects of learning, politics, and common life. I traversed the whole compass of his understanding, and . . . distinctly understood the peculiar and transcendent properties of his mighty and virtuous mind. I intended to write his life: I laid by sixty or seventy books for the purpose of writing it" (Parr's *Life and Works,* quoted in *Johnsoniana* [London, 1836], 326–27). The list of books that Parr gives as intended to be consulted in this task clearly points to some sort of "intellectual history" of Johnson.

Chapter One

1. It would be hard, however, to say what meaning there is in the phrase "literary dictator" applied to Johnson in some literary histories. He seems not to have exercised, or wished to exercise, any particularly "dictatorial" influence over contemporary literature. Smollett's amusing characterization of him to Wilkes as "the great Cham [i.e., Khan] of literature" (see Boswell, *Life of Johnson,* 1:348) has no claim to be taken seriously. Certainly neither Wilkes nor Smollett, as writers, would have obeyed his decrees, had he issued any.

2. *Rambler* 60; *Idler* 102; *Johnsonian Miscellanies,* ed. G. B. Hill (Oxford: Clarendon Press, 1897), 1:282; hereafter cited as *Misc.*

3. *Rambler,* 60.

4. *The Yale Edition of the Works of Samuel Johnson,* (New Haven: Yale University Press, 1958–), 1:3; hereafter cited as *Works* (1958).

5. James Boswell, *The Life of Samuel Johnson, LL.D.,* ed. G. B. Hill, revised by L. F. Powell (Oxford: Clarendon Press, 1934–50), 2:261; hereafter cited as *Life.*

6. James L. Clifford, *Young Sam Johnson* (New York: McGraw-Hill, 1955), 166, 171.

7. A valuable study of the evidence is given in M. G. Irwin, "Dr. Johnson's Troubled Mind," *Literature and Psychology* 12 (Winter 1963): 6–11.

8. *The Letters of Samuel Johnson,* ed. R. W.. Chapman (Oxford: Clarendon Press, 1952), no. 123; hereafter cited as *Letters.*

9. Clifford, *Young Sam,* 85.

10. *Life,* 1:445.

11. Ibid., 1:57.

12. Ibid., 1:74; Clifford, *Young Sam,* 337 n. 26.

13. *Lives of the Poets* (Edmund Smith), ed. George Birkbeck Hill (Oxford: Clarendon Press, 1905).

14. *Life,* 1:99.

15. The psychiatrist Edmund Bergler's phrase; see his "Samuel Johnson's 'Life of the Poet Richard Savage,' " *American Imago* 4 (December 1947): 42–63.

16. *Misc.,* 1:371.

17. *Diary and Letters of Madame D'Arblay,* ed. Austin Dobson (London, 1904), 1:117.

18. The story is told in Katharine C. Balderston, "Johnson's Vile Melancholy," *The Age of Johnson: Essays Presented to C. B. Tinker* (New Haven, Conn.: Yale University Press, 1949).

19. Sir John Hawkins, *Life of Johnson LL.D.,* ed. B. H. Davis (New York: Macmillan, 1961), 121.

20. Herman W. Liebert, "Reflections on Dr. Johnson," *Journal of English and Germanic Philology* 47 (1948): 86.

21. *Life,* 1:445.

22. Hawkins, *Life,* 256–58. There has been some controversy over the significance of this incident. See Chester Chapin, "Samuel Johnson's 'Wonderful' Experience," *Johnsonian Studies* (Cairo, U.A.R., 1962), 51–60.

23. *Letters* no. 559. This passage has sometimes been cited by students of Johnson as though it were intended seriously. But Mrs. Thrale's own marginal note should dispel any doubt: "This is very pretty Irony: He was always ridiculing Epistolary correspondence. . . ." (*The Rothschild Library,* privately printed, 1954, 1:323).

24. *Letters and Works of Lady Mary Wortley Montagu,* ed. W. Moy Thomas (London, 1861), 1:109.

25. *Letters* no. 61. The remaining letters quoted in this section are, successively, nos. 373, 970, 282.1, 238, 25, 78, 84, 133, 142, 147, 954, 262, 184, 61, 62, 172, 163, 185, 200, 435, 655, 715, 786, 197, 254, 293, 956, 860.

Chapter Two

1. Bertrand Bronson, *Johnson Agonistes, and Other Essays* (Cambridge: Cambridge University Press, 1946), 5, 51.

2. T. S. Eliot, "Johnson's 'London' and 'The Vanity of Human Wishes,' " *English Critical Essays: Twentieth Century,* ed. Phyllis M. Jones (London: Oxford University Press, 1933 [World's Classics]), 303–4. The essay was originally published in 1930.

3. Review of Joseph Warton, *Essay on the Writings and Genius of Pope,* 1756.

4. *Rambler* 154; *Rasselas,* chap. 10.

5. T. S. Eliot, "Milton II," *On Poetry and Poets* (New York: Noonday Press, 1961), 170.

6. Life of Gray.

7. This and the other pieces of Johnsonian verse in this chapter will be found in *Works* (1958), vol. 6.

8. Life of Milton.

9. See Chester F. Chapin, *Personification in Eighteenth-Century Poetry* (New York: Columbia University Press, 1955).

10. Wordsworth, preface to *Lyrical Ballads,* 1800.

11. Life of Milton.

12. On the text of this, see D. J. Greene, *Johnsonian News Letter,* March 1966, 11–12.

13. Joseph Wood Krutch, *Samuel Johnson* (New York: Holt, 1944), 63.

14. T. S. Eliot, "The Metaphysical Poets," *Selected Essays* (New York, 1950), 243. Eliot thought these lines the epigraph to a chapter in one of Scott's novels. They are in fact the conclusion of the text of *Ivanhoe.*

15. George Saintsbury, *History of Modern Criticism* (reprint, New Haven, 1955), 1:96–97.

16. Eliot, "Johnson's 'London' and 'The Vanity of Human Wishes,' " 309.

17. *Life,* 4:5.

18. See Bronson, "Johnson's *Irene,*" in *Johnson Agonistes and Other Essays.*

19. Eliot, "Milton II," 180.

20. Some passages in this chapter earlier appeared in Donald J. Greene, " 'Pictures to the Mind': Johnson and Imagery," *Johnson, Boswell, and Their Circle: Essays Presented to L. F. Powell* (Oxford: Clarendon Press, 1965), 137–58.

Chapter Three

1. For numerous recent suggested additions to the canon of Johnson's journalistic writings, see Donald J. Greene, "The Development of the Johnson Canon," *Restoration and Eighteenth-Century Literature: Essays in Honor of A. D. McKillop* (Chicago: University of Chicago Press, 1963).

2. For a more detailed account, see D. J. Greene, "Johnson's Contributions to the *Literary Magazine*," *Review of English Studies*, n.s. 7 (October 1956): 367–92.

3. "Observations on the Present State of Affairs," *Literary Magazine*, no. 4, 1756.

4. Introduction to the Political State of Great Britain," *Literary Magazine*, no. 1, 1756.

5. See Boylston Green, "Possible Additions to the Johnson Canon," *Yale University Library Gazette* 16 (July 1941): 70–79.

6. See Allen T. Hazen, *Johnson's Prefaces and Dedications* (New Haven, Conn: Yale University Press, 1937).

7. *Letters* no. 124.

8. See, for example, Arthur Sherbo, "The Electronic Computer and I," *University College Quarterly* 9 (November 1963): 18–23.

9. A useful account of Politian is given in a "Profile" by Alan Moorehead, "The Angel in May," *New Yorker*, 24 February 1951, 34–61.

10. A unique copy of the "Proposals" was recently discovered in the John Rylands Library, Manchester; see J. A. V. Chapple, in *Bulletin of the John Rylands Library* 45 (March 1963): 340–69.

11. See D. J. Greene, "Some Notes on Johnson and the *Gentleman's Magazine*," *PMLA* 74 (March 1959): 83–84.

12. *Revue Internationale de la Croix Rouge* [Geneva] 33 (December 1951): 969–71.

Chapter Four

1. Plutarch, *Lives*, trans. Aubrey Stewart and George Long (London: Bell, 1929), 1:393 (life of Cimon).

2. Lytton Strachey, preface to *Eminent Victorians* (London: Chatto and Windus, 1918).

3. Life of Addison; *Misc.*, 2:3; *Life* 4:65; 2:17; Life of Morin (footnote); *Life* 3:155.

4. *Life* 4:53; 1:433.

5. *Life* 5:79.

6. *Letters* no. 116.

7. See Allen T. Hazen, "Samuel Johnson and Dr. Robert James," *Bulletin of the Institute of the History of Medicine* 4 (June 1936): 455–65; Lawrence C. McHenry, Jr., "Dr. Samuel Johnson's Medical Biographies," *Journal of the History of*

Medicine and Allied Sciences 14 (1959): 298–310. These attributions, however, have been recently disputed. See O M Brack, Jr., and Thomas Kaminski in *Modern Philology* 81 (1984): 378–400.

8. See E. L. McAdam, Jr., "Johnson's Lives of Sarpi, Blake, and Drake," *PMLA* 58 (June 1943): 466–76.

9. See Montague Pennington, *Memoirs of Mrs. Elizabeth Carter* (London, 1808), 1:70–94.

10. Richard Ellmann's fine biography of James Joyce (New York: Oxford University Press, 1959) seems to me to be in the Johnsonian tradition. Some reviewers felt that it was "hostile" to its subject because (for instance) Ellmann meticulously recorded the details of Joyce's consumption of alcohol. Ellmann properly denied this charge in a succinct and convincing letter to the *Times Literary Supplement*, 11 December 1959. "It is . . . your reviewer, not I, who finds some romantic impropriety in the fact that artistic grandeur can live with human weakness," he concludes, in words that Johnson would have applauded.

11. In *New Light on Johnson*, ed. F. W. Hilles (New Haven, Conn.: Yale University Press, 1959), 257–84.

12. *Life* 1:76–77.

13. A large number of new readings were added by J. D. Fleeman, "Some Notes on Johnson's Prayers and Meditations," *Review of English Studies*, n.s., 19 (May 1968): 172–79.

Chapter Five

1. *The Plan of an English Dictionary*, 1747; *Life* 3:204, 200.

2. Lionel Trilling, "Manners, Morals, and the Novel," *The Liberal Imagination* (New York, 1950).

3. *Lives of the Poets* (life of Milton; life of Watts).

4. *Life*, 5:61; preface to *A Voyage to Abyssinia;* life of Cheynel.

5. *Life* 3:407; 2:103–5.

6. *Sermon* 6.

7. Krutch, *Samuel Johnson*, 1.

8. See Jean H. Hagstrum, "The Sermons of Samuel Johnson," *Modern Philology* 40 (February 1943): 255–66.

9. See Donald M. Lockhart, " 'The Fourth Son of the Mighty Emperor': The Ethiopian Background of Johnson's *Rasselas*," *PMLA* 78 (1963): 516–28.

10. See Kathleen M. Grange, "Dr. Samuel Johnson's Account of a Schizophrenic Illness in *Rasselas*," *Medical History* 6 (1962): 162–68.

11. See M. G. Irwin, "Dr. Johnson's Troubled Mind," *Literature and Psychology* 12 (Winter 1963): 6–11.

12. R. M. Wiles, "The Contemporary Distribution of Johnson's *Rambler*," *Eighteenth-Century Studies* 2 (December 1968): 155–71.

13. *Montagu Letters*, ed. Thomas 2:279.

14. E. L. McAdam, Jr. "New Essays by Dr. Johnson," *Review of English Studies* 18 (April 1942): 197–207.

15. Cf. *Rambler* 89: "In order to regain liberty, [the self-centered man] must find the means of flying from himself; he must, in opposition to the Stoic precept, teach his desires to fix upon external things; he must adopt the joys and pains of others."

16. *Misc.*, 1:293.

17. An excellent exploratory study of Johnson as "psychiatrist" is given in Kathleen M. Grange, "Samuel Johnson's Account of Certain Psychoanalytic Concepts," *Journal of Nervous and Mental Disease* 135 (August 1962): 93–98.

Chapter Six

1. *Taxation No Tyranny.*

2. Ibid.

3. For a detailed study of these, see Donald J. Greene, *The Politics of Samuel Johnson* (New Haven, Conn: Yale University Press, 1960).

4. And generally, the student should pay attention to the two following statements: "Dr. Johnson said of himself, 'I am not uncandid [malicious], nor severe: I sometimes say more than I mean, in jest, and people are apt to think me serious' " (Arthur Murphy, in *Misc.* 1:357); "It is much to be wish'd, in justice to Dr. Johnson's character, that the many jocular and ironical speeches which have been recorded of him had been mark'd as such, for the information of those who were unacquainted with him" (Frances Reynolds, in *Misc.* 2:271).

5. *Life* 4:117.

6. For a bibliography of modern post-Namierian historiography of eighteenth-century Britain, see Greene, *Politics of Samuel Johnson*, 288 n. 7.

7. A useful study is Benjamin B. Hoover, *Samuel Johnson's Parliamentary Reporting* (Berkeley and Los Angeles: University of California Press, 1953).

8. *Life* 1:504.

9. Ibid., 502.

10. The most fiery and memorable debate, that in the House of Commons on 13 February 1741, has never been reprinted in any collection of "Johnson's debates." It will be found in the *Gentleman's Magazine* for February, March, and April 1743. The long delay in publishing it may have been due to fear of the possible consequences of printing such violent invective against Walpole.

11. Reprinted in Hoover, *Samuel Johnson's Parliamentary Reporting.*

12. Hawkins, *Life of Johnson*, 227.

13. *Life*, 2:348—*not*, as a number of college anthologies say, the *Dictionary.*

14. Oliver Goldsmith, *The Vicar of Wakefield*, chap. 19.

15. For a short study of Johnson's economic views, see John H. Middendorf, "Dr. Johnson and Mercantilism," *Journal of the History of Ideas* 21 (1960): 66–83. Professor Middenford is perhaps a little too biased toward Adam Smith's views to be completely just to Johnson.

16. "Further Thoughts on Agriculture," 1756.

17. See E. L. McAdam, Jr., *Dr. Johnson and the English Law* (Syracuse, N.Y.: Syracuse University Press, 1951).

18. Which it still insists on. In recent years, individuals heading the poll in a British election have been disqualified by a resolution of the House, and the candidate obtaining the second-largest number of votes declared elected, precisely as in the case of Wilkes. The latest such instance was that of Anthony Wedgwood Benn, returned for South Bristol in 1961. The House emended the return in favor of an opponent who had secured a smaller number of votes (*House of Commons Journals,* 31 July 1961). One wonders why historians and literary critics still go on saying that Johnson's constitutional position in *The False Alarm* was mistaken.

19. It still goes on, the Argentine Republic having inherited the claim of Spain. The history of it is given at length in Julius Goebel, Jr., *The Struggle for the Falkland Islands* (New Haven, Conn.: Yale University Press, 1927).

20. *Life* 4:15.

21. *Letters* no. 329.

22. *Life* 5:106.

Chapter Seven

1. James H. Sledd and Gwin J. Kolb, *Dr. Johnson's Dictionary: Essays in the Biography of a Book* (Chicago: University of Chicago Press, 1955).

2. H. W. Donner, "Dr. Johnson as a Literary Critic," *Edda* [Oslo], 54 (1954): 325–37.

3. Yvor Winters, *The Anatomy of Nonsense* (Denver: Alan Swallow, 1943), 240.

4. "Johnson as Critic," *Scrutiny* 12 (1944): 187–204.

5. Edmund Wilson, "Reexamining Dr. Johnson," *Classics and Commercials* (New York: Farrar, Straus & Giroux, 1950), 244–49.

6. But see a dissertation (University of New Mexico, 1968) by Shirley White Johnston, "Samuel Johnson's Critical Principles: A Chronological Study."

7. See Arthur Sherbo, *Samuel Johnson, Editor of Shakespeare* (Urbana, Ill.: University of Illinois Press, 1956).

8. They are now available in *Johnson's Notes to Shakespeare,* ed. Arthur Sherbo (Los Angeles: Augustan Reprint Society, 1956–58), and in Arthur Sherbo, ed., *Johnson on Shakespeare* (*Works* [1968], vols. 7, 8).

9. See D. Nichol Smith, *Eighteenth Century Essays on Shakespeare* (Oxford, 1903; 2d ed., 1963).

10. The notes cited are, successively, on *2 Henry IV,* 4, 5: 80; 5, 3: 124; 3, 2: 300; 4, 1: 176; *Measure for Measure,* 2, 3:11: *Hamlet,* 5, 2: 84; *Measure for Measure,* 3, 1: 33; 3, 1: 115.

11. Helen Gardner, ed., *Twentieth-Century Views: John Donne* (Englewood Cliffs, N.J.: Prentice-Hall, 1962), 4.

12. *Diary and Letters of Madame D'Arblay,* 1: 183–184.

13. _Sermon_ 11.

14. _Rambler_ 92.

15. _Letters_ no. 116; Preface to Shakespeare.

16. Review of Soame Jenyns, _Free Enquiry into the Origin and Nature of Evil,_ 1757.

17. Preface to Shakespeare.

18. _Life,_ 1: 428; Life of Prior; Life of Dryden.

19. _Adventurer_ 137.

20. Life of Collins; Preface to Shakespeare.

21. See Hoyt Trowbridge, "Platonism and Sir Joshua Reynolds," _English Studies_ 21 (February 1939): 1–7, for a refutation of the widespread notion that Reynolds's criticism advocates generality in this sense, a notion that has rubbed off to some extent on his friend Johnson as well.

22. Review of Warton's _Essay on Pope;_ Essay on Epitaphs (1740); Life of Rowe; Life of Roscommon; Life of Milton; Life of Pope (essay on Pope's epitaphs).

23. Keats, _Lamia,_ Pt. 2, lines 229–32; Life of Cowley.

24. Virginia Woolf, "Mr. Bennett and Mrs. Brown," _The Captain's Death Bed_ (London, 1950), 105–6.

25. Ezra Pound, _Instigations_ (New York, 1920), 199; originally printed in _Poetry_ (1917).

26. For a vigorous and uncompromising defense of Johnson's critique of _Lycidas,_ see Warren Fleischauer, "Johnson, _Lycidas,_ and the Norms of Criticism," _Johnsonian Studies,_ ed. Magdi Wahba (Cairo, 1962), 235–56.

27. _Misc._ 2: 229.

28. The passages quoted in this section and not identified in the text are, successively, from _Works_ (1958), 1: 3; _Letters_ no. 316; review of Russell's _Natural History of Aleppo_ (_Literary Magazine,_ 1756); (second) review of Jonas Hanway, _Journal of an Eight Days' Journey and Essay on Tea_ (_Literary Magazine,_ 1757); McAdam, Jr., _Dr. Johnson and the English Law_ (1951), 107; dedication (to King George III) of Charles Burney, _Account of the . . . Commemoration of Handel_ (1785); Life of Blake (1740); _Letters_ no. 61.

29. W. K. Wimsatt, Jr., _The Prose Style of Samuel Johnson_ (New Haven, Conn.: Yale University Press, 1941); _Philosophic Words_ (New Haven, Conn.: Yale University Press, 1948).

30. _Life,_ 4: 320; _Johnsoniana_ [ed. J. W. Croker] (London, 1836), 439; _Misc.,_ 1: 185.

Chapter Eight

1. _Times_ [London], 10 October 1884, 7; _Westminster Review_ 3 (January, 1879): 39.

2. Donald J. Greene, ed., _Samuel Johnson: A Collection of Critical Essays_ (Englewood Cliffs, N. J.: Prentice-Hall, 1965), 2.

3. Anna Seward, quoted in _Life,_ 1:40, n. 3.

4. Oliver F. Sigworth, "Johnson's *Lycidas:* The End of Renaissance Criticism," *Eighteenth-Century Studies* 1 (Winter 1967): 167–68.

5. *Time,* 15 November 1968, 110, review of George Orwell's *Collected Essays, Journalism, and Letters.*

6. *The Cocktail Party,* in T. S. Eliot, *Complete Poems and Plays* (New York: Harcourt, Brace, 1952), 348.

Selected Bibliography

PRIMARY WORKS

The Yale Edition of the Works of Samuel Johnson. General Editor Allen T. Hazen, later
   John H. Middendorf. New Haven: Yale University Press. Vol. 1, *Diaries,*
   Prayers, Annals. Edited by E. L. McAdam, Jr., with Donald and Mary Hyde
   (1958) (the first complete collection of Johnson's surviving private papers).
   Vol. 2, *The Idler and The Adventurer.* Edited by W. J. Bate, J. M. Bullitt, and
   L. F. Powell (1963). Vols. 3, 4, 5, *The Rambler,* Edited by W. J. Bate and
   Albrecht B. Strauss (1969). Vol. 6, *Poems.* Edited by E. L. McAdam, Jr., with
   George Milne (1964). Vols. 7, 8, *Johnson on Shakespeare.* Edited by Arthur
   Sherbo (1968) with an introduction by Bertrand H. Bronson. Vol. 9, *A Jour-*
   ney to the Western Islands of Scotland. Edited by Mary Lascelles (1971). Vol.
   10, *Political Writings.* Edited by Donald Greene (1977). Vol. 14, *Sermons.*
   Edited by Jean H. Hagstrum and James Gray (1978). Vol. 15, *A Voyage to*
   Abyssinia. Edited by Joel J. Gold (1985). Other volumes in progress.

The Works of Samuel Johnson, LL.D. 11 vols. London; 1787. (Vol. 1 contains Sir
   John Hawkins's *Life of Johnson*). Supplementary vols. 12 and 13 (1787) (contain the Parliamentary Debates; incomplete, however). Supplementary Vol. 14
   (1788). Supplementary Vol. 15 (1789) (contains *A Voyage to Abyssinia* and
   other items).
   Numerous reprintings of this first collection appeared throughout the re-
   mainder of the eighteenth and in the nineteenth century, the last being apparently Troy, N. Y.: Pafraets Book Co., 1903. Some revision went on: in 1792
   Hawkins's *Life* was replaced by Arthur Murphy's *Essay on the Life and Gen-*
   ius of Johnson. In 1806, 1816, and 1823 Alexander Chalmers added various
   small items not hitherto included and deleted a few discovered to be not
   Johnson's; in some later printings, the "Sermons Left by John Taylor" (originally published separately, 1788–89) were included. But all these are essentially the same—highly unsatisfactory—edition, incomplete and full of
   errors. The Pickering edition (Oxford, 1825) is sometimes referred to as the
   "best," but it is no better, and sometimes worse, than the others. Students
   should use the texts in these with caution; for the *Parliamentary Debates* and
   miscellaneous works that have not yet appeared in the Yale edition, they are
   advised to consult their first appearance in the *Gentleman's Magazine, Liter-*
   ary Magazine, and other journals.

The Lives of the English Poets. Edited by George Birkbeck Hill. 3 vols. Oxford: Clarendon Press, 1905.

Samuel Johnson's Prefaces and Dedications. Edited by Allen T. Hazen. New Haven, Conn.: Yale University Press, 1937.

Rasselas. Edited by R. W. Chapman. Oxford: Clarendon Press, 1927. Edited by Warren Fleischauer. Great Neck, N. Y.: Barron's Educational Series, 1962. Contains an excellent introduction.

Life of Savage. Edited by Clarence Tracy. Oxford: Clarendon Press, 1971.

The Poems of Samuel Johnson. Edited by David Nichol Smith and Edward L. McAdam, Jr. Oxford: Clarendon Press (2d ed.), 1974. Edited by J. D. Fleeman. Harmondsworth: Penguin, 1971.

A Course of Lectures on the English Law, 1767–1773 . . . Composed in Association with Samuel Johnson, by Sir Robert Chambers. Edited by Thomas M. Curley. 2 vols. Madison: University of Wisconsin Press; Oxford: Clarendon Press, 1986.

The Letters of Samuel Johnson, with Mrs. Thrale's Genuine Letters to Him. Edited by R. W. Chapman. 3 vols. Oxford: Clarendon Press, 1952. A new edition in 5 vols., edited by Bruce Redford, is in preparation.

Samuel Johnson. Edited by Donald Greene. Oxford: Oxford University Press, 1984 (The Oxford Authors). The most comprehensive one-volume anthology of Johnson's writings.

SECONDARY WORKS

Bibliographies

Chapman, R. W., and **Allen T. Hazen.** "Johnsonian Bibliography: A Supplement to Courtney." *Proceedings of the Oxford Bibliographical Society* V (1939): 119–66. Chiefly details of descriptive bibliography.

Clifford, James L., and **Donald J. Greene.** *Samuel Johnson: A Survey and Bibliography of Critical Studies.* Minneapolis: University of Minnesota Press, 1970. A revision and enlargement of James L. Clifford, *Johnsonian Studies, 1887–1950,* and James L. Clifford and Donald J. Greene, *A Bibliography of Johnsonian Studies, 1950–1960.*

Courtney, W. P. (and D. Nichol Smith). *A Bibliography of Samuel Johnson.* Oxford: Clarendon Press, 1915; reissued 1925 and 1968. Badly out of date. A revision by J. D. Fleeman is being planned.

Greene, Donald J. "The Development of the Johnson Canon." In *Restoration and Eighteenth-Century Literature: Essays in Honor of A. D. McKillop.* Edited by Carroll Camden. Chicago: University of Chicago Press, 1963. A summary guide to the very numerous attributions to Johnson since Courtney (some certain, some implausible, many of them needing further study), as well as some earlier ones not listed in Courtney.

Greene, Donald, and **John A. Vance.** *A Bibliography of Johnsonian Studies, 1970–1985.* Victoria, B.C.: University of Victoria English Literary Studies, 1987.

Biographies

Bate, W. Jackson. *Samuel Johnson.* New York and London: Harcourt, Brace, Jovanovich, 1977.

Boswell, James. *The Life of Samuel Johnson, LL.D., with A Journal of a Tour to the Hebrides with Samuel Johnson.* Edited by G. B. Hill. Revised by L. F. Powell. 6 vols. Oxford: Clarendon Press, 1934–64. Standard scholarly edition. Students should be careful, when using other editions, to avoid Boswellian errors, such as the statement that Johnson left Oxford in 1731—it was actually 1729, as the annotation in the Hill-Powell edition will inform them. *The Correspondence and Other Papers of James Boswell, Relating to the Making of the Life of Johnson.* Edited by Marshall Waingrow. New York: McGraw-Hill, 1969. Contains much Johnsonian material excluded by Boswell.

Clifford, James L. *Young Sam Johnson.* New York: McGraw-Hill, 1955; London: Heinemann, 1955. Now the standard biography for Johnson's early life; supersedes Boswell's inaccurate account. Draws largely on Reade and other modern research.

————. *Dictionary Johnson.* New York: McGraw-Hill; London: Heinemann, 1979. Deals with the "middle years," 1749–63.

The Early Biographies of Samuel Johnson. Edited by O M Brack, Jr. and Robert E. Kelley. Iowa City: University of Iowa Press, 1974. Reprints fourteen early biographical accounts of Johnson appearing between 1762 and 1786.

Hawkins, Sir John. *The Life of Samuel Johnson, LL.D.* Edited by Bertram H. Davis. New York: Macmillan, 1961. Earliest full life, by a friend who knew Johnson much earlier than Boswell did. Still excellent; Boswell's attacks on it, as a competitor to his own book, should be ignored. This edition is a slight abridgement of the original, which is obtainable only in the two editions first published in 1787.

Johnsonian Miscellanies. Edited by G. B. Hill. 2 vols. Oxford: Clarendon Press, 1897. Reprints Mrs. Piozzi's *Anecdotes of Samuel Johnson,* Arthur Murphy's *Essay on Johnson's Life and Genius,* excerpts from Hawkins's *Life,* and much other early biographical material. A new edition of Mrs. Piozzi's *Anecdotes,* edited by Arthur Sherbo, Oxford: Oxford University Press, was published in 1974.

Krutch, Joseph Wood. *Samuel Johnson.* New York: Holt, 1944. Now a little dated, but perhaps the best single introduction to Johnson (both "man" *and* "writer") for the beginning student.

Reade, Aleyn Lyell. *Johnsonian Gleanings.* 11 vols. Privately printed, 1909–52. This astonishing work, the product of the spare-time labors of an amateur scholar over half a century, may be regarded as the beginning of modern "scientific" biography of Johnson. Vol. 10 sums up what Reade has been able to discover about the first forty years of Johnson's life; the earlier volumes provide the massive documentation for it.

Wain, John. *Samuel Johnson: A Biography.* London: Macmillan, 1974; New York: Viking, 1975.

Special Studies

Alkon, Paul K. *Samuel Johnson and Moral Discipline.* Evanston, Ill.: Northwestern University Press, 1967. Excellent treatment of Johnson's moral thinking.

Balderston, Katharine C. "Johnson's Vile Melancholy." In *The Age of Johnson; Essays Presented to C. B. Tinker.* New Haven, Conn.: Yale University Press, 1949. An important article, establishing the clinical nature of Johnson's "masochism," a secret apparently known only to Mrs. Thrale.

Bate, Walter J. *The Achievement of Samuel Johnson.* New York: Oxford University Press, 1955. Stimulating essay, although by no means an adequate account of Johnson's "achievement" as a writer.

Bronson, Bertrand H. "The Double Tradition of Dr. Johnson." *ELH: A Journal of English Literary History* 18 (June 1951): 90–106.

_____. "Johnson Agonistes." In *Johnson and Boswell: Three Essays.* Berkeley and Los Angeles: University of California Press, 1944. Also entitled *Johnson Agonistes and Other Essays.* Cambridge: Cambridge University Press, 1946. Perceptive presentations of a modern view of Johnson.

Brown, Joseph Epes. *The Critical Opinions of Samuel Johnson.* Princeton: Princeton University Press, 1926; New York: Russell & Russell, 1961. Valuable index to Johnson's critical dicta.

Chapin, Chester F. *The Religious Thought of Samuel Johnson.* Ann Arbor: University of Michigan Press, 1968. A competent, if limited, study.

Eliot, T. S. Introduction, *London* and *The Vanity of Human Wishes.* London: Etchells & Macdonald, 1930. Reprinted in *English Critical Essays: Twentieth Century.* Edited by Phyllis M. Jones. London: Oxford University Press, 1933 (World's Classics). One of Eliot's most brilliant pieces of criticism; an indispensable introduction to Johnson's poetry.

Fleeman, J. D., ed. *The Sale Catalogue of Samuel Johnson's Library: A Facsimile Edition.* Victoria, B. C.: University of Victoria English Literary Studies, 1975.

Folkenflik, Robert. *Samuel Johnson, Biographer.* Ithaca, N.Y.: Cornell University Press, 1978.

Grange, Kathleen M. "Samuel Johnson's Account of Certain Psychoanalytic Concepts." *Journal of Nervous and Mental Disease* 135 (August, 1962): 93–98. Shows the remarkable modernity of Johnson's views on mental health, especially in the *Rambler* and *Rasselas.*

Gray, James. *Johnson's Sermons: A Study.* Oxford: Clarendon Press, 1972.

Greene, Donald J. *The Politics of Samuel Johnson.* New Haven: Yale University

Press, 1960. Reprint, Port Washington, N.Y.: Kennikat Press, 1973. 2nd ed., Athens: University of Georgia Press, 1989.

————, ed. *Samuel Johnson: A Collection of Critical Essays (Twentieth Century Views)*. Englewood Cliffs, N.J.: Prentice-Hall, 1965. Reprints essays and excerpts from books.

————. *Samuel Johnson's Library: An Annotated Guide*. Victoria, B.C.: University of Victoria English Literary Studies, 1975. Describes the works listed in the sale catalog.

Hagstrum, Jean H. *Samuel Johnson's Literary Criticism*. Minneapolis: University of Minnesota Press, 1952. 2d ed., Chicago: University of Chicago Press, 1967.

Hoover, Benjamin B. *Samuel Johnson's Parliamentary Reporting*. Berkeley and Los Angeles: University of California Press, 1953.

Irwin, George. *Samuel Johnson: A Personality in Conflict*. Auckland, New Zealand: Auckland University Press, 1971. Interesting psychological study.

Johnson after Two Hundred Years. Edited by Paul J. Korshin. Philadelphia: University of Pennsylvania Press, 1986. Essays from the bicentenary conference at Oxford.

Johnson, Boswell and Their Circle: Essays Presented to L. F. Powell. Edited by Mary Lascelles, James L. Clifford, et al. Oxford: Clarendon Press, 1965.

McAdam, E. L., Jr. *Dr. Johnson and the English Law*. Syracuse, N. Y.: Syracuse University Press, 1951. Contains the text of Johnsonian portions of the Vinerian Law Lectures.

McGuffie, Helen Louise. *Samuel Johnson in the British Press, 1749–1784: A Chronological Checklist*. New York: Garland Publishing, 1976. A great many entries are extremely hostile, making one wonder how many of his contemporaries regarded him as "the Great Cham."

Naugle, Helen Harrold, with Peter B. Sherry. *A Concordance to the Poems of Samuel Johnson*. Ithaca, N.Y.: Cornell University Press, 1973.

New Light on Dr. Johnson. Edited by F. W. Hilles. New Haven, Conn.: Yale University Press, 1959. Anniversary collection of essays; uneven in value.

Samuel Johnson: Commemorative Lectures. Edited by Magdi Wahba. Beirut: Librairie du Liban, 1986. Lectures delivered at the bicentenary conference at Oxford.

Schwartz, Richard B. *Samuel Johnson and the New Science*. Madison: University of Wisconsin Press, 1971.

————. *Samuel Johnson and the Problem of Evil*. Madison: University of Wisconsin Press, 1975. Important discussion of the review of Soame Jenyns.

————. *Boswell's Johnson: A Preface to the Life*. Madison: University of Wisconsin Press, 1978. Argues that it is more a life of Boswell than of Johnson.

Sherbo, Arthur. *Samuel Johnson, Editor of Shakespeare, with an Essay on "The Adventurer."* Urbana: University of Illinois Press, 1956.

Sledd, James H., and Gwin J. Kolb. *Dr. Johnson's Dictionary: Essays in the Biography of a Book*. Chicago: University of Chicago Press, 1955.

The Unknown Samuel Johnson. Edited by John J. Burke, Jr. and Donald Kay.

Madison: University of Wisconsin Press, 1983. Nine new essays on lesser-known aspects of Johnson.

Vance, John A. *Samuel Johnson and the Sense of History.* Athens: University of Georgia Press, 1984.

Voitle, Robert. *Samuel Johnson the Moralist.* Cambridge, Mass.: Harvard University Press, 1961. A useful exploration.

Wimsatt, W. K., Jr. *Philosophic Words: A Study of Style and Meaning in the Rambler and Dictionary of Samuel Johnson.* New Haven: Yale University Press, 1948.

————. *The Prose Style of Samuel Johnson.* New Haven: Yale University Press, 1941.

Index

The Prefaces, Chronology, Notes, and "Recapitulation" (Chap. 8) have not been indexed.